ID0955480

THE ANGER
Advantage

THE ANGER Advantage

The Surprising Benefits of *Anger* and *How It Can Change a Woman's Life*

Deborah L. Cox

Karin H. Bruckner

Sally D. Stabb

Broadway Books
New York

BROADWAY

The Anger Advantage. Copyright © 2003 by Deborah L. Cox, Karin H. Bruckner, and Sally D. Stabb. All rights reserved. No part of this book may be reproduced or transmitted in any form or by any means, electronic or mechanical, including photocopying, recording, or by any information storage and retrieval system, without written permission from the publisher. For information, address Broadway Books, a division of Random House, Inc., 1745 Broadway, New York, NY 10019.

Broadway Books titles may be purchased for business or promotional use or for special sales. For information, please write to: Special Markets Department, Random House, Inc., 1745 Broadway, New York, NY 10019.

PRINTED IN THE UNITED STATES OF AMERICA

BROADWAY BOOKS and its logo, a letter B bisected on the diagonal, are trademarks of Broadway Books, a division of Random House, Inc.

Visit our website at www.broadwaybooks.com

First edition published 2003

Designed by Fearn Cutler de Vicq

Library of Congress Cataloging-in-Publication Data

Cox, Deborah L.
The anger advantage: the surprising benefits of anger and how it can change your life / Deborah L. Cox, Karin H. Bruckner, Sally D. Stabb.
    p.   cm.
ISBN 0-7679-1160-1
1. Anger. 2. Women—Psychology. I. Bruckner, Karin H. II. Stabb, Sally D. III. Title

BF575.A5 C67 2003
152.4'7—dc21   2002034290
              10 9 8 7 6 5 4 3 2 1

*For Joe and A. J., who have my
whole heart*

Deborah L. Cox

*

*For my children,
my greatest blessing,
Lorin, Benjamin, and Gailynn*

Karin H. Bruckner

*

*For my parents,
who showed me that love and anger can coexist,
I finally get it; thank you.*

Sally D. Stabb

Contents

Introduction

Seven years ago, we began a collaborative project to study women's anger. Our interest in the subject came from both our own personal experiences with anger and the experiences we saw our friends and clients having. We remembered, as little girls, being scolded for making angry faces. We remembered thinking at times that we were selfish for feeling angry. We remembered being scared when our parents were angry. We shared our perceptions that while anger was at the heart of our knowing ourselves, ironically, it was the one emotion that people did not want to see in us as women.

Through our own internal explorations and late-night conversations with each other, we discovered that we had, as a group, some very similar and some very different experiences concerning our anger. As women, we shared remarkably similar training from our families and schools—we learned that we each had been taught to put others' emotional needs ahead of our own, particularly if those needs had anything to do with anger. We realized together that one outcome of this rule to keep ourselves last in line, or muffle our voices and needs when they clashed with those of others, was that we had absorbed beliefs about ourselves that were not only biased, but were standing in the way of our connection with the goals and dreams we each held. But as products of different families, religious backgrounds, and communities, we each had learned some uniquely individual ways of handling anger. The ways we had come to know and use our anger were varied, complex, and reflected all the personal stories of hurt, triumph, disagreement, connection, and loss we had experienced as little girls, as adolescents, and as women.

As the months and years passed, the three of us became closer as friends and colleagues. A very big part of our connection was the energy we felt together as we hammered out our own framework for understanding what we saw in our own lives and in the lives of other women and girls. The hammering process was long and complicated. We looked to our psychotherapy clients, other researchers' findings, our friends, our relatives, our children and partners, anywhere we could turn to find information that would help us see more clearly what women do when they are angry—what they do on the inside and what they do on the outside—how people in their lives respond to them, and the emotional repercussions of those responses. We found important background in the writings of Harriet Lerner, Deborah Tannen, Sandra Thomas, Jean Baker Miller, Janet Surrey, and others. We found patterns in the many chronicles we heard, read, and watched. Those patterns resonated with our own private battles. Sometimes we women fight for cherished things, but sometimes we fight against ourselves instead.

Underlying all of these patterns and stories we found a power, a potency in women's claimed and spoken anger that took many forms but ultimately helped each woman to become a little more of who she is. We saw the raw, unfiltered, elemental health and opportunity for growth that lives inside women's honest anger.

We started to see that women who had experienced the traumas of rape, sexual abuse, physical assault, devastating bereavement, or even physical illness—things that would likely make any of us mad—seemed to benefit from openly expressing their anger. They got stronger. They assigned responsibility to the persons who had caused them pain. They freed themselves from feeling ashamed over things they could not control. We learned how to incorporate anger into the psychotherapy we did with these women and then witnessed their recoveries.

Thus, the Women's Anger Project was born. We approached our research from many perspectives. Since we believed it was important to look at anger and psychological symptoms as well as personality traits, we, along with some of our closest colleagues, surveyed over 1,000 women and girls across several different studies. We determined to find out more about the distress *and* the empowerment they experienced as it related to their feelings and expressions of anger. We asked, "How do women's anger styles affect their sex lives? Their depression and anxiety? Their recovery from trauma?" "Does anger ever lead to feelings of strength for women?"

Surveying women gave us certain kinds of information about their sense of agency or personal power, their relationships, their gender roles—all of which brought pieces to our colorfully developing mosaic. We knew, however, that to truly understand women's anger lives, we had to step outside of traditional numbers-based methods in psychology and adopt strategies based on interviewing and observation, long known to sociologists and anthropologists who study other cultures, but relative newcomers to psychology's research toolbox. We knew we had to hear women tell their stories in their own words—and incorporate their verbatim accounts into our existing frameworks, modify those frameworks, and come to understand the convergence of all these bits of priceless information. It would take years of interviewing and analyzing and discussing, but it would pay off in the richness of our participants' lived relationships with their emotions.

We learned much about the process of conducting qualitative research. We learned to find the questions to ask of our research participants—questions that would help to unlock their individual accounts of anger without imposing the definitions and assumptions we found in most other studies. We interviewed more than 100 women, individually, in focus groups, or with their families. As a group of researchers and therapists, we read nearly every published work we could locate on women's anger and conflict. We found studies that deeply informed our perspective and those that made us even more determined to uncover real aspects of women's emotional lives versus inducing an anger experience in our participants or taking unrealistic snapshots of their behavior in a laboratory. We agonized over the confusing definitions of anger and aggression in the literature and discovered that the mental health and behavioral science worlds were just as confused about these concepts as the general public. As a team, we strove to define those issues in ways that honored the separateness of feeling and outward behavior.

We discovered "heuristic research" (Moustakas, 1990) as a tool for answering questions like: "How do women use anger for the good of their children?" "How do women use anger to recover from the pain of a lover's infidelity?" and "How do women lose touch with their true outrage?" In this process, we listened to other women but always brought their words and insights back into our own group discussion, weaving it into the understandings we had of ourselves as women. "How do I use my anger to draw myself closer to my loved ones?" "How and when do I run away from my anger?" "When I run away, what do I lose?" "What do I gain when I allow myself to be fully conscious of my rage?"

During the evolution of our study and writing together, we became fascinated with the useful, productive, passionate ways in which some women use their anger. While the majority of our research participants talks about the problems they have with this feeling, always trying to hide or squelch anger in an attempt to regain control of their lives or protect others from what they fear will be monstrous rage, a small but significant portion of these women have learned to ride the waves of their hottest oppositional experiences, to welcome even the unpleasantness of feeling angry, and to channel that emotion into creative growth. These women use anger to promote their safety, protect their children, sharpen their concentration when it is needed to make a decision, enhance their love relationships, develop synergy in their friendships and work relationships, and ultimately free themselves to create identities and vocations that are consistent with their deeply held beliefs and values. It is in the spirit of these brave women that we present the findings of our ongoing work.

Ironically, we also approach this topic with sadness and concern, in light of the terrorist attacks of September 11, 2001. On this day, as a nation, we watched perhaps the most devastating misuse of anger that we had ever seen. The three of us held our breaths with the rest of the country and felt a mixture of difficult emotions, including anger. We were in the midst of writing this book when the whole world changed forever. We gathered together and wondered about the meaning of positive anger, in relation to these overwhelming events. Now, more than ever, we see the importance of knowing how to separate the emotion of anger from acts of aggression. If anger is denied or suppressed, it takes twisted, manipulative forms. If aggression is taught by any society as a way to handle anger, it creates tragedy. People need other options. All the things that legitimately make people angry—murders of their loved ones; social, political, and economic inequities; lack of appreciation for their religions, cultures, or worldviews; conflict over scarce and withheld resources—can be tackled in other ways besides killing and death; there are alternatives to teaching our children to hate and to link hatred to anger and aggression. These unfortunate links must be unlearned. We can't save the world with this book, but we hope it's a small step in the process of our society's enlightenment about its emotions. Anger must be brought out in the open, respected, and processed; the injustices it identifies must be addressed—with respect and commitment to solving problems instead of death and destruction.

———

Our premise for *The Anger Advantage* is this: When women attempt to *get around* their anger without fully acknowledging it, they lose a lot of valuable information and experiences that help them evolve into their full selves. They risk hurting themselves and/or others. On the other hand, when we attend to our anger, give it a place of respect in our consciousness, allow it to take shape and become spoken aloud, we increase the odds of our learning from it, growing through it, making important things happen in our lives because of it. We've seen both sides of this issue unfold in countless ways in the real lives and stories of the women we've worked with.

We sincerely hope our research will energize and inspire you to find your Anger Advantage.

ONE

Anger

From a Woman's Perspective

L et's face it. Anger isn't fun, and most of us would rather not ever have to deal with it. But the simple fact that you've opened this book signals you're ready to take a fresh look at anger and at how you ride out the storms of conflict in your life. To open this book, you had to reach past all the negativity commonly associated with this emotion to discover what anger might hold for you as a woman. Congratulations on a new beginning.

What's in store for you can result in the kind of powerful and positive changes that Marcy, a 55-year-old writer, shares below. After years of stuffing her anger toward her father and playing the dutiful daughter and the good wife, Marcy finally lets her outrage speak. The deceptively simple act of declaring her anger sets her free—free at last to recognize that her feelings are legitimate; free to declare that the insensitivity of others was, in fact, wrong and unjust; and free to connect with loved ones in her family in a new way.

> *I had a very recent experience with anger, and it ties in with my father, who was a social activist all my life. I think a great deal of him, but he's also an extremely difficult man, an artist, and extremely self-centered, and this has been a very painful relationship for me. Recently, because he's 91, I've been trying to be a really good daughter. He's writing an autobiography, and I'm a writer and I had agreed to do all this stuff for him; I went up and spent time with him for days on end, doing shit work with him, being the useful helping*

hand, working on his book. I was doing all of this with an open heart and was happy to serve. And my two brothers, he's completely alienated them; they would have nothing to do with him, they wouldn't cross the street to help my dad. So, on New Year's Eve, I'm reading the manuscript that he has left with me. I'm reading along through it, and he talks about my oldest brother being born and he talks about my next oldest brother being born, and then he talks about the baby after me who died, and he doesn't even mention me being born.

I went through a process over the next couple of weeks—it was really the stages of grieving. I went from complete fury through to the other end of it I guess, with some acceptance . . . but that was extremely painful for me. I was able, after working through it and after writing letter after letter after letter that I did not send, just to call him up and say how much it hurt my feelings. But what's been really interesting is that this opened up sort of a floodgate for me, because in the past it's been really difficult for me to express my anger.

Interestingly, my husband, who had known I was going through all this, feeling very disregarded and ignored, had made the mistake of standing me up on a date. What went through my mind, when I realized that he wasn't going to get home in time for us to have dinner was, "You know what, the universe is sending me a message. I've just been sitting and chewing on this thing with my dad, internalizing it, torment-ing myself for a month, and I obviously haven't got the mes-sage, and now the universe has sent my darling husband to give me the same message. This is going to keep happening until I finally <u>get it.</u>" And so I was able to address my husband when he got home, and the next day, to pick up the phone and call my dad, and express my feelings to him.

It was extremely gratifying and pleasurable, in a weird way, to <u>just spit it out</u> and to say <u>directly</u>, to these, the two most important men in my life, "I am so angry! I just am SO upset!" This has been a transformative experience.

Marcy's story dramatically shows how anger can spark so much more than guilt and self-recrimination for the woman who is ready to stop fearing her anger and to start using it to her advantage. She's still trying to get used to the idea that directly expressing her anger worked, and worked well, but make no doubt about it, she's very enthusiastic about the outcome of her new choice!

As a powerful and much misunderstood emotion, anger more often than not is avoided and denied. It is labeled as a sin, as unhealthy and destructive, and we are taught to be on guard against it. But working as researchers and therapists over the past decade, we have discovered and explored an exciting new way of looking at anger, one that highlights its constructive, beneficial side.

When we began our research years ago, we too were largely unaware of how anger might be helpful. We simply focused on how women handled their anger in light of the social pressure to hide it. Soon though, we were tracing the complexities of the stories we heard. The many layers of awareness, the subtle differences in how much anger women admit to themselves and others depending on the context and relationships involved, became clearer and clearer. Eventually, we came to identify themes in the ways women negotiate around their anger in different situations and with different people, and what the consequences of those decisions are. Real insight came as we realized the negative patterns we were seeing were all the result of *diverting* anger: whether by minimizing it, by shoving it under the rug, *or* by hurting other people through an explosion of rage, or even injuring others through passive hostility that we barely notice. In contrast, the really positive patterns we were seeing were the result of acknowledging, embracing, and acting constructively on anger. The result is our model of positive anger, which shows how anger handled well can become a powerful advantage for every woman, including you.

Based on the culmination of ten years of practice and seven years of research involving interviews, surveys, and other assessments of women, anger now emerges as a source of wisdom, clarity, and inspiration, offering support and solutions for women discovering the creative potential and growth opportunities in their own fury. But before you can harness this power, it is necessary to learn about anger in a new way. Because anger has been largely taboo for women, chances are you haven't had the opportunity or freedom to find out enough about this feeling, either in a personal way or even an informational way. As you develop a deeper understanding about what anger is and how it works, you'll be able to see how this knowledge relates to your own personal experience, whether that includes explosions of rage, a simmering temper, or a troubling absence of any angry feelings whatsoever. You'll also gain valuable tools for keeping your anger front and center and the skills to direct your anger into positive changes, both large and small.

ANGER AND WHAT WOMEN WANT

~~~I'd like to be a little bit more like Denise. She gets right to the point, doesn't leave things up in the air or anything for anybody to wonder about. Tell it like it is, and then it passes over faster.

—Leona (79; in praise of her daughter's anger expression)

Though each woman is unique, as psychotherapists, teachers, and researchers, we find that most of us want some key things. We seek intimacy and respect in our relationships at home, at work, and in our social lives. We want information about ourselves and the world that will help us grow and achieve things central to us. And most of us, on some level, seek to be conscious and responsible in our emotional lives. These desires make women both strong and vulnerable: strong because we tend to see the world in terms of its relationship potential; vulnerable because we sometimes mistakenly equate our own success with the suffering of those relationships. We fear that getting what we really want means someone else has to lose.

During the past decade, we have come to see that anger is not the problem; women's struggles really arise as we attempt to *rid ourselves of a feeling that was meant to be there in the first place.* So often, as we attempt to get what we want, we unknowingly disable aspects of our personalities that could most help us attain our goals.

Women *do* get mad, and often. We get the maddest about things of most significance to us, namely, being betrayed or abandoned in a close relationship, being blocked from accomplishing something we want to make happen, and being violated or witnessing our loved ones being violated. These kinds of assaults call up fierce, protective feelings that serve complex purposes. Women want to correct injustices, bring loved ones near, defend our rights, and have our ideas heard and taken seriously.

In contrast with most public attitudes and even therapist lore, our research suggests anger *benefits* us more than we once thought. It helps women do many of the things they need and want to do. Rather than posing an obstacle, anger endows its owner with emotional energy and intellectual clarity for making needed life changes.

We know this *sounds* great. Better than that, we know firsthand from the many women we speak with that *the advantages of anger are real and obtainable*. However, we also suspect you may be asking yourself, "But how do *I* get there?" or, "Where do *I* begin?" All changes require new knowledge and a bit of risk-taking to try out fresh ideas and different ways of interacting. They also require targeting those beliefs and actions that are no longer contributing to our well-being and figuring out how to undo them. We have spent years keeping up with the literature on anger from multiple points of view and across disciplines as varied as evolutionary psychology, physiology, social psychology, feminism, sociology, and, of course, psychotherapy. Through our scholarship, we have distilled this substantial material into what we consider the key elements of our model of adaptive anger. Information is power, and this is where it starts.

What You Need to Unlearn: Anger Myths

Let's begin with checking out what you believe about anger right now. Take the following quiz to see what kinds of attitudes you have about anger.

ANGER BELIEFS QUIZ

Rate each of the following statements as to how true it is for YOU.
(1 = rarely true; 5 = almost always true)

1. Anger is basically undesirable.   1 2 3 4 5
2. Anger leads to harmful or criminal behaviors.   1 2 3 4 5
3. Anger compromises my well-being   1 2 3 4 5
4. Anger usually hurts someone.   1 2 3 4 5
5. If you let it out, anger typically leads to more anger.   1 2 3 4 5
6. There is no good way to show anger to someone else.   1 2 3 4 5
7. There is probably something wrong with a person who gets
   angry very often.   1 2 3 4 5
8. Getting angry keeps others from taking you seriously.   1 2 3 4 5
9. Getting angry makes you look unattractive.   1 2 3 4 5
10. Getting angry ruins relationships.   1 2 3 4 5
11. It is usually best to avoid others who appear angry.   1 2 3 4 5
12. Holding in your anger makes for better relationships in
    the long run.   1 2 3 4 5
13. If you're angry quite a bit, it's likely that you have an
    emotional problem.   1 2 3 4 5
14. Anger should be avoided.   1 2 3 4 5
15. It's better to stifle your anger than to disrupt things.   1 2 3 4 5
16. Anger can be avoided if you work at it.   1 2 3 4 5
17. Getting angry and speaking your mind is unfeminine.   1 2 3 4 5
18. Showing anger means you are weak.   1 2 3 4 5
19. Anger makes a person think less clearly.   1 2 3 4 5
20. If you get angry, you just end up sabotaging yourself in
    the end.   1 2 3 4 5
21. You can't be all that helpful to anyone when you are angry.   1 2 3 4 5
22. Thinking is a better way to make decisions than feeling.   1 2 3 4 5

SCORES: *Total your responses by adding scores for 1 through 22.*

22–44: You have a fairly realistic view of anger most of the time and express it in healthy ways.

45–87: You're uncertain about anger, seeing both some positives and some negatives. You're in a good position to question or explore anger dynamics and myths to make room for a more productive style.

88–110: You believe many unfortunate societal myths about anger. You would probably benefit from an intensive look at anger's potential benefits in your life.

If you scored high or in the midrange of our anger beliefs quiz, don't despair. Many people do; you've just learned, as most women have, to think of anger as wrong and bad. People teach their children flawed ideas about anger, not because they wish their children to be unhappy, but mostly because they believe these notions themselves and feel obligated to pass them on to their children, who would perhaps be socially outcast as a result of not learning them. Some parents still teach their daughters mistaken notions about anger with the hope that they will become sweet women (read marriage material) and not wind up as dreaded spinsters; but most traditional parents remain unaware of the advantages of anger. It is all done with the best intentions, but our society—schools, peers, religious institutions, the media—is made up of individuals raised pretty much the same way, thereby reinforcing these misguided ideas.

Why do we believe these ideas are wrong? A decade of careful exploration, directly speaking with women and girls, individually, in focus groups, through our website bulletin board (www.anger-project.com), and via questionnaires, has convinced us that clinging to anger myths hinders our positive development. We've been in schools, homes, offices, and therapy rooms to listen to the stories of real women and their loved ones. We've looked at how women are trained in families and social circles to deflect attention away from anger. What we have found is that women who buy into anger myths repeatedly experience the repercussions of their fight against their own anger. In our interviews, women who habitually adopt these myths:

- lose valuable information that could help them make needed decisions.
- develop physical and emotional symptoms that could likely be avoided through clear use of their anger.
- become prisoners inside relationships that are unfulfilling and stagnant.
- miss out on opportunities to know themselves better through attention to what makes them mad and why.
- run the risk of hurting themselves and others, as they've lost touch with the internal signs of their anger and what it means in their relationships.

In our model of anger advantage, we call *all* the ways that women detour and bypass their oppositional feelings **anger diversions.** Operating under the influence of the anger myths greatly contributes to diverting anger. There are two big problems with diversion: one personal and one societal. The first problem is that anger diversion keeps us from personally feeling/acting effectively, as noted in the list above.

The second problem arising from diversion is the disempowerment of women at economic and social/political levels. This is why it is so important to be aware of anger myths; they often quietly serve those in power in maintaining their control over us. It's very convenient to encourage women to stay passive; uppity women might upset the apple cart after all! And you can't even imagine *having the choice* of being uppity if you don't know what's going on. Perhaps more than any other threat, anger's usefulness as a tool for gaining what we want and need threatens society—hence the threat of women's emotional honesty. Examining anger myths helps us break free of old limitations, thereby releasing us to make informed decisions about engaging anger's advantages. So let's look at seven core myths in a bit more detail.

Myth 1: Anger Is Destructive and Naughty

⸺Why does it seem like every time I start to raise my voice and talk plainly about something my husband recoils from me and says I'm being too pushy?

Anger and aggression are sadly intertwined in our national consciousness. Fear of anger has roots deep in our fear of the aggression that we typically associate with it. Only when we separate anger from hurtful aggression and violence do we develop a more realistic view of its role in our emotional lives. As many women well know, you can be angry and do absolutely nothing—so anger doesn't "naturally" lead to aggression. The truth is anger helps women in protecting and advocating for themselves. As a natural phenomenon, it arises in threatening situations or in the event of conflict, and it serves to assist us in responding appropriately (not necessarily aggressively). But somehow we omit this positive function in our perception of anger and, instead, believe the exact opposite. Women remain convinced by generations of stern warnings from our parents, teachers, preachers, and counselors that anger is destructive to the self and to relationships.

Myth 2: Anger Is Bad for Your Health

⸺I want my daughters to know they have rights, but my oldest, Kari, is always getting so worked up about things. It can't be good for her always to have herself in a twist about something that's not going her way.

Over and over, in myriad messages both explicit and hidden, women are warned against the dangers of becoming angry. These include the beliefs that anger breeds anger (once a woman allows herself to get angry, she will only become more and more enraged) and that anger makes us physically sick. However, a closer look at research supporting this view raises questions about its real-life application to women.

First, back to the anger/aggression connection: many studies that conclude anger contributes to ill health fail to note the differences between anger and aggression when collecting data (see Cox, Stabb, & Bruckner, 1999, for a deeper discussion). Second, the tests and surveys used in most anger research do not include *any* items that reflect adaptive anger. This makes it difficult to draw balanced conclusions about how anger can be beneficial *or* detrimental to our health, because it limits our imaginations to only those aspects of anger that are problematic. Also, most of these studies were done in a lab or through a survey of an hour or so. Such studies can't capture the positive benefits of anger consciousness that take place over months and years or that show up in unexpected parts of a woman's existence. Through our clinical work and in-depth interviews, which detail critical events and turning points in women's lives, we can see anger's broader influence on women's health and well-being as they describe the complexity of their everyday experiences.

It turns out that anger itself does not make you ill, but stuffing anger away—out of awareness—*does* makes us sick. For example, in one of our most recent investigations of sexuality and anger, we found that women who suppress their anger report more sexual dysfunction and pain than those who do not. The relationship between suppressed anger and depression, as well as a host of other stress-related illnesses, is well established. Suppressing anger *is* stressful; it takes lots of mental and physical energy. Some women try to bypass their anger by repeatedly pushing it out on others in agitated, antagonistic bouts of blaming. This kind of pattern—in which we disown our anger and dump it on another (called *externalization* in our model)—ignores the crucial positive aspects of anger's ability to connect us with others. Externalized anger pushes others away when we often wish to draw them near. Externalizing may lead to health problems such as high blood pressure and other cardiovascular difficulties. In contrast, adaptive expression of emotion has clear health benefits. Southern Methodist University's James W. Pennebaker studies men and women who express their anger through regular writing exercises and finds that they have fewer symptoms of illness than those who don't. It would seem that many women commonly confuse the health risks of deflecting their anger with anger itself.

Myth 3: Anger Equals Weakness or Emotional Instability

~~~I've learned better than to let the frustration show with any man. They look at me like "you're completely out of line here." No, I know what that will get me. They think I have a hormonal problem if my attitude is anything but pleasant.

Whether it's a radio talk show, your Sunday school class lesson, a prime-time TV show, or the latest issue of a family magazine, we find the same message coming through loud and clear—if you're a woman and you get angry, there's something wrong with you. This perception echoes through our focus group discussions with women. When we ask women how people perceive women who are angry, the number one response tends to be, "They think she's crazy." We also repeatedly hear, "They think she's a bitch," and "She has PMS."

Trivializing women's anger by equating it with weakness encourages us to question our own gut reactions. In that uncertainty, the reality of anger's power can be diffused. Powerful women are still perceived by many people as threatening. In contrast, recognizing our anger and acknowledging it brings a realization of our own individuality and separateness from others. It helps women come to understand just how we feel and what we want—significant parts of the sum total of who we are as people—and allows us the opportunity to see ourselves in more autonomous terms.

Our perception of anger as reflecting weakness or instability probably has its roots in our turn-of-the-century views that equated self-control with moral correctness. However, modern portrayals of extreme rage in movies such as *Fatal Attraction* or the ever-popular angry psychotic killer flick contribute to an oversimplified view of anger as linked to psychopathic violence and mental illness. It might surprise you to know that the vast majority of psychotic people are, in fact, completely nonviolent. Recognize that newspapers, TV, radio, and Internet news services have a vested interest in showing you the most outlandish stuff possible (to keep sales up), but that repeated exposure to such biased information can contribute to you buying into the myth that anger makes you depraved and unstable.

Myth 4: Anger Ruins Relationships

~~~ *My boyfriend and I broke up last month because we were constantly arguing. I'm really depressed because I miss him a lot. But we both decided that since we're always in some kind of fight, we probably weren't meant for each other.*

"If we're going to be in a relationship, I have to give up being angry with you." Women are trained to take responsibility in our relationships. Men are not typically designated or trained as caretakers and therefore tend to have more freedom to act on their own needs and wants without as much regard for the impact these have within a relationship. When it comes to anger, these cultural rules translate into a ban on anger expression for women, an ideal of anger-free feminine love, a true catch-22 for women. If our expression of anger is believed to be a fundamental threat to the relationships for which we are held responsible, *and* this same anger is crucial to our own sense of identity and self-advocacy, then we face the impossible choice between our well-being and the survival of the relationship.

Of course, this dilemma rests on the notion that most relationships are much too fragile to tolerate a woman's expression of anger, that expressed anger is a force that always drives people apart. But surprisingly, once we lose our fear of anger and learn how to deal with it directly, it actually helps to bring us closer to those we love and care about. This happens because anger allows us to recognize those things in a relationship that are painful, scary, or uncomfortable for us and to communicate truthfully about them. Instead of leaving these issues unresolved, we pay attention to what our anger is trying to tell us and use that information to form our relationships into more reality-based bonds.

This particular myth is a favorite in the popular media. For example, one women's magazine we reviewed advises women to "let him know that even if you don't agree 100 percent, you're still behind him." This flagrantly twisted message of self-denial leads us to believe it is more important for a woman to cushion her husband from the effect of her disagreement than to advocate for herself. Another article in a different magazine lists the steps women can follow in order to moderate their words and behavior (as well as attitude) carefully as needed in order to respond to the all-important boyfriend or husband's reaction. A parenting magazine gives tips on controlling anger to manage disruptive children, but no options for healthy anger expression between moms and kids.

Judging by this current sample of women's magazines, no shortage of discussion exists on how to manage conflict and anger in a variety of different relationships—with spouses, boyfriends, children, parents, friends, and coworkers. Although we find an abundance of reassurance that these arguments and fights are normal and fixable, one message booms out loud and clear: if you are a woman and you are angry, *you are the problem* in the relationship, and it's your job to fix it.

This means two things. First, because society characterizes women as sensitive, caring, and empathic, it also expects us to be accommodating, obliging, and conciliatory. The job of resolving conflict falls to women. As women, we are advised and encouraged to play peacemaker and to scrutinize our motives to weed out any self-centered impulse at the first twinge of anger. While this social control is meant to preserve harmony in relationships, it comes at considerable cost to women who eventually come to define every frustration as a sign of *selfishness*. This social obligation effectively keeps women from taking action on our own behalfs by imparting the dreadful fear of becoming an *angry woman*, or—horror of all sitcoms and soap operas—a *nag!*

Second, when we let our anger show, the topic suddenly switches from why we're irritated to what we're doing wrong. Her exclamation, "I can't believe you bought that $300 bike when we haven't been able to scrape the money together to get new tires for my car!" will be answered with his, "I'm so tired of your criticizing! I can't do anything without you coming down on me. You better figure out how to lighten up." This works for men because the subject shifts smoothly from his behavior to hers and her anger now becomes the issue, rather than his self-centered act. Focusing on her angry words provides a convenient distraction away from his misbehaviors. He regains the familiar offensive role rather than operating from the more vulnerable defensive position of acknowledging and responding to her hurt feelings. And she is primed to go right along with this because she's been taught all her life that it's wrong to be at odds with others. Couples can get stuck in a negative—"she nags, he withdraws"—pattern, whereas effective use of emotional energy can break through this impasse.

Myth 5: Anger Is Avoidable

Anger is kind of like slamming your head against the wall— it seems like a useless cycle that you have to get out of.

Every day we send our children to school for six or seven hours of hard work and stimulating play. We know they will be faced with frustrations and conflicts involving both classmates and teachers, so we instruct our kids to handle their emotions in such situations: don't hit, don't talk back, don't swear or break any of the rules. If the anger is directed toward a teacher or other adult, the difficulty mounts exponentially. Many trained professionals, teachers, and sensible parents expect that children will be able to tolerate the daily frustrations of life at school without releasing their anger at any point, even verbally. From our extensive experience in schools, this is quite unrealistic.

We have difficulty with children's anger because we have difficulty with our own. We seem to believe that we can always find some way to detour around our anger and not let it show. Trina (23) says, "Anger, even though it's natural, to me is a weakness. And that's been something I've been working on. Because I know when I have kids, patience is going to come in handy." Trina unfortunately sees anger as incompatible with patience, so she continues to view it as a liability and works to eliminate it.

We may believe that if we try hard enough, anger will go away. However, our research shows that anger doesn't disappear; if we try to force it to leave it sneaks back into our lives sooner or later. It may make a grand re-entrance, bigger than ever in a burst of pent-up, explosive raging. It may slither sideways into our relationships, reappearing as criticism or passive-aggressive inaction. It may burrow into our bodies, emerging as a migraine or a chronically upset stomach. Anger has a will, and it finds a way to make us listen. Anger is meant to be a part of each of us.

Myth 6: Anger Makes You Stupid

＊＊Given all the difficulties in my life right now, I really need to keep a clear head. I can't afford to waste energy being angry about any of it. I mean, I can't change anything but myself, so what's the point of getting angry?

Many of us buy into the time-honored belief that when we get mad we "can't see straight," that anger keeps us from thinking clearly. But recent research demonstrates that when people *suppress* their feelings, they may actually dampen their concentration and focus. Jane Richards and James Gross of Stanford University report that keeping one's cool may actually be costly in terms of memory. These researchers find that people who tend to hold their feelings in remember fewer details of a film or slides than those who tend to be more outwardly expressive. Similar work shows that anger helps people focus on information that is particularly relevant to the self, such as our goals. In this way, anger helps to remind us of our own needs and boundary lines in our interactions with others.

Studies such as these hold particular meaning for women's emotional health because women are most often accused of losing their heads or getting swept away with all kinds of illogical emotion when feelings are intense. It's true that in extreme situations some women and men experience a flooding of physical sensations when they're very emotionally aroused, and these individuals feel awash in a whole range of emotions simultaneously: fear, anger, nervousness, shame, or guilt. In the torrent of rushing emotion, some of these individuals say they have a hard time thinking clearly. However, these kinds of reactions differ from most everyday anger experiences. Our research suggests that women often think *more* clearly when they're truly furious, if only they grant themselves permission to seize the moment. We have heard many examples of women who tell of flashes of insight that come *only* when they are angry; these insights have been the basis of both profound positive changes in their lives and everyday triumphs.

A more subtle, but no less important point in understanding this myth is that our culture narrowly equates all thinking with rationality and logic (think of Mr. Spock on the old *Star Trek* TV series). This type of thought is trumpeted as an ideal for us all to achieve. There are old and deeply rooted value traditions in our country that link this type of thinking with men and superiority, while emotional knowledge is ridiculed as being feminine and therefore inferior. There is no ultimate truth or scientific basis to this idea. People in our society have *chosen* to value cold logic over the warmer knowledge of emotion, including anger. We choose to think differently, and so can you.

Myth 7: Anger Is Just a Cover-up for Other Feelings

~~When I'm angry at John, I can feel my fear. I know I'll have to talk to him, but I'm afraid that I'm not going to say the right words, even though I need to get this out.

Many women, and even many mental health professionals, believe in the myth that anger really just covers up some more important emotion, like hurt—and that we'd all be better off if we could just get beneath the anger and find out what else is there. While it is true that anger can be mixed with other feelings—guilt, fear, surprise, or sadness for instance—it's a mistake to assume that the anger piece is thus somehow invalidated. It isn't. It can certainly be a challenge for women to sort out mixed feelings; this is a complex skill. But to try to minimize or deny the anger component leaves an incomplete picture. For example, some women have told us that when they lose someone they love or go through some other kind of grief experience, they find themselves becoming angry (almost as if they put on anger and wear it like armor) as a defense against the more painful, vulnerable emotions they have inside. But all kinds of experiences, even the loss of a partner or a parent, involve being truly angry too—anger at the person for dying or leaving, anger at God or the universe for taking them away.

Unfortunately, many people feel guilty for giving this emotion much credence or examining it too closely.

And remember, pure anger can most certainly be experienced as well. It may not be mixed with anything else at all. Undiluted anger classically occurs in situations where we have been wronged or betrayed, when we have been violated, when someone intentionally sets out to hurt us, when an injustice has been done, or when we are blocked from reaching a desirable goal.

———

Now that you have a sense of the anger myths that must be challenged in order for you to rework the power of anger in your life, let's look at what else you need to know. If you're going to give up the mythology, you'll need new information that can help you construct a different foundation for action. Understanding how our anger emerges and is shaped over the course of a woman's life is a crucial piece of the puzzle.

THE GENDER JOURNEY

How do women come to discredit our oppositional emotions and lose touch with the very forces that could help us soar in our professional lives and create more meaningful relationships? It's a long and complicated journey that takes girls away from their true selves and into something more scripted and socially acceptable. Our research and that of others, such as the feminist scholars at the Stone Center at Wellesley College, support the notion that this journey is significantly different for women and girls than it is for boys and men. While both sexes start out hard-wired for emotional communication, the pathways traveled start to diverge almost immediately. Countless crossroads become marked with interpersonal signs that say "Girls, now you go this way" and "Boys, you head off that way." Gender thus becomes a defining feature in the landscape of anger experience and expression.

In the years of our focused study, we have come to see that

women's anger differs from men's in some important ways. Of course, we experience anger in response to some of the same things, and our nervous systems do similar things when we're very upset. But for women, just being angry produces a whole set of challenges not typically faced by angry men. Women and men seem to experience this emotion with similar frequency and intensity, but feel differently about their anger and show it differently on the outside. These differences are the result of years of social influence.

In carefully watching baby boys and girls, Ross A. Thompson of the University of Nebraska notes that infants of both sexes show basic emotions, including anger, within the first six months of life. In the second year, toddlers show more and more anger in their faces, but even by age two, young children know how to mask their emotions to a certain extent—that is, they can put on a happy face and show a different expression outwardly from what they are feeling inside. Why would toddlers do this? Relationships, especially the most important ones, shape our experience of feelings. Children at this age already pick up on the nonverbal signals from parents in reaction to the emotions they show with their bodies and in their play. These gestures actually increase, decrease, reroute, or delay a child's emotional reactions—typically based upon what is comfortable for the parents. Then, with the development of language, parents directly tell their children specific things about emotion. What do you remember hearing when you were a little girl? "Nice girls don't act mean to their brothers." "Pretty is as pretty does." "Don't mouth off to me." "No one likes to be around an angry girl." "Come out of your room when you decide to smile."

> *The first anger I remember was when I was nine years old and we had to go overseas where my dad was stationed. I felt confused and intimidated by leaving the United States. I didn't want to leave my home. When we got to England we were teased and crowds yelled, "Yankees, go home!" I was angry for having to live there. I felt I couldn't express my anger anywhere. If I did, I would get grounded and punished. My dad said children are to be seen and not heard.*
>
> —Eva (40)

We know from studies, such as those done by Robin Fivush of Emory University, that mothers avoid talking about anger with their girls and encourage their daughters from very young ages to make up with others if they get into conflicts. As kids get older, they get better and better at controlling the emotion they show others. They hide feelings, show feelings they don't really have, and identify feelings in others and themselves. Kids learn ways to regulate their emotions over time (for example, how to shift their attention away from a particular feeling, how to act differently to get different reactions from others), and learn ways to influence others and their surroundings in order to change their own emotional states.

From a girl's perspective, some very specific things begin to happen here. In our own research, girls hold their anger inside more than boys do. Roberta Buntaine and her colleague Virginia Costenbader of the Rochester Institute of Technology find that fourth- and fifth-grade girls read more of the social cues in situations that generate anger than do boys. Girls also place more emphasis on what such events mean for their relationships than do boys. They camouflage their anger more than boys, and distract themselves from anger more than boys—often by worrying over how attractive they appear. Girls have more anger about relationships; boys get angry about school and sports and have poorer memory for their emotions than girls do. Britt Galen and Marion Underwood of Reed College report that girls, but not boys, think that mean comments, dirty looks, and critical remarks are just as hurtful as actual physical aggression. Furthermore, preadolescent girls have more anger directed at themselves than do boys. In other words, girls start to take their anger—an emotion whose natural function is to tell us to engage with another person—and *reroute* it inside. Girls are encouraged to believe that they are bad or to blame for either their own angry feelings or for conflicts with others. So preteen girls learn to smile over their anger and send it underground. If this dynamic becomes a habit, girls are then set up for a lifetime of ignoring the important messages that anger carries in their relationships.

Girls' anger messages are repeated at school, where teachers punish them more often than boys for expressions of anger and assertiveness. In our study of elementary and middle school children, girls report that their teachers shame them for demonstrating disagreement, but reward boys' shows of anger by attending to the situations that aroused them. So the rules that little girls hear as toddlers become emphasized and elaborated in new ways during the school years. These rules also become reinforced when girls are rewarded with popularity and adult praise for being sweet. Girls get more and more unsure of their own reactions, and are encouraged to redirect their anger to the inside while showing a nice, agreeable face to the outside. The pressure to focus on others' feelings mounts, bringing with it the demand to avoid bothering anybody with one's hurt feelings or sense of being offended.

As girls enter their teen years, they turn a critical corner. Certain messages get louder as girls develop their sexual potential. Just when they need their angry voices most, direct expressions of outrage or disgust, which may have been tolerated to a certain extent in a younger girl, now become decidedly unladylike and unattractive. Even the engaging, quirky eccentricities that distinguish very little girls from each other now become things to assassinate. Girls' early socialization to maintain harmony in relationships and blend in—avoid showing too much passion about anything—grows hotter in the cauldron of peer relationships and the potential for beginning sexual exploration; the fear of being rejected or unpopular encourages adolescent girls to further suppress their oppositional emotions, something very different from what teenage boys are urged to do. Stacey, an energetic fifth grader in our school study, tells us that her younger brother, Cody, gets cheered on by their dad when he sticks up for himself. "Did you punch him?" her dad asks. Stacey knows very well that she must operate under a very different set of rules: namely, to avoid fighting and apologize or smooth over any misunderstanding she encounters with her friends or family.

Girls' sense of self develops through relationships with others to a greater extent than boys', whose social training demands that they separate and be independent of others to become real men. This means that people expect girls to care more about keeping those around them happy and avoid doing or saying things that might make others uncomfortable.

[I learned] that there are better ways to deal with a situation than looking at it through the dirty glass of anger. It's better to force yourself to calm down and back up, rather than let your anger control your actions. . . . When I was little, Zach was a terror of a brother, terrible, terrible! I would scream and I remember my mother saying, "Don't scream." The discussion of anger hardly ever came up except in that instant, when she would tell me not to scream.

—Carla (40)

I feel angry at her sometimes, but I can't tell her about it. I'm so afraid. I don't want to hurt her; I don't want to feel that awkwardness. She would take it in with those big brown eyes, and I just couldn't.

—Denise (31; speaking about one of her daughters)

Sometimes when people make me angry and they don't know it or they hurt my feelings, I'll just start crying. I just don't want them to see me so I won't talk to them, I'll get quiet and mad. I just cry. I'll keep my distance just so I'm not in that predicament anymore.

—Mary (19)

The emphasis on keeping others unperturbed often leads girls not only to suppress their anger and fear but also to become more critical of themselves at a number of levels. Adolescent girls experience lowered levels of confidence in their academic abilities as well as harsh self-evaluations of their bodies and attractiveness. Encouraged by family, friends, romantic love interests, and the media to buy into impossible ideals for feminine beauty and behavior, teen girls silence their own feelings of opposition and bury their sense of themselves in the process, in order to try to become what others want them to be.

In adolescence and young adulthood, the unwritten cultural rules for men encourage them to demonstrate that they are sexually competent and to assume the roles of seducer, initiator, and dominator. The socially prescribed story line for women encourages passivity and dependence—not opposition or anger. "I kind of like being the quiet one in the relationship," says Summer (22), a college student, about her role in relation to Kevin, who is 17 years her senior. "I think that's how it's supposed to be, you know? I wouldn't want to be one of these women who bosses her husband around." This is the kind of dynamic that women's studies expert Dana Jack of Western Washington University describes as "silencing the self"—losing your own voice in a relationship to satisfy the needs of others.

In middle and later adulthood, the cultural instruction to *not express or even feel* anger continues, even for those women who seem to be "angry all the time." These women suffer special kinds of shame and pressure to keep a lid on their feelings, often contributing to their tendencies to explode with pent-up frustration or engage in certain kinds of chronic whining that keep them from real interpersonal effectiveness and make them feel generally unheard and even avoided by others. As women, we are often ridiculed or teased for our anger or told that our anger reflects feminine weakness. Adult men's anger (particularly when it's *not* acknowledged as a *feeling*, as in, "I feel annoyed right now"), on the other hand, gets taken seriously. It is often admired as a vehicle for getting things done, keeping others in line, or as an expression of masculinity.

All kinds of anger experiences take on distinctive meaning for adult women. Women and men show about equal rates of verbal aggression when they're angry. However, a series of studies by Karin Oesterman and her colleagues of Abo Akademic University in Finland confirm that women tend to use *indirect* or relational aggression statements (e.g., criticizing or put-downs, often to a third party) rather than the more direct statements allowed to men ("I'm angry at you"). Sandra Thomas and her colleagues of the University of Tennessee study anger in both women and men. These researchers report on a fascinating series of interviews in which *men* discuss their anger, and they find that men talk about getting angry when they cannot *control* or fix things like inanimate objects (e.g., automobiles) or work-related issues, framing the situations as wrong versus right. The researchers conclude that men's anger is more often provoked by others' illogical behavior, in contrast with much of women's anger, which seems to come up when we experience a lack of support in our relationships and when we feel hurt.

Howard Kassinove and his colleagues of Hofstra University report that women experience more anger triggers in our love relationships and, compared with men, are significantly more likely to experience negative feelings *after* we are angry (irritation/annoyance, guilt/shame, concern, depression, sadness, anxiety, disgust, foolishness, regret) and are also more likely to cry than men when angry. Yet, ironically, this study shows that we also realize more of our own strengths when we're mad than do men.

We are more likely than men to describe our *feelings* when we're talking about a specific event or time in our lives. We also tend to express empathy for the people we're mad at—reflecting mixed feelings for them as we try to come to grips with our own needs. Trina (23) says, "I think about the other person *first*." This also tends to make us more worried about the possible consequences of our own actions and less concerned with the unfairness, stupidity, or insensitivity of the person who triggered our anger. These tendencies make many women focus almost exclusively on our anger behavior (worrying that we will do something we will later regret) and lose touch with the things that have caused us to feel pain. It keeps us much safer in terms of anger outbursts, but often turns our attention *away* from a situation that needs changing.

For these reasons, traditional "anger control" programs miss the mark with most women; they fail to take into consideration the fact that women balance many competing feelings and priorities when we feel we've been wronged. Most of us simultaneously consider ourselves as individuals *and* the relationship in which we feel our outrage or disgust or jealousy. We learn not to show our annoyance, at least not clearly. For some women, this learning is so thorough that we stop noticing it at all.

————

So the gender journey is one critical part of understanding how our anger has been shaped as women. But gender isn't the only factor that matters. What you need to know about anger in order to use it effectively also includes information about our evolution and an aware-ness of other cultural factors that play into our emotional lives. From the intricacies of the human brain that you share with all others on the planet, to the special influences of growing up in America here and now, to the unique details of your family and community, each strand has its place in weaving the tapestry of your own anger experience.

ANGER IN CONTEXT: FROM THE GLOBAL TO THE LOCAL

Anger Across the World: Our Common Human Heritage

One critical message that you need to incorporate in order to claim your anger advantage is that anger is natural and normal. It is not a bad emotion; *there are no bad emotions.* All emotions developed in our evolution as a species because they are helpful and necessary. Anger is not some by-product of your misguided upbringing or a character flaw. It is an essential part of being human. Acknowledging this reality can help to free you from anger myths and negative anger behaviors.

Regardless of culture or gender, human beings seem to get mad about similar kinds of things: being treated unfairly, or suffering an insult, a betrayal, or some other violation of one's boundaries. We call it different things, but we typically know it when we see it on people's faces or hear it in their tone. Paul Ekman's groundbreaking work on the cross-cultural facial recognition of emotion identifies anger as one of the six feelings that people in all cultures recognize, along with happiness, fear, sadness, surprise, and disgust. In fact, one recent study by interna-tional expert on culture and emotion Klaus Scherer and his research group of the University of Geneva in Switzerland shows that anger is the most recognizable of all the emotions across nine different cultures.

Evolutionary psychologists, such as Carroll Izard of the University of Delaware, believe that each emotion developed for a specific reason. Anger developed in the course of human evolution because it carries critical information between individuals about socially important interactions. Anger signals that something needs attention in a relationship between two people and, as such, serves an extremely important role in the give-and-take of everyday social behavior. In other words, anger helps us survive. Here, Margaret (58) talks about how her anger has helped her survive in both her work and love relationships.

> *When I'm angry, that causes me to make a change. And that's where I feel anger can be positive. If I get frustrated or angry with my business partners, then I think, "OK now, what's going on here and what can I do, and how can I prevent it from happening again?" So it causes me to move off dead center. I finally got angry enough to divorce my ex-husband. I realized that [the marriage] was not good for me . . . and I'm trying not to get myself into that position again. So, there are some aspects about getting angry that I feel are good.*

Margaret describes her anger as moving her *off dead center.* Dead center is the status quo, the norms that we are often so reluctant to disrupt. Yet when Margaret makes this shift, she experiences the life-sustaining and life-enhancing aspects of her anger, in sharp contrast to the stagnation that results for her when she fails to acknowledge and take action on her irritation.

According to Eddie Harmon-Jones and his neuropsychology colleagues of the University of Texas, all human beings have evolved with two basic types of brain activation patterns: one when we experience "withdrawal" emotions, such as fear and sadness, and a second pattern when we experience "approach" emotions, such as love and, yes, anger. This is important, because people have long mistakenly assumed that anger is a "withdrawal" emotion—that it keeps people apart or distances them from each other. But brain research shows that when people become angry, we are all equipped with a brain-based tendency to *engage others* in some kind of interaction (whether they actually do this or not). So biological evidence supports the idea that anger can actually help us stay connected with others and adjust social relations with those closest to us. Getting angry, like no other emotional experience, serves as a cue for us to engage with the people we care about, to resolve interpersonal problems with them, and to protect ourselves, all at the same time. Once we have followed anger's lead and explored our most important relationships, we may choose to stay in them or to leave—but the outcome isn't really the point. The point is that anger prompts us to explore our relationships more deeply. Our anger may then inform us that this relationship is workable or that it is not. Anger makes it possible for us to protect and defend the cherished relationships in our lives while keeping ourselves strong enough to participate in them and to make choices about them.

As we move away from universal aspects of anger, which are basically tied to our evolution and biology, what we *learn* is seen to play a dramatic role in our understanding of women's anger. Our cultural scripts and the ways in which we are socialized pose some specific challenges regarding anger from a woman's perspective. Understanding these influences is critical in discovering how and what you know about your own anger.

Closer to Home: Our Own Cultural Anger Legacy

Our own culture's unwritten anger guidelines did not just emerge out of nowhere. Knowingly or not, you have probably inherited a set of ideas about anger that are uniquely American. This is important, because it can be wonderfully freeing to understand that our everyday learning about anger is really out of date; an awkward set of baggage lugged along from the dusty attic of previous generations. These archaic views can certainly be unlearned, but *only if we recognize them,* allowing us to toss the old luggage into the Dumpster where it belongs and move ahead with new insights about anger's adaptive nature.

So how did we get into this difficult and ultimately dysfunctional position to begin with? Like many other stories, this tale of women's anger started once upon a time, in lands far away.

Picture for a moment the people from other parts of the world who initially came across the oceans, deserts, and mountains to be in this country. Historians and sociologists tell us that anger formed a part of their daily emotional diet. In general, anger was tolerated and freely expressed, and as long as the feeling did not lead to violent behavior, no judgment was passed and few restrictions applied.

Early emotional freedom in this country didn't last, however. Contrary to popular belief, we have *not* evolved into a more angry society, or even one that is more tolerant of anger. For at least a century past, people in this country have been characterized by a complicated ambivalence about anger that has singled out the need for *control.*

The rise of Victorian ethics in the home led to a focus on self-discipline, where any strong display of feeling by either men or women came to be seen as a sign of weak character. Quarreling between spouses and tantrums by children were portrayed as singularly dangerous conditions within the household, to be avoided at all costs. At the same time, the Industrial Revolution produced larger work groups, and management felt the need for control over their employees. Efforts to regiment the ranks first took aim merely on compliant behavior without demanding changes in feelings or attitudes. However, workplace sanctions against anger eventually grew to include the inhibition of the emotion itself. As a result, anger came to be seen as unprofessional.

The contemporary anger rules and regulations here in the United States have thus evolved into the following script—anger seems to be the *least* allowable emotion for girls and women. Men have their own taboos—don't be weak, don't cry, hide your shame, be tough, don't ask for help, and, whatever you do, never let yourself appear feminine. This script makes them squirm when they feel sadness or fear, but gives them a green light for anger (which may just be a green light for demonstrating aggressive problem-solving, not so much their *feelings*). Women's script allows them to show tender emotions like fear and sadness, but labels anger, or even stating a strong opinion, unfeminine.

Today, we continue our confused struggle with our American anger legacy, insisting on its ties to sin, moral failure, violence and aggression, selfishness, and a lack of femininity. Identifying it with all that we abhor, we continue to try to solve the violence problem by smothering anger, thinking that if we can convince ourselves we're not angry, we won't do things we'll later regret. We find ourselves bound on all sides by social conventions that expect perfection: we must *achieve* without appearing strident or rigid. We must keep our families intact without appearing hard. We expect ourselves to function creatively without the benefit of anger. We operate under the mistaken notion that our *disagreement* needs to remain hidden or snuffed out altogether if we are to do the things that matter to us. Though this folklore keeps us in line with our great-grandmothers' behavior, it forces us to miss out on so much that we have to offer ourselves and the modern world.

At age 40, Muriel speaks about her own struggle with the baggage she has brought with her over four decades of life.

> *I feel like I need to unlearn all the things that my parents taught me. I'm embarrassed to even bring this up but I've been in situations where I've been afraid and I'll see a man coming and he looks scary, but I don't want to reach out and lock the door because he might see me and be offended that I think he's a bad guy. I'm unlearning that, "Yes sir, Yes ma'am," making everybody feel good. I need to figure out what I want.*

Muriel shows us how our cultural system disempowers women in their work and personal relationships, as they must constantly disguise the parts of themselves that oppose, direct, manage, lead, or even keep themselves safe. Happily, Muriel is beginning to clean up her anger attic, leaving old patterns behind and embracing new feelings of opposition that are more grounded in her own sense of self.

In Your Own Backyard:
Examining Your Personal Anger Archives

Did you grow up rich, poor, or middle class? Has that changed? Did you grow up in the countryside, the suburbs, or in the city? Are you multiracial, white, black, Asian, Latina, Native American? Where did you go to school? Do you have the same religious beliefs now that your family had when you were a little girl? How are you the same or different from the family you grew up in? Why are we asking you all these questions?

We're asking because it isn't *all* about gender. We want to get you thinking about the anger messages you grew up with that are different from, but intertwined with, the gender role rules you have also learned. While gender is of key importance in understanding how our anger experience and expression have been shaped, other elements are powerful influences as well.

You have to be able to tease out the anger rules you grew up with in order to bend or break those rules and, ultimately, to create new guidelines for yourself. As one of our favorite writers notes, you can't think outside the box until you know what's in the box (Patton, 2002). Each of us has a box containing the archives of all our anger learning; we have files marked gender, but many others labeled with different aspects of our identities. And there may be papers in there that need to be shredded in order for us to access our anger advantage. But we'll never know unless we look.

Throughout the remainder of this book, you'll get a chance not just to look, but to re-evaluate, and ultimately change, if you so choose, how you approach your anger in many different settings. While we'll explore the contexts of family, love relationships, friendships, and work in detail later on, we want to give you a head start in considering these issues.

So let's start with some early family memories. What was it like to be you at the age of three? At seven? Who was there with you? How did people relate to one another? How safe was it for you to be a small child and express yourself openly? What did mom or dad or other family members do with their anger? Familial anger patterns form the most significant foundation for how we understand and experience anger. In hundreds of everyday interactions, we learn how and when to express our anger, and with whom, and if we should express it at all. We learn if we should yell and throw tantrums, if we should get whiney to get what we want, or if we should put up and shut up. We learn that our brothers and dads might express anger differently from mom or our sisters, aunts, and grandmothers. Kids are very keen observers of their parents' behavior; as little girls we were often monitoring when our parents weren't aware of it. The way our parents handled anger between themselves did not go unnoticed. But being children, as young girls we probably had few choices and little control over what happened at home; we just took it in and made it a part of ourselves.

To illustrate this process of learning across the generations, listen to how Nadine, a 40-year-old mother of two, describes the household in which she was raised.

> *When my mom would get mad, she'd throw things at my dad, and holler and scream. And you know, she'd hit him. She'd get mad at us for doing something, just for no reason. She was the disciplinarian. She'd line us up with the stick. We got it, but the last one got it the worst.*

As an adult, Nadine has become involved with and struggled to leave a highly abusive man. She's aware that her two daughters have been affected.

> *I've always tried to protect the kids from him. I took most of the brunt of it, but you know they still watched me. You know they heard.*

One of Nadine's two daughters, now age 19, says:

> *Sometimes when you're angry you say mean things that you wish you didn't say; it kind of backfires. Me and my sister probably do the same thing with anger. We sometimes just react. Like I'll explode.*

In this family, we can see the links in anger socialization from grandmother to mother to daughters. Your family may or may not have shown anger as aggressively as Nadine's, but the transmission of ideas and ways of reacting to anger in *your* family were surely handed down just as readily.

Our own religious background is another thing we each need to think about. Many women report that faith empowers and offers support, structure, and a set of ideas on which to base major decisions—without the added burden of guilt and self-recrimination that comes with some religious activities and backgrounds. However, for other women, religious training brings a particular emphasis on submerging anger, keeping it hidden, feeling shame about it, or attempting to avoid oppositional feelings altogether. For example, Bernadette, a 49-year-old divorced mother of three, speaks about how Catholicism and anger have intertwined over her lifetime.

> *Growing up, you didn't show anger. Anger wasn't allowed, it was like a sin. It would be a great disrespect to show anger to your parents. I also remember at my first communion, we were all dressed up in these beautiful dresses, and I was sitting in the pews playing with my dress—I thought I was the bees knees—and the principal of the Catholic school came up behind me, pushed my dress down, and said, "Don't think you're so special!" I was bewildered then, but later I was angry. But you couldn't show it. I also think back to the annulment of my marriage. I felt like I was an outcast from the church, being divorced. I didn't feel any acceptance from the church being a single parent, and I was really angry; they were saying, "Be THIS way" and I was THAT way. The anger I feel now is that I have a daughter who may be lesbian and she's afraid of coming out to the rest of the family because of the religious bigotry. I'm not really in the church now, but you're never really out of it.*

Bernadette shows how some difficult aspects of her religious upbringing are still strongly impacting her in the present. As with other childhood experiences, girls often have few choices in their exposure to religious training, but as adults, we can be more thoughtful about these influences. So ask yourself, how does religion play into your own anger experiences today? We're certainly not antireligious; however, we encourage a careful examination of your own religious upbringing, to consider what aspects of this training contribute to negative or unhelpful experiences with anger. This is always your call, not ours, and you will be able to use many of the ideas in this book without shifting your religious perspectives at all. You may wish to compare each concept or exercise we present with the important values and doctrines of your faith. Then you can decide which pieces of our model will work for you. If exploring your early religious messages leads you to question your faith, this may be one of the toughest processes you face as you consider working with your anger in a new way. Such changes may be challenging, but if you decide that a new perspective is where you want to go, stay true to your inner voice. Seek out others who are supportive and consider the wide range of spiritual options available in our country, where we have the right to religious freedom. There is much to choose from.

Schools are another prime domain for learning anger conventions. Childhood and adolescence are times of intense social learning for us, and our schools formed little microcosms of the outside world. Although rarely a part of the formal curriculum, a big part of our job in school was to learn to deal with others. As young girls, we practiced daily at school, evaluating our peers and being evaluated by them, forming connections with teachers, friends, and enemies, and learning the give-and-take of relationships. Inside these interactions, we learned what happens when we let our angry feelings show or when we shared them with other people. We also learned what social roles are acceptable and noticeable (e.g., Barbie doll, good student) and which ones are unacceptable or invisible (e.g., slut, tough chick, fat girl). If you can recall images of these roles from your own school life, you no doubt can recognize how these caricatures could put tremendous pressure on your developing sense of self. We often desperately want to be accepted and admired, and at the same time wish to avoid those images that are not so savory in our social lives. We feel the need to fit ourselves into some pleasing category while avoiding all those behaviors that could cause us embarrassment—and getting angry or showing opposition is likely to be on the list of don'ts.

The girls in our school study made it clear that when they get angry, they expect to be shamed or ridiculed by teachers and boys in particular. They also expect to have to play games with each other when someone is angry and for angry girls to pull away from their friends and parents. We believe that these kinds of expectations and roles translate into habits and ways of thinking that follow us into adulthood. Think about the pattern reported by the girls in our study: withdrawing, crying, getting quiet and expecting a friend to ask why. These behaviors follow stereotypical gender expectations for women and likely lead to depression, anxiety, and feelings of powerlessness in adulthood. In other words, by learning to take anger away to deal with it in isolation, girls may be preparing themselves for a pattern of avoiding conflict with important others, and also playing games that force them to be indirect with their feelings, rather than confident, deliberate, and open.

Other archival anger experiences also come from belonging to a particular cultural group or having a particular income level or living in a particular area of the country. As Lyn Mikel Brown of Colby College notes, women and girls of color, from lower socioeconomic backgrounds, or who live in rural communities in our country, often report different experiences and different sets of rules for anger within their own subcultures.

For example, we have conducted a number of focus groups with African-American, Arab Middle-Eastern, and Hispanic women to explore some of these issues. Each cultural group reports variations of anger conventions; some allowing for more anger expression than the perceived standard for white women, some even less. All of these women report anger at racism and prejudice. Our work is supported by other recent studies, such as that of Fields and her colleagues at the University of Tennessee, who conducted a study of African-American women in the southern United States. These women talk explicitly about having lived through school desegregation in the '60s and being treated differently by their suburban teachers. They speak about blatant racism on the job, being paid less than their white counterparts, and being stereotyped into less prestigious work roles because of the color of their skin. As a result of this kind of treatment by whites, these women learn to mistrust Caucasians in general. Alongside this mistrust, however, many of the women in this study describe trying to hide their anger when they feel powerless to make changes, especially at work. Lots of these immobilizing situations involve class race-related exploitation or harassment.

It makes me angry when people try to run over my family. Like they're upper class and come in and try to make my family look bad. I don't like it. We're a nice, loving, kind family.
            —Judy (middle-aged African American)

How does this kind of experience influence our overall anger style? When we must constantly hide our true feelings in order to survive an oppressive environment, those feelings don't simply go away. They remain active, though silenced, contributing to muffled rage or physical distress. Non-white, non-middle-class, and rural women remain poignantly aware of the middle-class white ideals. Many of these women report developing the ability to move in and out of different cultural roles, adjusting their expression of anger accordingly. In our current research, we continue to interview and survey women from many walks of life and from a diversity of backgrounds. In this way, we hope to be able to bring out stories that apply to all kinds of women, including you. In upcoming chapters, we present practical questions, quizzes, and other experiential exercises to help you identify the roots of your own anger patterns. You'll know your anger archives inside and out.

PUTTING IT ALL TOGETHER: THE ANGER ADVANTAGE MODEL

Anger myths, the gendered development of anger, the contexts of anger; how does all this learning and unlearning come together? Following the leads and insights of our studies, we have worked hard to synthesize the critical elements of women's anger experience into a coherent model. Our efforts are grounded in the poignant, inspiring, and sometimes brutally honest words of the girls and women we have interviewed and surveyed, as well as in our ongoing academic scholarship and clinical practices.

The model is important because it is, to our knowledge, the first and only framework that puts women's adaptive anger center stage and gives it the credit it deserves. The model pulls everything together in a way that illuminates the potent benefits of anger, including actual skills to help you obtain its strengths. It additionally gives you a systematic way to identify when you get off track and how to find your way back to the positive potentials of claiming your anger advantage.

The Anger Advantage

SELF-AWARENESS   ENERGY FOR POSITIVE CHANGE   SELF-DEFINITION

Balanced and Rewarding Relationships with Friends,
Family, Romantic Partners, and Coworkers

Anger Consciousness	Constructive Anger Talk	Listening	Think Tank
"I know what my anger feels like" "I know my anger archives" "My anger helps me know who I am"	"I feel comfortable expressing my anger" "I know how and when to choose to express my anger"	"I can hear and tolerate others' anger expression" "I know hearing you doesn't mean I have to agree with you"	"Let me hold my anger up to look at; then I'll decide what I need to do"

Adaptive Anger Skills

Positive Messages, Models & Choices

What We
Learn about Anger
•Family Emotional Models
•Values and Religious Teachings
•Gender Role Socialization
•Friendship and Romantic Experiences
•Influences from Our Cultures
•Our Own Choices
about Anger

Negative Messages, Models & Choices

Anger Diversions

Externalization	Segmentation	Internalization	Containment
"My anger doesn't allow me to be a good person, so I'll be a bad person" "My anger is your fault"	"I can't ever let myself feel angry" "I don't have anger"	"Conflict is all my fault." "I have to disown part of me to be liked by you"	"If I hold it in, it will blow over" "I can't show my anger when I feel it."

Symptoms of Anger Diversion

Low Self-esteem, Depression, Eating/Drinking/Substance Use Problems,
Anger in the Body: Headache, Chronic Stomach Trouble,
Sexual Difficulties, Chronic Pain and Fatigue

The model has a base in *what we learn* (development, context) *and the choices we make* about anger expression and experience. In its most bare-bones formulation, if we learn negative roles and rules (myths), we are likely to suffer the consequences in the form of multiple personal, professional, and physical difficulties. If we learn positive roles and rules, we are more likely to access the advantages of anger— an increased sense of who we are and what we want, better interpersonal relationships, physical health benefits, and enhanced professional effectiveness. So what we each bring in terms of learned ideas and actions is of major importance.

However, the role of *choice* is at least, if not more, essential. As young girls, our options were very limited. This is always true. Little kids don't choose when or where we are born; we don't choose our families, neighborhoods, and schools. We have very little true power or influence in our most formative years. But today, as adult women, we *do* have choices. We can choose to become informed and self-aware about our anger. We can choose to explore our family and cultural expectations and *decide now* if we want to discard them, modify them, or keep them. We can choose to learn new ways of taking action on our own behalf by attending to our anger. We can do it a little or we can do it a lot. It's up to us. It's up to you.

Our model also details what we call "anger diversions" and four adaptive anger skills. Anger diversion is problematic anger behavior that's linked to our acceptance of anger myths. In the next chapter of this book, we'll examine the complexity of anger diversion and the four main forms that it takes. In later chapters, we'll also track anger diversion across the different contexts of our lives: family, love relationships, friendships, and work.

The four adaptive anger skills noted in the model form the heart and soul of anger's advantages. We want to introduce these skills to you right away, so you can begin to explore them for yourself.

1. **Anger Consciousness: dive into the depths of your anger and learn about what's there.** You'll learn how to use your anger to become more conscious about who you are and what you like, want, and need.

2. **Constructive Anger Talk: express your anger consciously and powerfully.** You'll explore and learn new types of anger expression to find what works best for you in different situations.
3. **Listening: paying attention to your loved ones' anger.** You'll learn how to really hear people's feelings without absorbing unnecessary self-reproach or feeling like you have to agree.
4. **Think Tank: holding your anger up front while you decide what you want to do.** You'll learn how to keep your anger alive when you can't act on it the very moment it arises, how to keep its vital information with you to make decisions and take action when the time is right, without submerging it or spewing it irresponsibly.

Using these four skills day in and day out in your personal and professional relationships will lead to all the benefits of anger's advantage. These skills are your guide to identifying anger rules, breaking those rules, and then rewriting your own anger rules to help you achieve your unique desires and potentials. We'll talk about how to use these skills throughout the rest of the book, bringing them to bear on each major context of your life. So let's go!

GETTING STARTED WITH ANGER CONSCIOUSNESS

You'll notice that the first adaptive anger skill in our model is anger consciousness. Developing a deep awareness of your own anger is important; to know exactly what it feels like in your body when it comes; to know your past triggers and current hot spots as legitimate guides to significant issues that are asking for your attention. The next two exercises will help you begin to know your angry self better.

Know Me, Know My Anger

One step in developing your anger profile is to assess how much of it you currently have. However, keep in mind that testing people's levels of *anger proneness* poses a number of challenges. First, everyone gets angry and most of us get angry fairly often (e.g., at least mildly irritated more than once a week according to James Averill, a prominent emotion researcher). Therefore, it would be very difficult to diagnose some people as *angry* people and others as *non-angry* people. Also, some people are more aware than others of their emotional states. For example, Barbara, a 39-year-old freelance painter and sculptor, experiences a painful divorce after discovering her husband of 14 years is having an extramarital affair with her former neighbor. Barbara is extremely angry, but working hard not to notice or give credence to her anger because she believes it to be a waste of her time and energy. Therefore, when she takes an anger test, she answers questions in such a way that she receives a very low anger score. Her therapist and her sister express surprise at Barbara's low anger score, even though lots of other people in her life see Barbara as serene, calm, and slow to anger. Her sister says, "Personally I think she's about to blow on the inside. I really think she would kill the man with her bare hands if she thought she could get away with murder."

Since it's easy for some of us to convince ourselves we're not angry because we don't run around killing people, we get a more accurate picture of overall anger when we use multiple sources of information. For example, when you *look at both your own perceptions of your anger and the perceptions of someone you trust and love,* you discover those areas in which you have anger blind spots and need further exploration. This quiz is not a standardized test, but is loosely based on several widely used instruments in psychological research. Answer the questions as honestly as you can to get a rough idea of how much anger you tend to carry around with you.

Anger Inventory

Directions: Read each statement and, on a separate sheet of paper, *rate each from 1 (never; not at all) to 5 (all the time; very much) as it applies to you. On your paper, write answers to the open-ended questions following items five, ten, and thirty. Then, have someone who knows you very well answer the questions about you. Ask them to be very honest in their ratings. Instructions for scoring are at the end.*

Right now, I feel . . .	Not at all (never)			Very much (all the time)	
1. annoyed	1	2	3	4	5
2. like screaming	1	2	3	4	5
3. frustrated	1	2	3	4	5
4. like I'd like to tell someone off	1	2	3	4	5
5. like I could throw things	1	2	3	4	5

Right now, I'm most upset about _____

_____

These things have bothered me for (how long) _____

_____

Most of the time, I feel . . .					
6. frustrated	1	2	3	4	5
7. annoyed	1	2	3	4	5
8. like screaming	1	2	3	4	5
9. like I'd like to tell someone off	1	2	3	4	5
10. like I could throw things	1	2	3	4	5

Most of the time, I'm upset about _____

_____

This has been an issue for me for (how long) _____

_____

11. I'm angry because I don't feel respected by someone in my life.	1	2	3	4	5
12. I'm angry at other drivers on the road.	1	2	3	4	5

Right now, I feel . . .	Not at all (never)			Very much (all the time)	

13. I hate it when I work hard and then
get no credit.   1   2   3   4   5
14. I feel like I'm always having to make up
for other people's laziness.   1   2   3   4   5
15. It seems like I have more than my share
of hassles in a given day.   1   2   3   4   5
16. I struggle more than most people with
worries like money.   1   2   3   4   5
17. I'm angry because I've been betrayed
by someone in my life.   1   2   3   4   5
18. I have more than my fair share of
medical/health problems.   1   2   3   4   5
19. I have to work very hard to get
time to myself.   1   2   3   4   5
20. At times, I feel I've gotten cheated
in my life.   1   2   3   4   5
21. I often disagree with people.   1   2   3   4   5
22. I feel jealous.   1   2   3   4   5

In the past week, I have experienced the following:

23. felt angry   1   2   3   4   5
24. worried that I would just "lose it"
with someone   1   2   3   4   5
25. been angry about feeling physical
pain or discomfort   1   2   3   4   5
26. felt like I was being blocked from doing
something I wanted to do   1   2   3   4   5
27. been so upset I've had a headache
or stomachache   1   2   3   4   5
28. been so upset my heart
has raced   1   2   3   4   5

29. been so angry my muscles have

    tightened   I   2   3   4   5

30. felt insulted   I   2   3   4   5

Other physical, mental, or emotional aspects of my anger include_____

_____

Scoring: You will get two separate scores from this quiz: one is a tally of your responses and the other is a tally from your friend's/partner's ratings. You each need to do the same thing.

- *First, add up* your *numbers and divide the sum by 30.*
- *This is* your *average self-rating. If your average self-rating is four or five, you probably perceive yourself to be angry a lot of the time or to have a pretty high level of overall anger. If your average self-rating is three or less, you probably perceive yourself as having a low to moderate amount of overall anger.*
- *Next, have your friend or partner add up her/his numbers (her/his ratings of you) and divide the sum by 30.*
- *If your friend/partner's average rating for you is four or five, that person probably perceives you to be angry a lot of the time or to have a pretty high level of overall anger. If your friend/partner's ratings for you are three or less, that person probably perceives you as having a low to moderate amount of overall anger.*
- *Use your answers to the open-ended questions to shed light on your overall self-rating and your friend/partner's ratings of you. Your written answers will help you to determine how chronic versus occasional these angry feelings have been.*

As a follow-up to this exercise, ask yourself: (1) Are there any surprises here? (2) How different are my self-perceptions from my friend/partner's perceptions of me? (3) How do I explain the difference between my self-perceptions and my friend/partner's perceptions of me? Keep in mind that whatever you learned about yourself in this process represents a step forward in your anger consciousness. You're on your way!

Relaxing into Your Anger

This second exercise is a totally different approach to developing your anger consciousness from the inventory you just took. The basis for this method of raising your anger awareness lies in the traditions of meditation and works by allowing you to attain a deep state of relaxation. In such a state, feelings, meanings, and experiences that we don't give ourselves time to pay attention to often surface. The wording of this meditative exercise is tailored to help your mind gently access emotional awareness.

For best results, *read the following script aloud, slowly, into a tape recorder* so that you can listen to it later. Choose a time when you have lots of privacy at home. Sit in a comfortable chair or lie on the bed or floor. Remember, if you record this script, avoid listening to it while in the car. The kind of deep relaxation it encourages can make it difficult to drive safely.

Become very still and quiet. Give yourself plenty of time to become perfectly comfortable and to notice your breathing. Close your eyes or simply focus on a spot on the ceiling or the wall. Just become very aware of your breathing and spend a few minutes listening to it, paying attention to the rhythm of your inhaling and exhaling and the gentle feelings of relaxation that begin to wash over you. Take very deep breaths that move from the top of your head to the tips of your toes. Enjoy the way those deep, deep breaths fill every part of your body with oxygen and make you feel even more and more warm and content. Enjoy the warmth that spreads throughout your body, into every muscle and tendon, into both arms and both legs, into your feet and each of your toes, into your hands and each of your fingers. Just notice how nice it feels to enjoy the warm spreading of relaxation into your neck and shoulders and the way your back responds by softening and letting you be perfectly comfortable where you are. As you enjoy feeling warm and tingly and soft and heavy and loose . . . you probably notice thoughts rising to the surface of your consciousness

. . . and that it feels perfectly okay to let these thoughts come and go and wash over you as you continue to relax more and more deeply and profoundly. You let yourself glide and float around and through the thoughts as they help you to clear the way to notice what is important to you at this moment. Important things come easily to you as you breathe in the deep relaxation and exhale the cleansing breaths, in and out, in and out . . . the important parts of you become clearer and clearer and easier to see as you notice yourself focusing without intending to focus at all on the things that you need to know at this moment in time . . . the answers to the questions about your feelings. And these questions come easily and effortlessly to you. (1) What change do you want right now? (2) What do you need to help you solve the problem that you want so much to solve right now? (3) What are the feelings that wait to be noticed and given attention? (4) How can you save all the important feelings and give yourself the respect and attention that you need right now? Let the questions swirl around or float or simply fade away or remain there in your mind for as long as they need, or as little as they need. Continue to relax and enjoy the comfort and warmth of this place you find whenever you need to find it and wherever you need to wander inside to look and listen for signs of feelings that deserve your attention . . . and when you become ready to fully awaken, you find yourself reorienting to the surface under you . . . noticing that you are becoming a little more alert to the sounds around you . . . continuing to breathe deeply in and out . . . opening your eyes and looking around the room . . . five, four, three, two, one . . . feeling refreshed and ready to continue your day . . . or feeling ready to continue resting or sleeping (if you prefer).

What did you notice during that exercise (besides the fact that you probably need more relaxation)? What thoughts and feelings rose to the surface of your awareness? If you don't recall any, that's perfectly okay. Sometimes the important realizations happen later in the day, or in a dream you have tonight or next week . . . but rest assured that the answers to the questions you need live there with you, waiting for a good time to be noticed. Frustration, resentment, hurt, jealousy, outrage, indignation, and despair all may be feelings that need your attention, feelings you've lived with for a long time without really noticing. Give yourself all the time and space you need to reconnect with your internal experiences and the meanings they have for you.

REPRISE

Our hope is to offer you a constructive model for anger experience and expression, with both techniques for raising your anger awareness and concrete skills to take away and use whenever you recognize the need. This book is our way of helping you to use your anger effectively to bring about your own personal changes and to become empowered by your newfound abilities to make choices. And the more happy-with-their-anger, motivated, clear-sighted, energized women there are out there, the better. Our dream is that one by one, or through more collective action, anger's advantages will better the lives of women everywhere.

Once again, let's see what Marcy, the writer you met at the beginning of this chapter, has to say on the joys of expressing her anger with her dad:

> *My father is so proud of himself that he can cry, because he was raised in a generation when men weren't allowed to express emotions—and he can cry on demand. So when I confronted him about leaving me out of his autobiography, he started to cry. And I listened to that for a little while, and then I realized, "Oh well, here we go, he's turning this around to be all about him." And I just said to him, "You know, I didn't call to listen to you cry. I'm hanging up." And that felt great. I didn't even feel guilty.*

TWO

Me, Angry?

Disarming Diversion

For several years, I didn't know I was angry. I knew I was sad. I knew I felt worthless and unattractive and dumb. But I had no idea I was really furious with all those teachers and clergy who taught me to judge myself according to some pretty hollow but impossible standards and to hate myself for being female.

At 17, 18, 19, and 20, I thought I was fatter than I should be, more sensitive than I should be, and slow in general. I thought that even though my own thoughts seemed deep and meaningful to me, I must be dumb in all the areas that really mattered. Math, computer science, algebra . . . these were classes I did terribly in, and so I assumed it was because something was wrong with me. I never once considered that my male teachers could be treating me differently from how they treated the boys around me or that they could maybe even expect me to fail—or want me to fail, just a little bit. I remember that one teacher would read proverbs from the Bible that had to do with how women were a nuisance and should be kept in their place by men or how parents should beat their children. Then, he would start the lesson of the day. I don't remember feeling mad about this at the time. I just remember kind of going numb.

I had all the wrong thoughts at this point in my life. I was too dependent, too sinful, too sad, too serious—always too this or too that. I assumed that it was because I was at some kind *of disadvantage in my family or in myself. I was so vulnerable to all the bad things that happened to me in relationships too because I assumed I was behind in all the ways that mattered. I would think about how I desperately needed a boyfriend, because I felt that if I didn't have a boyfriend now I would always be alone. And alone—single—meant worthless. Getting married was the only way to be a worthwhile girl or woman.*

I was in my middle 20s, in college, before some of my sadness and anxiety began to melt away, leaving me to realize that I was so, so, angry . . . and that I had been angry for a very long time. I had professors who talked to me, who taught as if it was me they were talking to, not just the males in the room. Then something old that I had been wearing began to crumble and fall to the ground. Not only in the realm of academics and professional growth, but in the love realm too. Many of the smart, successful women I started to meet and learn from were single and happy. Some of them had relationships, and they expected things from their partners. They didn't just feel like they were lucky to be with someone. They had rights, needs, feelings. It was such an incredible awakening to watch these women. My new friends taught me that my style of thinking was every bit as worthwhile as the next person's. I started to excel in all kinds of ways. But with the growth came the awareness that I had so much rage inside for the lost years—the years I spent trying to hold myself back. The years I spent not being able to trust my instincts to tell me what was really going on.

I really started looking back at things—like my early boyfriend experiences, and how I had been emotionally and even physically abused in some of them. I remembered how the church and community indirectly condoned male violence toward women—and how no one seemed to notice my increasing shyness, withdrawal, and submissive behavior; my decreasing focus on creative pursuits. I was doing a good job at learning my role. No one cared to tell me that I had potential, rights, and a self that deserved respect. I remembered the tears and guilt and shame and incredible anxiety and panic—and I got really angry about being cheated and lied to for so long.

Somehow in the anger I discovered who I was. I put back some responsibility on those people who taught me to discredit myself (no matter how well-intentioned their efforts), and I began to see myself as more powerful and more capable than ever before. It became a loss of years and something to be angry about, rather than a bunch of personal flaws of mine. I could no longer tolerate things I had once thought were normal, like being ignored and belittled in my relationships; being expected to be submissive and docile and agreeable and sweet. I could suddenly see the value in my way of thinking and relating to the world. I could see the value in who I was. The me that was not always sweet, but sometimes fiercely opinionated. The me that was passionate about my work and that of others. The me that got angry. And that changed everything.

—Stephanie (30)

Does Stephanie's story sound at all like yours? In her personal journal, she describes a girlhood history of *not knowing* she was angry, feeling other emotions instead; emotions that cause her to blame herself for her problems and to feel inferior. Not knowing—not having conscious access to her righteous indignation—left her weak and less of an authority in her own life. Stephanie's depression comes from having to spend her creative energy hammering herself down, forcing herself to keep quiet and let important things go unnoticed and unnamed. The burst of growth she experienced in her 20s happened *because* she found the locked-up energy of her outrage, set it free, and stepped into the authority of her anger. Stephanie's anger tells her so many important things about who she is, what she wants, how she needs to be treated, and how she must treat herself. Can anger do all these things for you?

We hope this chapter will help you bring your anger out of hiding and prepare you to do something like Stephanie has done. But to get there, you first need to find the escape routes that have taken you away from your anger, the ones that have led you to neglect parts of yourself that scared you or seemed like a turnoff to other people. Why do we need to look for these routes? For most of us, running away from anger is so thoroughly learned that we barely know we're doing it. Our anger avoidance is almost invisible; a flash seen out of the corner of our eye—blink and it's gone. Anger escape routes are so well hidden and automatic that we have to make ourselves really slow down to find these well-camouflaged pathways. If we can't find our anger because it has run down a rabbit hole (often one we made for it long ago), we can't bring it out and use it to improve our relationships and give us the inspiration for new endeavors.

How do you escape your anger? Knowing the answer moves you closer to *anger consciousness*. And anger consciousness is a change in understanding and viewpoint, an adoption of a different approach and way of looking at the whole issue of anger. Anger consciousness doesn't just cause you to think differently; it *feels* different too. Your mind opens to what is going on in your relationship life, and your body gives you signals about what to do. We'll look at how and why. Now we look at some basic emotional escape routes and then follow them back to the source, identifying four ways to reconnect and *grow through anger*.

To say that some women hold anger in while others let it fly is too simple. Our research suggests that some of us hide our anger so effectively we forget it's there, while others of us keep tight-lipped in the presence of people we're angry with, but then really spew around folks who have little to do with why we're mad in the first place. Still others get a headache if they consider telling it like it is to close friends or family members. We may eat too much or exercise too much; not eat enough or exercise too little. We get overinvolved with work or church. We sometimes do one thing with coworkers, but something else at home or with our kids. There are many ways of holding anger inside and more than one way of moving it out into the open. Anger responses are complicated and they vary, depending on who we're peeved with, how entitled we feel to be angry, and our beliefs about anger in general.

There are also countless ways we use our anger to help us achieve important things like Stephanie used hers to renovate her self-esteem.

Lots of us talk about anger in our relationships, listen to its messages in our work and home lives, and notice positive changes happening as a result. However, there are also lots of ways in which we minimize our effectiveness by cutting off our anger consciousness. When we avoid talking about or thinking about our anger, we're usually *diverting* it, or bypassing our awareness of it in some way. To *divert* is to redirect something, to move it off its original path, to reroute it, so that it moves in another direction besides the one on which it was initially set. To divert anger is to move the emotion away from its primary course, the course on which it was initially and fundamentally traveling, and redirect it to another target or deflect awareness or consideration away from it.

Evidence also shows women may be more apt to divert their attention away from their true feelings when those feelings involve anger. In Cheryl Rusting and Susan Nolen-Hoeksema's recent investigation at the University of Michigan, women were more likely to try and distract themselves when they felt angry (as compared to other kinds of moods) rather than focus on the situation making them angry. As women, we're especially primed to think of our anger as a liability rather than an asset—because of our conditioning to be nice girls. Therefore, it's no wonder we insult ourselves (as witch, bitch, hag, or nag) when we're most angry.

> *Blind with rage.*
> *So mad I couldn't see straight.*
> *Beginning to see red.*

These phrases are common ways we describe ourselves when we are angry, and they seem to come from common but faulty thinking about what anger does to our abilities to think, reason, and solve problems, especially for women. And language shapes our experience, causing us to flee from feelings we see as pointless or hazardous.

Anger naturally comes with an agenda—a desire to right a wrong, aggress against someone who we perceive as hurting or threatening us, or make our needs and motives known to someone in a way that will change the current proceedings in a relationship. When we divert anger, we move our feelings away from their intrinsic, directional goals and force them onto some other, less natural course. We take something spontaneous and reroute it, so that it aims not at its original target, but at ourselves, at other non-target persons, or splinters into fragments of unclaimed discomfort that we're no longer able to identify or use with conscious, deliberate intention. We lose the value of our anger. In addition to lost opportunities for relationship change, we lose access to the creative problem-solving (though solving problems can be painful) and the specific kinds of focus that anger or irritation or frustration bring. When we buy into the popular falsehood that anger is a problem, we treat it as such, losing its meaning and value in our lives.

FLEEING THE SCENE: ANGER DIVERSION IN WOMEN

Through our clinical work and research with women of all ages and from all walks of life, as well as through our own personal experiences, we can identify at least four basic *diversions* or strategies by which we as women emotionally disappear from the scenes of our most intense feelings and avoid knowing about and acting consciously on our anger. These diversions protect us from some of the discomfort that goes with being angry, but they also keep us from being able to use our anger to effect change. Each serves a purpose, but each has a cost.

Mind Over Madness: Containment

> Sex with my partner really stinks lately. I notice that I totally shut down when he wants to get romantic. I can go through the motions and, if he's really into it, he won't even notice I'm not. I used to think that if you deny a guy sex, then you'd really lost him. So, I usually go along with it even though I'm dead inside. He enjoys himself while I try not to just hate him for not noticing that there's something I want to deal with here.
>
> —Madeline (39)

"I'm just going to go about my business as if nothing has happened," you think to yourself. Sometimes women use what we refer to as "containment," or keeping an anger response hidden inside themselves, even though they're pretty aware they're doing it. Containment is the collection of physiological responses that are necessary to allow for storage of anger; it's like physically pushing the feeling down. It takes forms like "swallowing my tears," or "biting my tongue." Women tell us that they often force down a feeling with sheer willpower. They fight the hot, angry tears or urges to defend themselves by physically exerting control over them, biting down on the words and sounds and outrage: putting it somewhere besides in public view.

Consider Barb (41), who teaches high school history in the same school her 16-year-old daughter attends. She takes her work seriously and grades students' essays on both content and grammar. When she returns the carefully graded essays to her class, she contends with attitudes of disappointment among the students who receive lower grades. On one afternoon, she returns student essays to receive a bombardment of angry student reactions, most blaming her for not telling them they needed to write in complete sentences. One student yells, "This is not an English class. Why should we have to get graded on our writing?" This student goes on to say to Barb, "No wonder your daughter is weird. You're so picky." Barb is angry, but handles this situation by maintaining a calm demeanor. She laughs the students' comments off, thinking, "If I show how I feel, I've lost the upper hand here." She bites down hard and finishes her day, wishing she could scream. Barb knows that her male colleagues demand the same attention to detail, but rarely get the protest and criticism she does. Later that evening, on the phone, as she tells a friend about the incident, her whole body shudders, she becomes sweaty, and feels her breathing become shallow.

Women who contain anger often know they're holding back part of themselves. Women report feelings like heat rushing through their bodies, chest tightness, shallow breathing, sweaty palms, waves of nausea, and diminished sexual desire and painful intercourse.

I get red. My heart starts beating fast. My stomach feels

empty. I grit my teeth. I feel like my nerves are just jumping around.

—Lynette (40)

Sometimes women talk about feeling nervous or anxious when they're angry—and these responses often peak during containment. Listen in on Mandy (27), Denise (53), and Bev (49) talking about what happens in their bodies when they're angry.

> *Bev: I will feel my heart pounding. If I get really angry or something that's the thing I notice the most—like your heart is bursting out of your chest like you see in those movies [makes the gesture of heart pounding through blouse].*

> *Denise: That's just how I react to it. My stomach tightens up and I probably create excess acid because I know that's frequently when I break out the Tums. And I think maybe I'm kind of tensing all over.*

> *Mandy: I don't notice myself feel—apparently because I'm so angry at the time. But I get real stiff shoulders afterward, especially if it's more of a personal/home type situation. But it's more of an aftereffect.*

In another interview, Ellen (39) talks about how her body responded when she contained anger.

> *I got hives. Big time. And people knew I was angry when I didn't speak. When I clammed up. And then the hives come out. They were three-dimensional. When I broke out in hives, I used to hold in a lot of anger. I don't do that anymore. I'm more direct with my anger now.*

We contain anger in order to hide it when we feel afraid to bring it out into the open. Sometimes that fear is quite valid. Fearing that we'll lose our jobs or that someone will retaliate is a good reason for containing anger in the moment. However, women often report being so good at containment that it's hard for them to even tell a trusted friend just how bad it is for them in their work, love, or family relationships. They stay perpetually furious at being devalued and keep the lid sealed shut around the pain, using up tremendous energy reserves in the process.

Containment is also related to some negative health and relationship situations for women. It's no small task to conceal years of anger behind a face that looks polite or sweet. The toll this storage takes is documented in a number of clinical studies showing patterns of problems like depression (Thomas & Atakan, 1993), breast cancer (Greer & Morris, 1975), and overall poorer health (Thomas & Williams, 1991) for women who contain anger rather than express it directly. Women are more likely than men to express their anger through physical illness (Haynes et al; 1978) rather than openly discussing it. Research also documents the links between suppressed or contained anger and other medical conditions, in both women *and* men. For example, a 1993 report describes irritable bowel syndrome, a disorder that involves abdominal cramping, diarrhea, and other gastrointestinal symptoms, as related to unassertiveness in expressing feelings (Nyhlin, Ford, Eastwood, Smith, Nicol, Elton & Eastwood, 1993). This unassertiveness often comes with other symptoms like blood pressure problems (Mills & Dimsdale, 1993; Thomas, 1997), and it's been suggested by some researchers that problems like overeating and smoking may be linked to suppressed anger in women. In other studies, contained anger has been linked to recurrent headaches (Venable, Carlson, & Wilson, 2001).

How does this work? Sandra Thomas, a psychologist and professor of nursing at the University of Tennessee says these physical problems most likely come from prolonged and intensified nervous system activity when we hold back our anger. We subject our bodies to more of those flight-or-fight responses—increased respiration, adrenaline release, and muscle tension—when we keep anger hidden for long periods of time.

It's easier to contain than you might realize. To illustrate how automatically you may be doing this, try the following exercise:

KEEP TRACK OF YOUR CONTAINMENT

Keep a daily journal of your anger, updating it every couple of hours. Keep this journal with you constantly for at least three days to remind you to notice when you are even mildly irritated. Notice and record each instance of frustration, annoyance, and intense anger, writing down the situation and your physical sensations. Also make note of the way you're behaving on the outside—what others around you would see or hear. If you tend to contain, you may discover you're holding back more than you realized. Becoming aware of containment heightens your awareness of the times when you could do something different, like talking or writing about your feelings.

Sometimes women contain anger because they don't have words readily available with which to express feelings. The term *alexithymia* (from the Greek, meaning "no words for emotion") is a diagnostic label given to people who have trouble identifying their feelings or distinguishing between them, have trouble using words to describe their feelings to other people, tend to have less ability to imagine or fantasize about things, and tend to focus on external objects or events rather than their internal processes (Bar-On & Parker, 2000). These people tend to conform to social expectations, seem flat or devoid of feeling, overuse substances like alcohol, and have a greater risk for developing problems like eating disorders (Taylor et al; 1997). Many women do such a good job of hiding their anger as little girls that by the time they reach adulthood, they lose many of the words they once could have used to talk about what's happening inside them.

It Must Be My Fault:
Internalization

I'm pretty certain that Jeff's seeing someone. The signs are all there. I've been an idiot to not see it sooner. And who could blame him? I've not been a very good person for him for the last three years. I make a lot of demands that he doesn't seem able to meet. I want to be able to spend time with him in the evenings and on weekends, to know where he is at night. I ask him to call me when he's going to be late and I know that feels like nagging to him. I wish I could just trust him and just let go of all my jealous need to control him or make him show me that he's committed . . . I'm just like my mother in this one.

—Claire (23)

I would hate to see a fat model in a Victoria's Secret catalog. It would make me sick. I don't want to see someone fat modeling underwear that I might buy. One summer I came home from college and my boyfriend said "looks like you've put on a few pounds." I was just crushed and I started swimming every day and doing aerobics in the evenings and watching what I ate. And the weight came off and I felt so much better about myself.

—Lisa (28)

What we hear in each of these scenarios is *internalization*. Internalization is the process of gradually absorbing anger meant for others, and it most likely happens when we contain anger. Go back and look at the two statements made by Claire and Lisa. What do you notice about their thoughts and feelings? In the first, read closely to see who is getting the blame for Jeff's indiscretions. This statement, made by a college senior, married for three years, shows a pretty clear example of someone directing anger toward herself, when it originally emerged (in her body and mind) as a signal that she was being cheated on.

What stands out about Lisa's statement? It's tougher to find the hidden message in this; a response from a young woman to a question about body image. Lisa holds some pretty strong, negative opinions about people who are fat and seems ready to transfer these sentiments to herself when someone calls her worth into question through an insult. Instead of being consciously put out with her boyfriend for his insensitive comments, she aims her anger at her own body and at those of other women, particularly those who happen to be fat. She feels disgust at the thought of women who are bigger than Victoria's Secret models. But unconsciously, she's furious with the people in her life who try to keep her in line by reminding her to focus all her energy on remaining thin.

Recall that when we divert we move away from one thing and focus on an alternative thing. Over time, as we contain our real feelings, holding back responses we'd like to make but are afraid to, we make sense of that holding back. We explain to ourselves *why* we're doing it and how it is necessary, given the relationships in which we're angry. First, on a conscious level, we may say things like "I need to keep my mouth shut because if I don't, I will really look like a bitch." "I have said enough about this matter. Any more from me and I will push him over the edge." Or perhaps, "I really should not be angry about this. It's no big deal."

However, as we consciously tell ourselves why it makes sense to keep our feelings hidden ("I should forgive her for doing this to me."), we're *unconsciously* telling ourselves a more complicated story ("I am overly sensitive."). As we tell ourselves that we must keep anger private, we must also explain to ourselves why this makes sense. These why messages tend to be dense and convoluted because they have to do with the reasons we should not, must not, ought not to declare or defend ourselves. The hidden why message is harder to find, but packs a punch. Behind "I need to back down" lies the assumption that some of our feelings are valid, while some are not. Some of our feelings must be irrational and without basis. If we're not careful, our anger could hurt someone or make us look stupid or crazy. We have the potential to say the wrong thing. We don't have a legitimate concern.

The conscious statements may appear benign, and even contain some logic. "I don't want to appear stupid or immature, I could lose my job." "Maybe I really *am* fat." "I'm boring him to tears. I'm driving him away."

But each statement carries potent messages that are communicated to our inner selves and reinforce our keeping quiet ("I *am* immature."). Of course, there are times when we *have* to contain anger. But even on those occasions, we must, and do, tell ourselves why we're doing it. If we keep the anger hidden from everybody, the conscious *why* of the situation translates unconsciously into our flaws or guilt. For example, if we live with someone who physically or verbally abuses us, we experience countless situations in which we must contain anger or subject ourselves to hurt. Gradually, what we tell ourselves about this relationship, and about our anger, tends to fall in line with holding back. "If I can just be quiet and agreeable tonight, maybe he won't get too upset about the VISA bill," leads to, "Since he lost his temper with us, I must have not done well enough at getting things in order," which leads to, "I can be really disorganized at times," or "I am a basket case most of the time." Over the course of time, people caught in these situations tend to absorb anger meant for others, bullying themselves with it because they are the only ones who will listen.

So, internalization can be immediate ("I'm making a mountain out of a molehill.") or long-term ("I'm not the wife I should be—he'll probably find someone he loves more."). Many women tend to second-guess themselves in each situation as to whether or not the event merits their being angry and then judge themselves on their feelings. Over time, these women simply come to feel negatively about themselves, their bodies, their worth, their intelligence, their competence, and so forth. Constantly telling ourselves that our emotions are out of line with reality eventually has an adverse impact on our sense of who we are.

Dana Jack of Western Washington University, author of *Silencing the Self* and *Behind the Mask*, studies and writes extensively about women's mental health. In her work, she describes the process whereby women gradually *lose* themselves as they become agreeable, compliant, sweet, and *not angry*. This process, which she calls *silencing the self*, leads women down a path to significant clinical depression as we are robbed of a sense of ourselves as whole persons with our own agendas, needs, and priorities.

According to our own research, many young girls absorb the mythology that anger makes you unattractive and less desirable to be around (recall Anger Myth 4) as early as the fourth grade. When queried about their anger, one group of preteen girls exclaims that when they are angry they look ugly. These same little girls mention throwing away their school lunches and refusing food at home when they are most angry, in addition to pulling away from friends and family. What does this mean in terms of their development and thought? It means that these girls have learned to internalize anger. When they become incensed at school or at home, they come to feel that *they* are the ones who should apologize. They harshly criticize *other* girls who openly display opposition ("she thinks she's all that"). And they feel guilty when they get mad—as if they have done something shameful by noticing a wrongdoing or offense. In addition, they constantly police each other to make sure no one gets too uppity with her anger.

So over time, many of us come to tell ourselves that we are fat or ugly, stupid or hormonally challenged, instead of furious. In a recent study by Leora Pinhas and her colleagues of the University of Toronto, women show *more* depression and *more* anger after viewing slides of female fashion models. These researchers believe this kind of exposure (which for most of us is daily) triggers binge eating in women who have eating disorders. No matter how thin or attractive we already are, we feel we *should* always be on guard about gaining weight or appearing unfit. Instead of feeling outrage at the fashion and entertainment industries, we internalize our anger by starving or hating ourselves for not measuring up to an impossible standard.

Jennifer, a 31-year-old Latina mother of two, believes she is fat, even though she wears a size 8. She feels pretty sure she's become totally repulsive to her husband, Jerry, so she makes sure to cover herself up when they're alone together. Jerry pursues Jennifer for sex nearly every night, but she has been uninterested for most of the past year, in part because she feels so unattractive. Jennifer also has a real estate license and a college degree in business. She currently has plans to begin selling with a local real estate agency but has twice delayed her start date because she thinks she is unprepared to do the work. Jennifer tells her therapist she has to work twice as hard as most people because she can't remember details. She also talks about how Jerry refuses to help with child-care and household duties, so she fears getting in over her head with work and home responsibilities.

Sometimes, like Jennifer, we tell ourselves that we are less competent instead of angry. Again, think of all the media images of beautiful, well-dressed women who not only have gorgeous homes, but keep them perfectly ordered, in addition to being competent full-time trial lawyers or physicians while raising young children. We reason unconsciously that we *must* somehow be at fault if we're unable to make ourselves look, feel, and act like those women. If they can accomplish these coveted things, there must be something wrong with those of us who cannot seem to get it all together and live our lives at that kind of peak. To complete the picture, when we are chronically angry with no safe outlet, many of us start thinking we need medication, we need to get a grip, we have a problem. We pin the blame on our own imperfection, rather than the other persons at whom we're angry.

What's the relationship impact of internalizing? Ironically, while we may think we are protecting our relationships by holding opposition inside, this act makes us less available to our friends and loved ones. Jennifer *disconnects* from Jerry as she keeps her feelings hidden. She further removes herself as she begins to feel unworthy, incompetent, and unattractive. Were she to begin telling him about her resenting their distribution of home responsibilities she would initiate *contact* between them. Yes, they would likely argue. But the alternative, for Jennifer, is to keep Jerry at arm's length by feeling too overwhelmed and disgusted with herself to want closeness.

Take note: Are you punishing yourself?

Answer the following questions honestly to explore your tendencies to internalize anger.

1. **Think of the last time you were really angry with someone.** What thoughts ran through your mind at the time? Were those thoughts familiar?
2. **Try to make a list of all the areas in which you feel guilt, embarrassment, regret, or shame.** Look carefully at this list and ask yourself if any of those things involve anger. For instance, if you feel guilt about not being the kind of mother or daughter you wish you could be, is it possible that part of that guilt is connected to feeling a resentment of some kind? In these situations, do you ever feel as if you've been taken advantage of? By whom? How?

3. How many of these thoughts and feelings apply to you?
   - feeling too fat or too skinny; disliking your whole body
   - disliking some specific part of your body or appearance
   - feeling constantly as if you aren't measuring up
   - experiencing chronic anxiety regarding your house/apartment (neatness, decor, etc.)
   - feeling pressure to prove yourself at work
   - feeling pressure to prove you're a good mate or mother
   - feeling pressure to prove you're a good daughter
   - feeling pressure to prove you're a good friend
   - feeling pressure to be all of these (above) at once and if not, feeling totally worthless ("nothing I do really matters")
   - having a sense of always being behind
   - making to-do lists that are always too long
   - feeling guilty about not finishing the things on your to-do list (or not finishing them quickly enough)
   - feeling a need to apologize all the time
   - losing sleep at night thinking about any of the above; waking up early and anxious
   - spending excessive time putting on makeup, exercising, doing your hair, tanning, or getting manicures (e.g., you find yourself unable to get other things done because of the time devoted to your beauty regimen)

If you recall lots of experiences that fit with item number two above, or if you find you have more than two or three of the experiences in item number three, consider how internalizing anger may be contributing to these issues.

I'm Not the Angry Type: Segmentation

> *I don't want to be angry. I want to turn that frown upside down. There is nothing pretty about being angry.*
>
> —*Trina (23)*

Jane, a 52-year-old mother of two, works as a leasing agent for a large property management company in a metropolitan area. She has devoted 20 years to a company that barely acknowledges her contributions (which were once quite strong). She gets passed over time and again for promotions and raises, only to watch younger, less experienced agents receive these rewards. However, she articulates none of this to her company's owner or managers. Any feelings she might have about being overlooked she camouflages by being pleasant.

Yet, interviews with her peers tell us they experience constant confusion and guilt with regard to Jane because of her inconsistent but ingratiating behavior. She often calls in sick on days that are scheduled for grand openings and other events, for which her help is needed. These absences leave them scrambling to perform their designated roles and hers as well. Jane has such an enduring reputation for missing these events and falling behind on paperwork that her team has come to expect her unavailability and her lack of contribution to important projects and they cover for her. Why? On the flip side, Jane flatters her coworkers by noticing their unique interests and bringing gifts (like a set of beautiful glass beads for a peer who loves to make jewelry) or surprising the staff with glazed donuts in the morning. At times, one of her coworkers, Angie, feels so furious with Jane for shirking work responsibilities that she plans ways to confront her about her behavior and its impact. However, Angie finds herself feeling torn between protecting Jane and their amicable relationship and being honest about the strain she experiences when her peer fails to show or make deadlines. Angie feels guilty at times for her secret dislike of Jane. Jane always has a smile and a friendly greeting for everyone she meets and she usually appears to put the needs of others ahead of her own. When opportunities arise for Angie to talk to Jane about feeling dumped on, Jane typically launches into a story about how tired, overwhelmed, and stressed out she is.

She seems unwilling to consider anger in others, says it is very important to be positive about things, and speaks disapprovingly about people who argue and express opposition. This makes it hard for Angie or the others to really come out with their true feelings. In fact, everyone around Jane tends to resent her a lot of the time, but they also feel paralyzed by her niceness.

In *segmentation*, women sever their angry selves from their conscious identities and disclaim this aspect of who they are. If you bought this book for yourself and you identify with the description of women who segment their anger, you may have some trouble maintaining intimacy in your close relationships—or perhaps you get the sense that people at home or work are frustrated with you but don't quite know what to say. However, many women who are experts at anger segmentation may have difficulty seeing their anger clearly because they perceive it to be about something that either does not affect them or something about which we should not spend so much time talking. They see anger as a *trait* or a character flaw. "Anger is so negative."

While containment is a mostly conscious process, segmentation seems to be much more *un*conscious: "Who me, angry?" Anger makes these women so uncomfortable and afraid that they learn to keep it hidden from themselves virtually altogether.

These women lose touch with the parts of themselves that can behave forcefully and see assertiveness and force as purely selfish. They absorb messages in their environments teaching them that anger is harmful, sinful, or ugly. Sometimes the messages are conveyed by a parent, clergy, teacher, or other significant person who becomes rejecting and cold if oppositional feelings are displayed, creating a painful reminder to keep one's anger contained or hidden ("nice girls don't act like that in public"). Over time, learning to keep anger hidden because it is dangerous, a person sometimes develops such a hatred of her own anger (and others') that she forgets its signals in her body. These women seem to literally *unlearn* their anger responses and act on them unconsciously.

Being angry, yet unaware, puts us at a distinct *dis*advantage. We experience the emotional response and its related thoughts, but keep our awareness of these things to a minimum. Since we don't allow ourselves the conscious opportunity to process this information, decide what it's about, and choose an appropriate action, we experience great risk of acting *unconsciously*. Since the anger is there, regardless of our awareness, it naturally fuels behavior that is self-interested. We may suddenly become motivated to protect ourselves by resisting another's demands or requests, but have little awareness that we're resisting or why.

Often, we use segmentation as an anger diversion when we are in low power positions. Usually, segmentation starts early in life, but becomes full blown in adulthood, when a woman finds herself in a work or other situation that mirrors her family: she feels undervalued and must use creative strategies (maybe unconsciously) to protect her integrity. When she is angry, she disowns the actual feelings, as they are too painful or unacceptable to her. Instead, she feels compelled to act them out in a way that puts another person in the powerless position she herself experiences daily. She still acts on her anger, but she is not fully aware that she is acting on her anger. It's important to remember that anger *always* expresses itself, no matter how hard we try to hide it or neutralize it.

Historically, people who express themselves through hidden hostility have been called passive aggressive. Mental health professionals use this term to describe behavior that is unhelpful, rude, insensitive, or mean, but which is unacknowledged. While smiling at you, the passive aggressive person stabs you in the back. If you ask her: "Are you angry with me?" "Is there something I have done to offend you?" you likely get reassured that she is not angry, despite the hostile energy she sends your way. You may wind up feeling crazy and wonder if you are imagining things or being too reactive ("maybe I have the problem here").

These are the hallmarks of segmentation: denial of anger accompanied by actions that hurt others but appear to be accidental, done in ignorance, or done without knowing that others will be injured. For instance, women who segment often cite religious reasons for avoiding anger, teaching their children to keep their anger hidden too. They may say things that indicate that they abhor political activism when it appears angry or strident (unfeminine). They may say things like why can't we all just get along? Women who segment anger can also seem to be brooding, but not allowing their anger to have a voice in any direct kind of way. The anger behind the brooding is valid and deserves recognition, but the anger becomes misshapen in the woman's attempt to disown it.

In fact, if you think segmentation sounds like the stereotypical traditional woman, you're right. There's evidence that women are more likely than men to use indirect, manipulative, or hidden forms of aggression when they're angry, behaviors that do get them something, but in the long run sabotage their effectiveness at cultivating relationships (White & Kowalski, 1994). Why do they act out anger "under the table"? Dana Jack's research suggests that for some women, even *thinking about* taking a stand feels like an act of aggression. Segmentation may be cultivated in girls much more readily than boys. Conduct like raising one's voice, saying "I'm mad at you," or looking someone straight in the eye while asking for something to be changed tends to be discouraged in girls and rewarded in boys.

Containment, internalization, and segmentation are all kinds of diversions in which our anger tends to stay inside us, being squashed down and pulled out of shape by our mental or emotional gymnastics. In the fourth type of diversion, anger gets redirected out, rather than in. This last form of diversion, externalization, is often the most visible to others as raging violence or vicious verbal assaults.

Get Out of My Face: Externalization

Janice (28) considers herself a good partner, daughter, mother, and friend. However, she sometimes "lose[s] it" with her three-year-old, Ashley, and feels that Ashley really knows how to "push [her] buttons." Ashley becomes very agitated when it's time to get ready to leave for day care in the mid-morning and then again when it's time to get ready for bed at night. When she's agitated, she cries incessantly, refuses to cooperate in having her clothes changed, and insists on getting into the refrigerator or the toilet. Janice finds this behavior completely inexcusable and often screams back at Ashley to "shut up" or hits her forcefully on the behind. Afterward, Janice feels embarrassed, but tells herself that Ashley has to learn.

Shannon, a 24-year-old student, is engaged to be married in six months. Tim, her fiancé, has a number of expectations of Shannon, some of which she has difficulty meeting. For instance, Tim likes Shannon to avoid going to the university li-

brary alone. He reasons that since her ex-boyfriend works there, she should only go when Tim is available to go with her, in order to reinforce the solidity of their relationship to her ex. He also becomes upset if Shannon is late to meet him, worrying that other men are flirting with her or trying to pick her up. Shannon finds these expectations unreasonable but tolerates Tim's lectures. She feels like she owes it to him to make sure he feels secure in their commitment. However, she has no problem yelling at her mother, Rosemary, when she perceives that her mother is advising her against marrying Tim. Recently, Rosemary told Shannon that she was worried about her daughter repeating a family pattern, ending up with a man who is controlling and manipulative. Shannon became totally infuriated with her mother and told her to mind her "own goddamn business." She went on to tell the older woman that she (Rosemary) was the one who was controlling and manipulative and should just keep her mouth shut if she had nothing intelligent to say.

When we become angry, we typically feel this emotion within the context of a relationship. A person's behavior stands in the way of our getting what we want. We feel anger at that person. To be aware of this connection we share with others, even others with whom we're not well acquainted, raises some alarming issues. Other people have impact on our lives. We become attached to them and they leave us. We come to trust them and they let us down. We work with them and they fail to show us signs of appreciation or respect. We share highways with them and they put our lives in peril. These are relationship issues, and it can be threatening to notice how much our emotional lives are affected by the behaviors of others.

Instead of being conscious of these relationships and their impact, some of us use a tactic that lets us escape full awareness of the *implications* of our anger at these others. A diversion style that some people get into the habit of using, *externalization*, allows them to project angry feelings outward, often in an abusive way. This blaming position often, but not always, leaps out against a third party—not the actual target of the original anger (as in the case of Shannon's mother, above). In indirect externalization, the recipient is often a less-powerful other (in the case of a child like Ashley, above) or one with whom the externalizer feels more relationship security.

But even in direct externalization, when we dump anger irresponsibly into the laps of people with whom we're actually angry (as when you hurl an insulting remark at your partner as he arrives late for a date), the act of dumping *detours* an honest expression of our feeling because it focuses solely on the behavior of the other person. Externalization involves the escape from awareness of one's angry feelings through an immediate burst of blaming, insulting, or even violence. So, while it may seem that the externalizing person is getting their anger out, they're actually bypassing full awareness of their anger-in-relation-to-another-person by moving immediately into a blaming position. Bypassing awareness of anger leads to an expression that does not fully satisfy or lead to productive resolution because it is amputated from the source of its energy, the relationship. In other words, by throwing anger *away* from yourself and at another person, you lose touch with the fact that you have a *connection* with that person: a connection in which there is pain. On the other hand, dealing consciously and respectfully with the pain *inside your relationship* could give you some self-definition as you deal with this other individual and possibly help both of you grow closer as two people who share a bond.

Sometimes anger becomes projected at its target and sometimes at other people besides the target who happen to be in the way. Look back at Shannon's comments to her mother. What is it about her words that make them externalization, versus constructive expression? Here is another sample of externalization-based thought. Look at this statement and see if you can identify the key ingredient that makes it an externalized kind of anger statement: *They just totally sent me over the edge. Those little brats! How could they be so selfish?*

The statement above represents externalizing thinking because the person blames her reaction on her children, instead of claiming her feelings as hers and dealing with the anger as her property instead of the product of her children's flaws. If she had said, "I really felt pushed over the edge when my kids were acting out today," we would hear her talking about her own reactions in relation to her children's behavior. Although the difference between the two scenarios seems small, it's extremely powerful.

Hitting your child or calling her an ungrateful brat severs a connection. It also fails to fully acknowledge the relationship dynamic, one in which you automatically possess much more power and influence than does your child. When she does something inconsiderate and leaves you feeling afraid and angry you are obligated to help her learn to do things differently. But if you teach her that her behavior warrants an aggressive response, not only do you cause separation between the two of you, you also put her at more risk for both behaving violently in her adult relationships and being victimized in them (Swinford et al; 2000).

To externalize anger requires that we shut off our awareness of the connection between ourselves and others, at least long enough to hurl an insult, strike out physically, or reject them out of hand. Kate (42) externalizes by getting rid of people in her life who hurt her. Sometimes, her rejection of people is much needed, like when she ends relationships with men who cheat or take advantage of her. However, at other times, Kate banishes those she'd really like to work things out with.

> *I think that when I'm really, really, really angry at somebody I discount their importance in my life. If that happens several times over—I'll cut you off. I'll cut you off and ice you out. You know how, when you're in a relationship and you break up with somebody you don't have half the pain as if they dumped you? Well I've never been dumped. I'm going to dump you first. You will not dump me. I think that's what it is. So I can feel superior. I can rationalize anything.*
>
> *When I'm mad I think about how awful that other person is. What's wrong with them. Look how that person does that. It's all about them. You know, I'm not involved here. How dare they do that to me. In my male relationships, I would not let them engage me in the argument. I would avoid the argument at all costs and make them suffer.*
>
> *But they're not the only one who gets cut off. I get cut off too. And then I do not get to do stuff in a relationship with that*

person that I once did. But that has happened so seldom. You know, I have all my high school girlfriends still. And it's pretty much only happened with men, except my sister and I are not doing our thing right now. And she's pregnant, so it's particularly sad, because I'm nine years older. I've always been kind of like a momma-sissy to her. But she has behaved very badly many times in the past couple of years and said very, very hurtful things. She's very judgmental, very holier-than-Roman-Catholic right now. She's been such a judgmental person, and I cut her off last fall. So it's a loss of support for me, but at the same time I'm still furious with her, because she got me to that point.

Did you catch how Kate gives credit to her sister for "getting me to that point"? Kate knows she feels angry and can talk about these feelings very clearly. She also possesses a great deal of awareness of her behavior in relation to others. However, Kate has trouble owning responsibility for her part in a process and engaging in the necessary arguments that could heal her relationships with people. The arguments might involve talking about feelings of vulnerability, outrage, fear, or other feelings that would take her *down deep* into the thick of the connection between herself and her sister or her partner: this kind of expedition is off limits because it's just too scary.

Women who externalize often have trouble apologizing. This is because doing so would involve hearing the pain of another person, and that would trigger empathy (an experience that has *relationship* written all over it). Empathizing with another person keeps us from hurting them when we'd like to. But the woman who's triggered to lash out remains fairly unconscious of certain aspects of her anger. She doesn't fully connect with the impact of being in a relationship and getting hurt. Should she decide to become more conscious of her anger and the impact she is having in relation to her loved one, she would likely face a painful crisis—the crisis of being both furious and open to change, as well as hurt, fearful, and disappointed. On the other hand, such a crisis might help her begin to heal her relationship and begin using her anger deliberately to enhance and protect it (yes, anger can enhance and protect relationships!).

We mentioned earlier that when women hold their anger in, they are more likely to be depressed. But it may surprise you to know that the *opposite* seems true as well. One of our most recent studies, conducted with Patricia Van Velsor of Southwest Missouri State University, shows evidence that women who *externalize* are more at risk for depression and certain kinds of anxiety symptoms, including obsessions and compulsions. Women who habitually abandon their experience by lashing out or cutting people off may find relationship-building extremely frightening. These same women may also feel laden with guilt and worry about the disconnection they face in their interactions with loved ones. In this study we also explored *somatization*, or expressing psychological problems in physical ways. These kinds of physical or medical problems include fainting, dizziness, heart or chest pain, stomach upset, breathlessness, hot and cold spells, numbness or tingling, and weakness in parts of the body. We found that when women reported *more* somatization, they also reported diverting anger through *both* internalization and externalization. So holding back an anger response *or* pushing it out aggressively on others may actually leave women at greater risk for having these types of symptoms.

In sum, women use at least four different strategies to flee their anger, none of which really help them in the long run. If you opt for containment, you risk the physical, intellectual, and emotional consequences that come with this misuse of energy. If you internalize, you blame yourself in subtle ways that keep you feeling less powerful than you really are. If you segment your anger, you develop a shield around yourself that may protect you from immediate discomfort, but probably costs you in your relationship life. If you externalize, you risk hurting others with your unclaimed anger and probably set yourself up for increased anxiety as you sense the negative impact you have on people.

Note that you probably divert your anger in more than just one way. In our focus group research, women most often describe using a combination of diversion styles, like containment with segmentation or containment with internalization. For example, we sometimes use one style with our coworkers and a different style with our family and romantic partners. You shouldn't try to force yourself into one category if it doesn't always fit for you. The important thing is to gain awareness of how, when, and with whom you divert your anger.

Remember that if you divert your true feelings by containing, internalizing, segmenting, or externalizing them, you leave yourself *more* vulnerable, not less. You're probably at greater risk for certain kinds of problems like anxiety, depression, eating problems, cardiovascular symptoms, diminished sexual desire, and unsatisfying relationships. You jeopardize your career satisfaction and goal attainment by dulling your senses to important emotional information. You block future opportunities by ignoring messages from your environment and your inner self. But starting to explore your diversion marks the beginning of your change.

BEYOND ANGER DIVERSION: FOUR ADAPTIVE ANGER SKILLS

Once women acknowledge how they have learned some variation of the anger diversions and/or anger myths, they often begin to question how they might do things differently when their perceptions and emotions go against the grain. One of our most recent studies suggests that women who feel more effective in their relationships tend to express anger openly, particularly with those they care most about (Cox et al; forthcoming). Toward this end, we need to be aware of the following ten anger traps. These traps set the stage for anger diversion and make it more likely a woman will miss an opportunity to use her emotion purposefully.

Ten Anger Traps to Avoid

Trap #1: Confusing anger with violence, aggression, or any other kind of external behavior.

Trap #2: Thinking you must justify your position if you're

angry; assuming that you must make logical sense to yourself or someone else.

Trap #3: Going more than a few days without talking to someone about your feelings; letting your emotions incubate in isolation.

Trap #4: Assuming anger will go away on its own if you give it enough time.

Trap #5: Assuming you can't love someone and be angry with her/him simultaneously.

Trap #6: Associating your anger with things about yourself that you do not like (e.g., "my bad temper," "my period," "my tendency to look at the negative side of things").

Trap #7: Being unable to hear and appreciate other people's anger.

Trap #8: Assuming you can't be loved if your loved one is angry with you.

Trap #9: Assuming the person who is angry with you must be right (or wrong).

Trap #10: Trying to force yourself to forgive and forget.

Sidestepping anger traps is only a part of the picture. Diversions can keep us from experiencing and expressing anger in helpful ways. The result is a considerable loss, individually and collectively, of voice and emotional energy. But there is a different approach to anger that leads to empowerment and emotional wholeness. What do the women who tell a more positive anger story have to report?

> *Well, if I didn't show my anger the way I do, I wouldn't be Cecile. I'm just plain outspoken, and I believe it's best to let a person know where you're coming from, how you feel, rather than hold it in.*

We agree. And the anger model we described in chapter One is the result of what we have learned so far from women like Cecile about adaptive, healthy anger. We want to share four critical tools for change from our model that we call Adaptive Anger Skills. By choosing to use these skills instead of diverting your anger, you can experience the kind of anger advantages that we know some women already embrace, all to their benefit. Let's take a closer look at these four key abilities and the opportunities they offer for turning anger from a negative into a positive experience.

Anger Consciousness: Wake Up and Smell the Anger

You're lying in bed. Pick a time or place when you can remember arising from sleep to the scent of your favorite breakfast. Maybe someone's fixing pancakes or baking rolls. Maybe you've peeled a fresh orange and are sitting down to your own little table, the flowers you picked yesterday opening in their vase. The tang of citrus is sharp against the delicate air of honeysuckle or roses. We rejoice, often without even thinking about it, in our natural ability to experience the sense of smell.

We have a similar built-in aptitude for experiencing all kinds of emotions, including anger. Anger consciousness means having access to your angry feelings. It means being able to name them and choose deliberate ways to handle them as they arise. Anger consciousness is the *opposite* of anger diversion.

The first step in claiming your anger advantage is to get in touch with your anger and become fully aware of it when it occurs. Actually, developing a sophisticated understanding of all your emotions is a critical life skill. Women are often encouraged to know our emotional selves better. However, in the case of anger, emotional awareness is typically disapproved of and even, to some extent, forbidden. The process of emotional regulation is labeled many different ways, such as emotional intelligence (as in Daniel Goleman's work) or meta-emotion awareness (from John Gottman). However, regardless of what you call it, understanding your anger in the context of all your emotions is a critical life skill.

Achieving anger consciousness means you have moved past your fear of anger, past the idea that you might be overwhelmed by your anger, past being threatened by your anger. It means you have realized that even if your anger was forbidden, punished, or shamed earlier in your life, you're okay with it now. When you're feeling mad, you tell yourself the truth about it.

Does this sound appealing to you? If it does, then you are already on your way. Just by exploring the issues and sifting through them in your own mind until they start to make sense, you enter into a whole new level of anger consciousness. In addition, we suggest the following exercises to make some of these abstract emotional concepts more concrete and realistic to you.

Finding Your Anger

- *Find an angry voice.* Practice speaking into a tape recorder. Talk as if you're having a conversation with someone who triggers your indignation. Tell them how you feel and what they do that elicits these feelings in you. Go back and listen carefully to your recording. What do you hear (e.g., giggling, apologizing, placating)? What are all the subtle things being communicated with your tone of voice? Practice this until you hear clear anger along with respect and feel at ease with the combination. What will this voice sound like? It will probably be a bit different for each woman. Sometimes it helps to watch movies about women who speak their anger out loud, or ask a friend to share her angry voice with you. As you practice your own words, think *strength* and *caring*.

- *Find an angry face.* Practice speaking in front of the mirror. Talk as if you're conversing with the target of your frustration. Write a script before you start to help you concentrate on your facial expressions. What do you see? Are you tempted to laugh or smile? What reactions do you have to seeing your reflection? Practice until you become accustomed to seeing yourself talk about what makes you cross.

- *Find an angry posture.* Again, in front of the mirror, talk about being annoyed. This time, pay attention to the rest of your body. What are your hands doing? Comfort is key: find a position that feels solid and easy. Practice talking, listening, and watching your body movements until you feel comfortable with the whole package.

- *Find your responsibility.* Start noticing the things you do when you're angry, and assess the consequences of your actions. Are you consistently careful not to mix aggression with your anger? Are you accountable for your misbehavior with others when it occurs, or do you choose to walk away without apology? When arguments occur, be willing to talk about both sides of the issue. Open yourself up to the possibility that you may have made a poor choice, but be careful to hang on to your version of what happened and why. It matters. Be-come responsible to yourself, by noticing each time you feel anger in a day, and keep a notebook handy to write down your emotions and thoughts. Consciousness brings the responsibility of being truthful with yourself and those around you while accepting the consequences of your honesty.

Mind, Body, and Anger

Making your anger visible brings it to the surface, showing on the outside what you feel on the inside. Psychologists and therapists call this achieving "affect congruence," and not only does it feel better than hiding, it's good for you too. The exercises above help your out-side—your face, voice, body language, and energy—match what you are feeling on the inside. Starting with the outside and working inward is one way to get past traditional barriers and find a connection with the anger that is stored there. It's generally better to do this work on your own. That way you won't have to worry about feeling self-conscious in front of others or get caught up in their reactions to you.

There are lots of additional ways to do this kind of anger work, so all you need is the courage to explore until you find the ones that work best for you. Basically, this type of anger expression falls into two categories, physical and verbal. Women usually have a preference for one or the other, but almost always end up using something from each.

Physical activities allow your body to help you connect with your anger. You can choose a sports-related exercise, such as running, or slamming a tennis or soccer ball against a wall. There are also a lot of unstructured physical activities that can be useful, such as pounding pillows, tearing newspapers, or dancing hard with the stereo volume on high. We've heard of women bringing bags of ice into the backyard to throw at a fence (it has a satisfying breaking glass sound to it), whopping curtain rods on bed mattresses, and reducing old phone books to scraps. Anger seems to generate a strong feeling in our bodies to *do something*—something active with some force behind it.

However, important research by Brad Bushman of the University of Iowa sends a cautionary note. In his study, college students (both women and men) got angry when they read negative evaluations of their essays. They were told that another student had evaluated them. After having their anger triggered, one-third of these students were asked to sit quietly. Another third were told to beat up on punching bags that had photos attached to them of the students who had supposedly criticized their essays. Participants in this latter group were instructed to think about their critics while punching. The third group also punched the bag, but were shown a fitness video and given no instructions about focusing on the target of their anger. The results of this study showed that people in the second group (punching bags with the photo while thinking about the person who criticized their essay) became the most physically aroused, the angriest, and the most aggressive. Bushman concludes that self-help advice encouraging people to get their anger out in physical ways is misguided. What are we to make of this study, especially in light of the fact that women in our own research talk about sometimes needing a physical outlet for their anger?

First, keep in mind that being angry—even very angry—is *not* negative in and of itself. Anger is valid *and the emotion itself cannot hurt another person*. As psychologists, we find ourselves concerned with aggression, however, and must make it clear that we do not support violence or verbal assault as an appropriate way of expressing anger. Second, the conditions Bushman set up in his laboratory differ vastly from the conditions of our real world. In our interviews, lots of women tell us they get a huge benefit out of physically declaring their opposition through venting strategies and even visualizing the person with whom they're mad. This kind of private *acting out* helps women feel relief from the intensity of their physiological arousal and focuses their thoughts on productive action. So our fieldwork as clinicians and qualitative researchers shows us a different side of the issue, pointing to some inherent value for women in "blowing off steam."

Still, we suggest that given Bushman's findings, as well as others in this area, you should think of these physical release strategies as ways to help you *ultimately lower* your physical arousal: to let you breathe more deeply, slow your heart rate, allow your muscles to contract and then release, allow yourself to verbalize or growl or make whatever sounds and movements help you feel some immediate release. Once your body is physically calmer, you can decide how you want to handle the interpersonal aspects of your anger, *without violence*. A parent who can also teach alternative ways of expressing anger should monitor children doing these exercises.

For those of you who don't *feel* your anger at all, but know intellectually that you *are* angry deep inside, you can use this kind of strategy to find a connection with your raw emotion. You don't have to feel angry to start. That's the beauty of this kind of exercise—you are using your body to help you open the door to an emotion you've been taught to avoid for a long time. Keep in mind the task of *searching for what's inside*, and avoid doing anything that would hurt yourself or anyone else. Research shows that you can maximize the benefits of this kind of anger expression if you involve your cognitive abilities too. Spend some time putting words on your thoughts and feelings after your body has finished processing through anger in its own way.

If you feel inclined to let those words come out as either spoken or written comments, then you'll be working in the second category of anger exercises, verbal expression. Anything involving words, including written journals, diaries, letters, stories, poems, songs, etc., can become a vehicle for bringing your anger outside of yourself and into the world. By making emotion concrete and visible, you allow it to become real and allow yourself to fully examine all of what you feel. This is a way to begin rebuilding a natural connection between your logical, thinking self and a feeling that has been off limits to exploration for most of your life. In addition, there's one final but important arena of awareness you can cultivate in order to grow in anger consciousness.

Gender Socialization—Another Layer of Awareness

Who originally made the unwritten rule that you should be a nice girl who doesn't make waves? Who enforces that now? In mainstream Western culture, rules are determined by those in power, meaning, for the most part, white men who are at the top of the political, social, legal, and economic scene. It's a fact of life that when you are sitting pretty at the top of a mountain of money and influence, you don't want to give it up. And powerful women are starting to do some climbing, which makes those at the summit nervous and defensive.

So consciously or not, complex and subtle efforts to minimize women's power are embraced by most men *and many women*. Since anger has wonderful motivational power and often encourages action and change, it is often seen as a threat. It takes some time and energy to realize just how many ways there are in which women are told to stay in their place, keep quiet, and not be angry. As a quick exercise in gender and anger awareness, read through the following checklist to see which of these experiences you have had (if any):

Scenario   **Have I seen or experienced this?**

Baby talk: being called "girl, baby,   Yes____ No____
darling, honey," or any other word—especially at work—that indicates
   you are not a grown woman who knows what she is doing. This kind
   of language implies that your emotions are the immature responses
   of a little girl and not to be taken seriously. Note: this kind of talk
   between lovers is fine as long as it's not deliberately degrading.

Calm down!: being told to not upset yourself,   Yes____ No____
to not get worked up, that you're blowing things out of proportion at
   home or at work. Others find your anger threatening and want to
   shut you down.

I know you're hurt: being told you are disappointed   Yes____ No____
or sad when you are actually angry. Perhaps you feel both, but are encouraged to focus on your hurt. This one is tricky, because it comes
   across as supportive, but it bypasses your anger and can make it
   harder for you to acknowledge it. It makes it more likely that you
   will do nothing (sadness decreases energy for change) and less
   likely that you will take action (anger increases energy for change).

You'll ruin everything!: being warned that if you use   Yes ___ No____
your anger to try to make changes in your relationships or in your
   workplace you will endanger your connections with others or your
   job. While risks need to be assessed in these cases (Will I really get
   fired? Will my partner hit me?), these warnings are often more
   about others' need to maintain the status quo.

You're too sensitive—you're too emotional: Yes ___ No ____
being told that whatever you're feeling, it's too much, for too long, or at
    the wrong time and place. This kind of message makes us want to
    keep our feelings hidden inside for fear we won't be taken seriously.

If you answered yes to any of these questions, you are recognizing how
unspoken gender rules play into the diversion of women's anger. This
critical aspect of anger consciousness involves keeping our eyes open
to social forces that pressure us to divert anger rather than own and
use it for our own good. Only by coming to an understanding of why
we've chosen to deny our anger up to this point can we begin to
accept it as an integral and valuable part of who we are.

Constructive Anger Talk: Putting It All on the Table

Anyone who wants to be more verbal about her anger will need
some new ground rules for communication. So we'd like to propose a
few guidelines for how you can match words with your angry feelings.

Let's start from the perspective that others may very well feel in-
timidated or uncomfortable with your honesty. While holding firmly to
the message you want to put across, you can lessen their discomfort
and increase the chances you'll really be heard by describing your own
experience while avoiding criticism, judgment, or accusation. Even
though your emotions may be raging at the time, try to keep the
following in mind:

1. Begin by using "I" statements. This means starting your sentences with "I feel . . ." instead of "You are . . ." In this way,
   you make yourself the subject of the message. You are sharing how *you* feel, so you're getting to talk about your anger;
   and you are *not* talking about what others have done wrong,
   which keeps them from feeling attacked. Don't worry, they'll
   figure it out for themselves. But the fact that you've allowed
   them to do so, instead of informing them of their mistakes
   or faults, shows your respect and good intent.

For example, saying "I am so annoyed that you forgot Valentine's Day," or "I felt betrayed because I wanted you to be there for me yesterday," sounds vastly different from, "You were so mean to me on Valentine's Day—you just don't care, do you?" and "You totally blew me off yesterday. It's just another example of how selfish you can be." Although you may feel all these things, you can be judicious in the ways you express your feelings and still be true to yourself. One further note: be wary of the following formula—"I feel that you are . . . (lazy, lying, etc.)" Sorry, but this won't work. Keep your focus on sharing your own experience so others can understand where you are coming from and what you would like to have changed.

2. Be specific. Let others know the concrete details about what is making you mad and why. Think of constructive anger expression as a way to pass on information crucial to resolving the issue. If you are yelling "This always happens and I hate it," there's not much specific information for anyone to work with when it comes to making changes. But if instead you yell "I hate it that you spent $700 before we could even talk about it!" your partner then knows beyond a shadow of a doubt what the issue is.

3. Respect boundaries. Avoid any name-calling or verbal assault, and learn how to recognize when you slip from anger into verbal aggression. Be careful not to use your angry voice and face as weapons to intimidate or instill guilt. You can talk about your perceptions or your gut feelings, but be sure to label them as yours. For example, you might say, "I feel like I'm being taken advantage of," but avoid, "You're exploiting me and you haven't got the guts to admit it."

Remember, others are likely to be much more uncomfortable with your anger than you are at this point, and they may need to walk away from the conversation and take a break. Allow them space and time if they request it.

4. Be honest. This means not hiding your own vulnerability. Speaking your anger is one of the most vulnerable acts you

will commit in a relationship, because it lets others see how intensely you feel about something and how much you need and want things to be different. Talk about all the sides of your anger, even the sad, hurt, and afraid sides.

5. Avoid apologizing for your anger (e.g., taking care not to say things like, "I know I shouldn't be mad about this, but . . ."). This is important for two reasons. First, being true to your experience bolsters your credibility *with yourself*. Remember that if you feel mad, you have every right to feel mad. Second, being unapologetic about your emotions helps you avoid sending mixed signals like "I think I might be angry, but perhaps I'm just imagining things."

The Emotional Think Tank

Sometimes it helps to give yourself a little time and intensive focus on your anger while you learn about it. This focus lets you choose a strategic course of action and prevents the kinds of mistakes that happen when we either ignore our feelings or impulsively act them out. Think-tanking is often a way to achieve more detailed anger consciousness and to think of creative solutions in conflict situations. If you're at work, you need a safe place to put your anger while you consider what to do about it. If you're furious at your friend, but also confused about why, you need a way to study those feelings before selecting words that truly match your experience. You need an emotional think tank. Here's how it works:

You feel furious but you're afraid to say the words that are coming to mind. Or maybe fear is not the issue, but you are concerned about the consequences to yourself or someone else if you let it all come out. Maybe you're completely baffled as to how you can turn a rotten situation into something positive. You're stuck: the person who's triggered you doesn't seem to care or is not willing to talk. Take some deep breaths and . . .

1. Imagine that you hold a large, clear container, something like a crystal ball, in your right hand. Inside this ball, you can see yourself, your anger, and your situation—like you might view

a scene in a souvenir snow globe. Just allow yourself to watch from above as you hold this crystal ball. Your anger can take any form. It can be a bright color or a specific shape. You can see your anger through the glass so you always know where it is, until you have the opportunity and safety to give it your undivided attention. Try to give yourself this time within the first few hours—don't put it off for very long.

2. When you have some privacy and are in a better position to examine your anger, picture yourself going *inside* the crystal ball. Try to tolerate the discomfort you may feel in looking at your anger *up close*. What does your emotion look and feel like: a porcupine, a ray of light, or perhaps a red sports car? Sometimes imagining a trusted buddy going with you inside the emotional think tank will help you uncover parts of your resentment you didn't see before. Choose someone you know very well, who will be genuine and honor your right to feel the way you feel. Imagine asking this person what s/he sees there ("Larry, what do you think I'm doing here?"). Getting this person's (albeit imaginary) read on the situation will help you empathize with yourself and prevent tendencies you may have to be overly critical of your reactions.

3. Study the entire contents of your anger and become familiar with what triggered it and why.

   - With whom do you feel most angry?
   - What does this person mean to you? Is this someone you love or care about deeply? Is this someone who holds power in your work or family life?
   - What are the real risks you face by being honest with her/him? Ask yourself about the implications of your anger.
   - What's being threatened: your sense of what's right or maybe the stability of your relationship? Is your career on the line, or maybe your reputation?
   - What tender or prized parts of you are being hurt?
   - What words best describe how you feel and what you want?
   - How can you be as genuine as possible without putting yourself in danger (i.e., of a lawsuit or being fired from your job)?

4. Take all the time you need to study your anger both by diving *into* the think tank and observing it from above. Promise yourself to *do* something with it when you've reached some conclusions. Use your think tank to write a script, write a letter, make a video, or rehearse a conversation. Now, where will you go from here?

Listening to Others

Listening well takes courage. Why? When we open ourselves to others' experiences we risk hearing things that hurt or trigger defensive anger or fear in us. But caring about people requires that we hear their side of the story. Typically, an anger situation involves at least two people, so get ready for some self-examination as you exercise your listening skill. You can invite others to share their anger with you, in the hopes of achieving a greater understanding and coming to some kind of resolution on an issue. Here's how.

1. Pay attention to the person sharing their position. Most important, listen for the *feelings* they express. Realize that your partner might be afraid to say "I'm mad at you" because of how our culture views anger. Be willing to read a little between the lines and be sure to check out your conclusions with your partner to be certain you're on the right track (see #3 below). Listening is really hard because often our first impulse is to interrupt, defend ourselves, or break in with our own side of the story. Good listening means splitting your attention; keeping track of what *you* want to say and what *you* are feeling *while still focusing on the other person's communications*. It takes a bit of practice. Consciously practicing these skills when you're calm will allow you to get the hang of it when you're not overwhelmed with emotion and make it easier to keep the habit even when you're feeling angry.

2. Repeat what you heard the person say. "So in other words, you feel cheated when I work all weekend instead of going out with you." "It sounds to me like you feel really sad and

angry because I let you down." Be sure to repeat it without adding your own opinion ("and it's hard for you just to realize that I have to put in overtime")—just give it back the way you hear it. Don't add your own analysis or critique. This allows the other person to realize you really are tracking their message.

3. Check to see if you're on target. "Did I get the picture?" "Is there anything else that I need to hear?" "What did I miss?" Few things escalate a conflict faster than making incorrect assumptions. By letting your partner know what your understanding is, based on their statements, you can avoid painful detours on your way to working things out.

4. Remember, respecting boundaries is a mutual obligation in any relationship. If someone becomes aggressive or abusive with their anger, it's important to clearly draw the line. Be sure to let them know you are okay with their angry feelings, just not with the way they are choosing to express them. You can set limits on time—"I can handle about ten more minutes and then I'll need to take a break. This is really intense."—or volume—"You're getting so loud that it's frightening me. Can we go back to normal conversational voices?"—or content—"I don't mind that you're mad at me, but I do mind the language you are using. I really want to talk about this, so can you clean it up?"

The significant thing about being willing to listen to anger is that as you begin to respect others' rights to voice their disagreement and frustration with you, you contribute to your own freedom. You are building up a tolerance for anger that will go a long way toward loosening the binds we all feel around this emotion. As you listen effectively to others share their frustration or fury, you model for them how anger, when expressed with respect and honest intentions, can be beneficial. Apologize for disallowing others' anger in the past. Let them know you'll be doing things differently now.

———

In conclusion, making big changes takes time. Give yourself plenty of space, time, and self-care as you begin to work with the tools above. You need to support yourself with rest and rewards during this process because it can push you to the limits of your comfort zone.

When you make adaptive anger skills a part of your everyday life, you get to know yourself in a new way. You understand where your ideas and reactions about anger developed, you identify your anger patterns, and you no longer try to divert your true feelings. You welcome your frustration and resentment as adaptive and natural, and that gives you the sort of inner peace and calm that comes with accepting all of who you are—not just the sweet, agreeable girl but also the furious woman who has her own mind.

The women in our interviews tell of how they struggled over time to find the authority of their anger. Their relationships began to change, both at home and at work. They became attracted to stronger people and found themselves drawn to jobs that better suited them. They changed their relationships with family and healed old wounds. They solved thorny problems and achieved impressive goals. They became more of who they really are.

The next few chapters take us into these women's lives so that we can look closely at how they moved from diversion to creative action. Shayla is a wonderful example. She's a young African-American woman who already has a good deal of anger consciousness; she knows her own anger and can tell which situations are in her control and which are not. Today, she uses her anger to move ahead in the world, without apology:

> *I get quiet at first, but then I have to let it out. I shake. When there's nothing I can do about it, I cry. If there is something I can do about it, I say what's on my mind. I'm outspoken. Anger helps me express the way I feel without having any regrets about it. When you're angry, that's when the truth really comes out. It helps you speak the truth; you're really trying to say what's on your mind because you're angry. When I get angry, it's because people tell me "you can't"—and that's what makes me want to go ahead and try even harder. I can say, "I've done it!"*

THREE

Loosening the Ties That Bind
Anger in the Family

*M*y mother was very physical in her discipline. I remember many whippings that, knowing what I know today, would be considered child abuse. In my family, children were not allowed to express anger . . . ever. I remember one time in particular that my mother had humiliated me in front of friends and I yelled "I hate you!" She took a jump rope and she beat me until her arm got tired. I had welts from my shoulders to my ankles. Then she would always tell me to stop crying or she would whip me again!

I learned early on that it was not safe to show you are angry if you are a girl. And if you make someone angry, you deserve what you get. It was better just to pretend you weren't angry . . . stuff it!

When I was younger, I played the game. It was all I knew. It was about as dysfunctional as it gets. Then, when we were older, my sister and I moved down the street from one another and we started talking, much to my mother's dismay. We talked about our childhood, how we were raising our children, about how my mother played us one against the other, and we started reading books and discussing child rearing, discipline, and alternatives to what we had known as children.

Now I am vocal about my anger, but in an informative and curious way. With my mother I got very direct, asking, "OUCH! Are you trying to hurt my feelings?" or when she is *manipulating guilt I will confront her, and many times we end up laughing because what she said is so ridiculous. I get clarification if I think someone is being hurtful or is upset about something, and many times it has nothing to do with me. Taking time to figure out what is going on with me, communicating that clearly and without rancor, and taking the risk of learning the truth instead of assuming I know what happened or what someone's motivation is, has set me free from all that anguish.*

When I get upset about something, or something doesn't feel right, I get very introspective. I have to figure out what is going on with me first, then I can go to anyone in my family and be clear about what I am upset about and why and talk it through. It is great! This works in all aspects of my life. It is really about self-examination and figuring out what it is that is causing your discomfort, pain, hurt feelings, or anger and then confronting it.

I have also been determined that my children, Justin and Shane, would be allowed to express their anger, even though it was disapproved of by the rest of my family. I didn't beat my boys, but I yelled. When Justin was in the third grade, we discovered that he had ADHD (Attention Deficit Hyperactive Disorder). I went to a child development specialist; I learned a lot about how to discipline, reward, and get creative with child rearing. I also learned that the disparaging remarks made by teachers and us as parents were doing more damage than the disorder he had! I was devastated that I was contributing to his angst, especially when I had thought that by not beating him I was doing such a good job.

I realized that what I was doing was personalizing everything the kids did. I felt it was a direct reflection on me! How egocentric is that? As I changed and started doing things differently, the boys started reacting differently (duh!). I would let them say that "It sucked!" and agree with them that life could be very difficult and unfair. They openly expressed their anger, knowing that it wouldn't change anything. They knew they didn't have to agree with me, and if they had a logical, valid argument I would listen and possibly compromise or acquiesce. If not, at least they felt heard.

One of the things that most amazed my current partner, Aaron, when he first met Shane and Justin was how open they were with their anger with me. He expected me to hit or get upset or scream because that is what would have happened in his home. But I explained that I had come from a place where stuffing anger almost made me lose my mind, and that would never happen to my children. I did teach them appropriate ways to voice their anger and appropriate times, but they always knew they could ask "Can I speak to you in the other room?" and I would get up and go. They could express whatever they were feeling and it was alright. I am so glad they didn't stuff their anger and let it eat at them physically and mentally.

I think I have taught my kids that anger is not something to be afraid of and that it is okay for them to express it respectfully, and when they don't, they can do a lot of damage to the other person. They are years ahead of where I was at their age. Anger has fueled so much of what is right with my life!

—Kira (51)

So how can you get as comfortable as Kira with your anger? How can you make your anger work for you as well as it works for her and her family? How do you overcome the unhelpful ways of handling emotion that may exist in your family as Kira did in hers?

Creativity often comes from setting loose old ideas that once held us in, restrained our thoughts, made us wonder about our worth when we felt livid, or when we were the object of someone else's wrath. You look back to understand how your family first shaped your anger. You look at the present to examine the way family anger patterns exist in your current life and to make new decisions about which ones to keep, change, or do away with completely. You look forward to how you can embrace different ways to interact around anger with your family members and others now and in the future. You can watch the benefits firsthand as they emerge. Breaking free means re-evaluating the subtle relationship lessons learned in our youth—and passing on new ways of being passionate, determined, and, yes, angry, with the ones we love.

To begin in a helpful mind-set, take a moment to contemplate. You can sit or stand, but either way, get your body involved too:

REFLECTION ON SELF, FAMILY, AND ANGER

- Be still for a moment. Breathe deeply.
- Today, right now, you are at a point in time. Say the hour, day, month, and year out loud. State your name and age. Close your eyes and create a vivid picture in your mind as you answer these questions: Where am I? Who is with me? What does my anger look like now?
- Open your eyes and look behind you, over your shoulder. Hold that position while asking yourself: Where did I come from? Who was there at my childhood beginnings? What did my anger look like then?
- Look ahead, setting your eyes at the farthest point on the horizon you can see. Keep your gaze steady. Now respond: Where am I going? Who is likely to be with me as I journey onward? What do I want my anger to look like a year from now?

Your reactions to this exercise will be unique. What was *your* experience of these short moments of focus on anger and your family? You may have had memories or images float by; you may have answered "I don't know" to some of the questions. Maybe it was hard to look back for a long time without it becoming uncomfortable (physically and emotionally). Perhaps you felt annoyed or foolish keeping your eyes locked on the vanishing point in your view—after all, who knows how the future will go? Note your reactions. They are clues to what aspects of anger are important to process in your family. To go deeper into the usefulness of anger in the family, let's start at the same place you did.

LOOKING BACK TO UNDERSTAND
WHERE YOU ARE NOW

Building Blocks for Life

We learn the most about anger in our families. Our family-of-origin is the first setting in which we learn how others respond to our own anger and in which we see how others express and experience their anger. The very essence of our adult personality is etched into every memory of this feeling and the ways in which our significant caregivers reacted to us when we showed it. How we structure relationships with our peers at work, our bosses, our lovers and partners, our kids, and our friends leaps out of the past—mirroring our most defining moments of oppositional feeling at home.

The first three concepts we'll explore are how anger relates to *attachment,* to *boundaries,* and to *triangulation.* These are fundamental ways to understand our connections to others, and while they get their start in our families, *these dynamics factor into all relationships throughout our lifetime.* We have chosen to present them here in the chapter on anger and the family, but we hope you will carry them with you as you read on about lovers, friends, and coworkers, and as you explore your anger in each of these different settings.

Attachment

Attachment refers to the basic emotional bonds formed between children and their caregivers, as well as to the bonds in our most intimate relationships throughout our lives. As the founder of attachment theory, John Bowlby, states, attachment is critical throughout the life span, not just in childhood. The essence of attachment is that when you are in distress, someone will not only be physically there, but will be emotionally responsive to you in a comforting way. When this process occurs on a regular basis in childhood, kids develop attachment security: a sense that they are worthy of love and that the world is an essentially safe and trustworthy place. A great deal of research supports the fact that secure attachment has potent interpersonal benefits across our life span in terms of social competence, effective use of our emotions (including anger), and healthy, satisfying relationships.

However, for some kids, early childhood is a time of insecurity; they are not comforted, or their caregivers are negligent or inconsistent—or, in worst-case scenarios, actually abusive. Children predictably show protest—anger—as they desperately try to reconnect with their parents. "Bad" behavior from a child is almost always a way to get a caregiver's attention, and from an attachment perspective, negative attention is better than no attention. Thus, it is invaluable to keep in mind that anger in the family often signals disconnection and an underlying need for reconnection.

Boundaries

The line where you stop and another person begins, both physically *and psychologically*, is a boundary. Throughout this book we talk about anger's power to help women learn more about themselves and find out who they really are. So how does anger help us to accomplish this?—by bolstering our sense of who we are both as autonomous beings and in relation to others.

Our feelings, including anger, give us information about ourselves (i.e., self-knowledge—what turns us on and what turns us off) and about how we interact with others and the world around us. Imagine that each of the circles below represents an individual. The circles can provide us with a visible model for how we relate and intersect with others in a variety of situations.

Curiosity: one circle moves toward the other

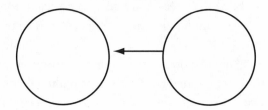

Fear: one circle moves away from the other

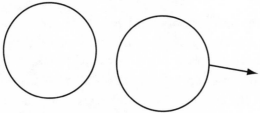

Love: the circles move together

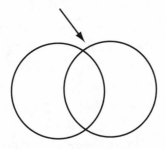

Every one of our feelings allows us to see ourselves in relation to other individuals with whom we interact. Now take a look at the two circles below. You can see that they are touching, but not overlapping.

Anger: reveals our boundary points

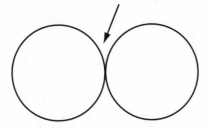

This is how we envision anger in a relationship—as *a point of intersection with another person*. Two circles, or individuals, bump up against each other and anger arises at the point of impact. The lines of the circles represent personal boundaries: "I need this. You need that." Here's where patterns of diversion learned in our families can lead us down an unproductive path or where the choice to use adaptive anger skills can assist us in defining who we are while improving our relationships within and outside the family.

Clear boundaries are considered by many family therapists to be central to healthy relationships and a strong sense of self. Anger helps us find out exactly where our borders lie. When we bump up against another person, we not only feel irritated, but we discover where we end and the other person begins. This is important because when we feel perturbed we receive an unmistakable message about what we need—part of the essence of who we are as a person—and how those needs are being met. Opposition helps us to understand how we differ from someone else and how important any given issue is to us. The antagonism that flares up when we fight over holiday plans with family or disagree with a friend or colleague furnishes important feedback about our outer limits. What's more, *no other emotion can do this for us.*

How Anger Diversion Creates Boundary Problems in the Family

What kind of long-term impact results when people cannot develop healthy boundaries with each other? When we say that someone has "boundary problems," we usually mean that he or she either tries to fuse with another person as completely as possible (as if you could make your two circles overlap and actually *be* the other person) or that he or she refuses to communicate at all with another person (physically or psychologically makes their circle unavailable). For example, being completely wrapped up in protecting others from your anger or expressing anger through violence are both boundary problems.

In the professional literature, we use the terms "enmeshment" and "cut-off" for these two processes. Cut-off means you shut down and decline to interact. In terms of our diversion model, you externalize your anger so that others are afraid to approach you or segment your anger so that it is unavailable to you or others. This stifles your anger advantage because your anger has nowhere to go; you've lost the connection that could lead to resolution. You don't even really get to escape the situation—you just prolong the tension of your unfinished business. Enmeshment means you end up diverting by turning your anger inside; you stuff your anger away in order not to cause waves or upset anyone else; presenting that pretty, smiling, always pleasant exterior makes it so much easier to accommodate others. You prioritize others' emotional needs over your own. But enmeshment is a huge sacrifice; you don't leave yourself options for acting on the important messages that anger is sending you. Let's look in more depth at some of the complex ways in which boundaries, diversion, and family anger rules are intertwined.

Externalizing and Cut-off Boundaries

Do you find yourself lashing out at your kids, your partner, or other adults in your family? When we push our anger out on others, we seal off chances for relationship growth with inappropriate blasts of fury. Here, Pam (married, in her early 40s, with two young children) describes how she and her sister use their anger to hurt each other, resulting in a long-term cut-off between them:

> *Two years ago was the last time I saw my sister. She comes to visit and she's the guest from hell. You try to get along. You try to fit in. Two years ago I weighed 30-some pounds more than I do right now. So I've struggled with my weight for a long time and it's still an ongoing battle. My sister's never had a weight problem. She's a size eight . . . until the day she dies. Well all of this stuff is building and "Her Honesty" is finally getting off the plane. She hasn't seen me in six years, and she has to mention my weight first thing. Well aside from feeling like I got stabbed right through the heart, there's a part of me that wanted to grab her scrawny little neck and throttle her. I thought, "Okay, that's a real sore spot with me . . . I'm going to go for the jugular . . . because I know her sore spots also." One of her issues is her skin. She's younger than me but she looks older. The sun has really done a wicked number on her. Normally I wouldn't feel compelled to say anything about it. But since she felt compelled to tell me how I looked, I said, "Well, you know . . ." It has now been two years since I spoke with my sister.*
>
> (Pam's family rule: Anger should be used to
> hurt and silence others.)

Pam and her sister have pushed their anger so far out on each other that they have created a wall between themselves through their rigid cycle of conflict. By following old family rules today, Pam's anger stays unresolved and the disconnection from her sister thwarts any possibility of honest dialogue.

Pam has used one of the most common ways of creating cut-off: invoking the "I'm never going to talk to you again" decree. Another typical strategy is to geographically relocate so that contact is severely curtailed between family members. Because the *intention* behind these actions is often to punish others, such actions reflect externalized anger. Family members are left in a frustrating standoff, sealed away from each other by their impenetrable boundaries.

Enmeshed Boundaries and Inward Diversions

Do you find that it's hard for you to challenge people who take advantage of you? Are you afraid you'll be seen as mean and nasty if you say, "Hey, I didn't like this"? Look back to your family rules to see if you can find out why. For example, listen to Connor (48), who works in her family business. She has a long history of protecting her other family members from her anger. She pays a high price for this containment and internalization:

> *I think that I've been holding back my anger for several years toward my mother, and probably my dad too, and my sister. I really think that there's a very good possibility that it sparked my depression; I think that's how it manifested itself in me. I was the person who was supposed to keep the family together and I think that it ended up making me depressed. Well, it could have been the drinking too. Because I remember when I got put on Zoloft, the doctor asked me, "Were you depressed and that's why you drink? Or do you drink and that's why you're depressed?" And I didn't have a clue.*
>
> *(Connor's family rule: I have to submerge my anger to keep everyone else happy.)*

What does it cost Connor to run away from her anger as her family rules have dictated? She uses lots of energy and huge amounts of time trying *not* to be mad at her family, trying to keep all of them on an even keel while falling into deep sadness and blunting her annoyance with alcohol. Connor loses chances for intimacy with her family, as anger diversion prevents all of them from really getting to know each other.

So how do we create better boundaries? Through adaptive anger skills and understanding how good boundaries and healthy anger are intimately related to each other.

Identifying, Developing, and Maintaining Good Boundaries

Girls who receive early family confirmation that all their feelings, including anger, are valid have a firm foundation to build on when it comes to being able to talk about their emotional experiences as adults. A recent study conducted by Joanne King at the University of Oregon and her associate Brent Mallinckrodt at the University of Missouri suggests that unclear boundaries in children's families relate to alexithymia, or difficulty identifying and labeling feelings later in life. On the other hand, growing up in a family that encourages autonomy and feeling expression shows the reverse pattern. Straightforward communication about anger not only makes for healthier family dynamics, it is necessary for healthy identity development. Why? Because anger talk helps us form the boundaries that teach us where we stop and others start.

Good boundaries mean you can say no to another family member who makes a request that angers you and maintain a positive relationship at the same time. You can stick up for yourself without resorting to one of the two main escape routes we mentioned earlier: cut-off or enmeshment. You don't divert your anger. A good boundary is when you recognize what is your stuff and what is their stuff. Read the story below to see how one woman has used her anger awareness to make the move from fuzzy to forthright boundaries.

Edie:
Building Better Boundaries

Edie (46) is a nurse with two teenagers at home. Her anger is a response to her mother's assumption that it's okay to visit her daughter indefinitely. As Edie comes to know herself better and to be clear about her own needs, she begins to maintain firmer boundaries with her mother:

> *One of the things that I've noticed, particularly as I've gotten older, is that I don't like sharing my space. The thought of houseguests is my least favorite thing. My mother sleeps very, very late. She likes to stay up all night. Well, that's lovely. She doesn't have anything else that she needs to do, so she can do that. But at our house it doesn't work so well. My feeling is like good old Ben Franklin's; you should kick company out after three days. Her feeling is she's coming 700 miles for two to four weeks. I go over this and over this and explain and explain and every time it's tears and, "It'll be different this time." [I say] "How? Tell me how it will be different. How are you going to be different? How am I going to be different? How are we going to be different together? I don't see any changes. Let's just make it easy on ourselves." In other words, not openended—as long as you like. I just don't do well with that. I like three days . . . a long weekend.*

> *(Edie's new family rule: I can use anger to help me take care of myself.)*

While Edie accommodated her mother's wishes for many years, she has recently allowed her own feelings of opposition to help her define who she is in relation to her mother and to stand her ground. Do you have a similar history with a parent, sibling, or other important relative? Do you find yourself continually trying to work around their demands and decisions so that you won't have to confront or disagree with them? If you're ready to make a change into healthier adult ways of relating to your family and others, check out the ways to make progress with boundaries in the "Breaking Family Anger Rules, Roles, and Patterns" section later on.

Along with boundaries, the second key building block in understanding how your early family anger experiences affect all your current relationships is triangulation. This complex dynamic is one that has both valuable and detrimental sides.

Triangulation

If your family-of-origin rules include the one about "Tell someone else when you get mad, don't tell the person you're mad at," then you have lots of company. Triangulation (a term first coined by one of the founding fathers of family psychology, Murray Bowen) means introducing a third party into an interaction between two people in order to dilute some of the tension involved. The Johnson family shows this indirect anger pathway clearly. Denise can tell Leona (her grandmother) or Margaret (her mom) about her anger with her sister, but she won't tell her sister face-to-face. She may know—or hope—that these other women in her family are likely to carry her message for her.

> *Denise: It bothers me that . . . they [her sister and brother-in-law] don't go to church all the time. And it's fine that they don't, but I don't want them to tell me a lie Saturday night, when we ask them, "Oh, are you going to church?" They'll just lie: "We've got the house to work on" or "I've got papers to check." That just bothers me, because my priorities are different from Betsy's, and so I get angry with that. But I don't tell her. I'll tell other people. I won't tell the person. I'm too afraid of conflict.*
>
> *Leona: It'll come around.*
>
> *Margaret: Yeah. I was thinking of something to say the other day.*
>
> *Denise: Maybe, well sometime, if we're ever talking about it. But I don't think I can tell her.*

Denise is struggling to define why it is she can't seem to bring herself to talk directly with her sister about her angry feelings. The family rule, unspoken up to this point, dictates that someone else needs to communicate it first. Denise, her mom, and her sister are in a triangle. Sometimes grandma substitutes for mom, but the triangle remains.

Triangulation and Anger Diversion

Some families keep triangulation in place in order to prevent any direct confrontation between family members. In these families, confrontation and anger are often viewed as dangerous and detrimental. As we saw with boundaries, in such families anger diversion through keeping quiet, giving in, or avoiding the expression of irritation is the norm.

Other families triangulate anger due to power differences between family members. The family rules state it's not acceptable to express anger to someone higher up in the family hierarchy. Therefore, family members develop a pattern of passing anger down through the ranks. When a person feels angry, they usually seek out someone less powerful, threatening, or intimidating than the one they are angry with.

For women, this pattern most often involves redirecting the anger we feel toward our father or husband/partner to someone in a less powerful position—typically a child or sometimes a female relative such as a sister. When we take our anger out on someone else, we are usually diverting through externalization or segmentation.

The negative results of triangulation can include distortion of your message by others, failure of others to even deliver your message (so no helpful action even has the chance to occur), or retaliation by the person who got the message but feels insulted that you didn't come to him or her first. In more extreme situations, triangulation can even lead to abuse of another family member—for example, shaming a child when you are really angry at his or her father ("You're just like your good-for-nothing dad!").

If triangulation seems complicated, that's because it is. The beautiful thing about learning adaptive anger skills for tearing down triangles is that it significantly *uncomplicates* your life. Imagine not having to spend all that time and energy going through multiple others to get your point across!

Breaking Free of Triangulation

Cora (15) and her mom have been working on anger in their family in therapy for some time. Here, Cora's mom has pulled herself out of a triangle between her daughter and Cora's father. Cora now has to confront her anger with her dad directly. The story is told from Cora's perspective:

One time me and my mom were in a fight. I don't remember what the fight was about, but she said "I'm not going to cover up for you with your dad this time. He sounds hurt. You know, if you want to tell him you don't want to go with him, then you tell him." And I called him up, and said, "I do not want to go with you." And he said, "Why?" My dad always guilt-trips me. So that's why it was such a big thing to tell him that I didn't want to go. I said "I don't want to go with you. I do not want to see you right now. I am not going to see you. I'm furious with you." And he said, "Okay," but then he called my mom and she told him, "I don't know, it's between you and her." So I told him . . . It was kind of like taking a weight off my shoulders.

(Cora's new family rule: Dealing directly with anger helps relieve tension.)

To Cora's surprise, dealing directly with anger at her father comes as relief. You can find many ways to change *your* family geometry too. The upcoming section on "Breaking Family Anger Rules, Roles, and Patterns" tells you how. But before we get there, let's look at some other aspects of your family history that are critical to your awareness of anger patterns.

Understanding Your Earliest Anger

Take a look at the conversation below, from the interview we conducted with four generations of women in the Johnson family, from great-grandmother Leona to toddler Joanne (you met them briefly earlier). Think about what the youngest member, three-year-old Joanne, who is present in the room, is hearing about anger in her family:

Leona (79): I just keep it inside. I try to forget it; I don't think about it too much and try to keep myself busy with things.

Margaret (58; Leona's daughter): I don't ever stay angry very long. I have witnessed situations where anger has just consumed a person, and I don't like that. If I get angry about something, I will say it, I will get it out, and I'm not angry anymore.

Denise (31; Margaret's daughter; Leona's granddaughter): I'm not angry with my mom often, but when it comes, I get really scared. I can't tell her I'm angry with her. For example when Joanne was born, I had her in the bouncy seat and she was uncovered. I was exhausted, lying on the couch. Mom comes in and says, "Oh Denise, should she be in that seat? She should be covered, don't you know she's cold?" I was so angry, and I just went into the other room and cried. I don't want to have to stand up to my mom; I don't want to feel like I'm hurting her. (To Margaret) I don't want you to know I'm angry. I don't want that confrontation stuff.

Margaret: I knew she would be angry. It was interesting trying to figure out how to communicate with Denise when she had Joanne. The only way was to keep my mouth shut. I didn't realize how insecure she felt. This is a little child's fear, but it stays with you—she always tried to be so good because she didn't want to make Mama worry.

What is Joanne learning about anger from her mom, grandmother, and great-grandmother, even at the tender age of three? Will she learn that "good girls" don't get angry and thereby worry their mamas? Or will she come to express it, albeit with hesitation, like her grandmother?

Just like Joanne, all tiny tots give and receive lots of important communications about their emotions every day. Simple daily living provides children with plenty of opportunities to practice giving and getting angry responses. But at these early ages, children lack the adult ability to reflect on the logic of the messages they receive. The messages are swallowed whole and, without examination or questioning, become part of who we are.

As little girls, we logically put together the cause and effect relationships that have impact on our lives; we get scolded, we feel sad; we feel sad, we cry; we cry, we get a hug from someone big. However, in some families, just being aware of the connections between events and feelings puts us at risk. Many women talk about growing up in families where it was considered disloyal to show anger even when you are hurt or insulted ("How could you hurt your father that way?"). Perhaps showing emotion was punished in an "I'll give you something to cry about" kind of way. Fear of reprisal teaches us to avoid noticing when we are slighted and perhaps teaches us to hide any anger we do notice or risk worse consequences.

In our research, many of the women describe family backgrounds in which expressing anger was discouraged or unsafe. Was it like that in your family? Later, although you may have come to realize intellectually that anger is a valid human emotion, you still are likely to have a haunting sense that it's unwelcome between loved ones or unattractive in women. This family-of-origin fear/anger template becomes automatic, causing anxiety should you attempt to break the rules. This set of well-learned childhood dynamics creates a "don't ask, don't tell" kind of adult environment down the road.

Taking Stock of Your Anger Ancestry

While it may seem like a no-brainer to assume we learn rules of anger expression in our families as we grow up, tracing these influences is harder than you think—one of those forest-for-the-trees situations. Rummaging for our familial anger patterns takes some work because we're so close to our own families, and our reactions and experiences within our families are often so automatic and embedded. One systematic way to do this is with a genogram. Genograms graphically help people see the patterns in their families and have been used by family therapists for the last two decades. To trace your family's anger patterns, try creating your own genogram:

YOUR ANGER GENOGRAM

A genogram is a little bit like a family tree. Use a big sheet of paper to draw at least three generations of your family; if you have kids, make sure to include their generation. Males are shown by squares, females by circles. Marriages are shown by horizontal lines; children by vertical lines. Other symbols that are helpful include:

− − −   is an informal relationship, such as an important family friend
        or an affair
/   a single slash across a marriage line indicates a separation
//   a double slash across a marriage line indicates a divorce
X   an X in a circle or a square means a death

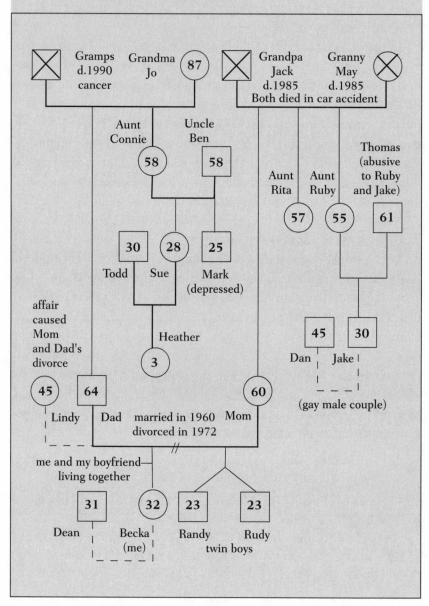

Fill in a circle or a square halfway to show alcohol or substance abuse. Usually, people also write in things like ages, birthdates, marriage dates, death dates, and information about who really likes each other (draw double or even triple lines between these people if they are enmeshed) and who is in conflict or even abusive (draw jagged lines or lightning bolts between these people). An example of a genogram is presented above. After you make yours, answer the following questions about patterns of anger in your family and write your answers directly on your genogram next to the appropriate people.

1. Who comforted you in your family? Who could not or would not?

2. What did you learn about anger from the other women in your family?

3. What did you learn about anger from the men in your family?

4. Who knows the most about your anger? Who knows the least? Why?

5. How do different people in your family express their anger? What results do they get? With whom?

6. Can you see any triangles in your family? (Who talks to whom when they are angry? Is it direct communication or is someone in the middle? Who's usually in the middle?)

7. Who in your family diverts anger by using:

    a. containment (knows they're angry, but tries to stuff it)

    b. internalization (doesn't seem aware of their anger, but blames self a lot)

    c. segmentation (claims no awareness of their anger, but others may see it)

    d. externalization (bypasses ownership of anger by just acting impulsively aggressive)

8. Can you identify who has good boundaries and who doesn't? (Who can hold their ground appropriately when angry? Who just totally cuts others off when angry? Who seems like they are always in each other's business when angry and has to get half the family involved in it?)

9. What messages about anger and gender, religion or your culture/ethnicity did you receive growing up?

10. How are you carrying any or all of these messages into your own relationships today?

What are your reactions to completing your anger genogram? Many women report that drawing this picture and going through the process of labeling anger patterns in their families is immensely helpful. The genogram can help you pick key places to start in using some of the strategies we'll mention for working with your anger constructively in your family.

One thing that may have come up in your genogram that we haven't discussed yet is abuse. Too many girls and women experience these devastating violations for us to let this chapter go by without addressing abuse, its role in the development of anger diversion, and ultimately, how anger provides a remarkably healing power for survivors of abusive family relationships.

Special Cases: Sexual and Physical Abuse in the Family

I was starting to get pissed, because at ten o'clock the dishes were still not done. I said, "Do the dishes." And when I was young and my dad said, "Do the dishes," it meant mop the floor, clean off the stove, clean the countertop, put the fresh tablecloth on, wipe down the walls—it was the whole kitchen. Anyway, she (my daughter) goes in there and starts throwing my dishes around. And I whipped her around, and I got in her face. And she raised her hand to me. And I was blind with rage. And I thought, who does she think she is? I will kill her. I said, "Oh no you won't!" And I smacked her in the face. I slapped her good, because one little drop of blood came down. And then I said, "Who do you think you are? I fight every day not to beat you like my parents beat me. You don't know what I fight every day. Because it's absolute instinct to beat you every time I'm mad at you, because that's what I was raised with." She was great for the next nine months. Not a snotty little word out of her, and I thought I should have slapped her earlier. She totally challenged me, and I was going to take her down if I had to beat her with my fist. You will not ever, ever raise your hand to me. I've done too much for you.

—Kate (42)

(Kate's family rule: Parents are allowed to control their children, even if it means using brute force to do it.)

Kate's story illustrates how cycles of violence can be perpetuated in families, and how the use of physical aggression teaches children dysfunctional rules about emotionality and respect in families. Abuse gives the message that when adults are angry with their children for whatever misbehavior their children are committing, the grown-ups have the right to cause their children physical pain. Abuse teaches you that you deserve to suffer physical pain. Your behavior takes away your rights for physical safety, integrity, and respect. Abuse communicates that if you are a child, your body deserves less respect than that of an adult. Abuse models permission for you, when you become a parent, to cause your own child physical pain if you are angry. It validates the idea that adults should enforce ways of thinking and behaving at all costs; that to be an adult means to be in control of your children's thinking, feeling, and behaving. Abuse means that controlling children's behavior is more of a priority than being honest with them.

Some women report having been hit in their families-of-origin and surviving this experience unscathed. For others, there are more obvious, serious, long-term consequences to self-esteem, self-confidence, and the development of anger skills. The line between physical discipline or spanking and abuse is subjective and highly controversial. Certain segments of U.S. society so widely accept the practice of hitting children as a means of discipline that many people assume one should not be upset about it. However, our perspective is that the negative effects are the same no matter how *hard* one hits a child. Thus, we disagree with the practice of using physical discipline altogether.

Adults in our clinical practice who externalize their anger by abusing others often come from families in which anger at others wasn't permitted unless it came from a parent or other authority. Therefore, little girl anger that came up at being mistreated has to be stored underground. As trauma expert Collin Ross notes, abused children get caught in the dilemma of "loving the people who are hurting them and being hurt by the people who love them." The natural anger a child feels toward her or his abuser cannot safely be expressed, and the child instead comes to believe that he or she is profoundly bad and unworthy. What other reason could exist in a child's young mind for being on the receiving end of such behavior?

Sexual abuse is one of the most devastating experiences a child can have. As Sue Johnson, a cofounder of Emotion-Focused Therapy notes, childhood trauma, especially sexual trauma, creates profound difficulty in attaching to loved ones, feeling secure, and trusting—and promotes problems with shame and anger. A large body of research on women and sexual trauma highlights the intense struggles around anger that victims contend with.

Women who experienced incest in their families-of-origin learn to submerge their own needs in the service of their perpetrators' needs. This practice trains them to unlearn their natural physiological responses to anger. So anger often presents a frightening dilemma for women who are survivors of sexual trauma: it's scary, because feeling anger can trigger memories of abuse that have been neatly repressed, and that repression has been very adaptive (it helps us simply survive abuse as children), yet acknowledging anger about past abuse is critical to the healing process. Moving into anger sometimes triggers the unnerving feeling of being out of control. Women often say they feel like they will continue feeling and expressing anger in a wild frenzy if they allow themselves to consciously feel and talk about anger at all. Ironically, it is exactly such open expression that is curative.

The Healing Power of Anger for Abused Women

Learning to express anger openly and consciously helps many survivors of sexual trauma feel more empowered and diminishes the devastating effects of certain traumatic stress symptoms. Through case studies of women survivors, we've found that anger boosts the healing process by helping women place responsibility where it belongs— on the perpetrator. The self-definition that comes with constructive anger talk helps us see ourselves as, in many respects, separate from the people who caused us harm. It validates our immense feelings of resentment at our undeserved hurts. It gives us new options for expressing ourselves that don't repeat the violent patterns we were exposed to early on. Yes, it breaks family rules—rules that desperately need to be broken.

Take Alana, for example. Now in her early 40s, Alana has a history in which she was physically abused by her biological mother and later by her foster mother, exposed to strip poker games and pornography by her stepfather, and raped at 16, resulting in a pregnancy. She explains how learning to handle her own anger differently empowers her to break old family rules:

> For a long time, my anger was more like what my birth mom and foster mom had modeled for me. Just after I left my second marriage my ten-year-old son said one day, "Nobody loves me." That made me so angry that I slapped him across the face and left a handprint. When I realized that is the way my moms would have treated me, I broke down and cried. It was an epiphany . . . a life-changing experience.

Alana then remembered and made a conscious effort to bring forward different ways of handling her anger. She had learned some good things from her grandparents, who modeled healthy boundaries:

> My grandparents raised me when I was 16 and pregnant, and I learned a whole different life through their nonviolent ways. I knew what was expected and I knew they loved me. I still have anger at my parents for not role-modeling healthy relationships for me. But I have developed and opened up. I have different levels of anger. I can choose what's important enough to fight for, and not everything is a battle. I will say no if I'm not comfortable.

Alana is now in a stable ten-year marriage, where she and her husband both express their anger directly and constructively. Anger doesn't linger.

We gripe, and it's gone.

This is a striking transformation, given Alana's history. She has worked hard at understanding and using her anger differently from her abusers, and it shows.

Whether you experienced abuse or trauma in your past or not, you can benefit by looking back to your early anger patterns in your family and figuring out how those first lessons affect you in the present. Having considered boundaries, triangulation, and anger rules in your family, think about how you feel now about breaking rules from back then. While we have zero choice about the families we're raised in, as grown-ups we get to make different choices about what we do with anger. We have the capacity to understand and interrupt early family patterns if they hurt us or the other people in our lives. When you were four, it was vital that you learn to follow family rules. But finding out who you really are *now* requires that you break them. Here are some ideas for putting these new choices into action.

Breaking Family Anger Rules, Roles, and Patterns

For Better Boundaries and Clearer Connection
Here are some additional skills and ideas for developing better boundaries. While the examples below deal with family, these tools are likely to be useful in all your relationships.

Anger Consciousness:
- *Face the issues:* It's time to start being more honest about how you really feel and what you really want. When you find yourself in disagreement with your family members, don't brush it aside or gloss it over. Make the decision to voice your opinion and your input, even when it goes against what you are hearing from others.
- *Realize what is possible:* Expressing your anger is not a guarantee that you can change another person's irritating behavior. Many women ask, "What good is using anger to set boundaries if I can't

make the other person act or feel differently?" The urge to control others and to try to get our own way often gets confused with anger expression. Don't forget that *your only real, obtainable goal can be to let the other person know what you are experiencing and where your own boundaries lie.* Letting others in on your feelings, especially the more vulnerable ones, encourages them to do the same. Of course we'd all love to be able to make others conform to our desires. But the truth is that we don't have that kind of power; others are free to act as they wish, and trying to control them is a set-up for disappointment. It is possible, however, to control your own actions. So being angry and setting a boundary that involves your *own* behavior is much more likely to lead to success. It's the difference between telling your party-animal sister, "Stop calling me so late at night! You're so inconsiderate!" versus "I'm angry that you call so late at night and I'm going to turn off the ringer at ten P.M. and let the answering machine pick it up." The first request is one that your sister has the option of ignoring, and you can't do anything about that. The second not only expresses your anger appropriately, but it draws a boundary line that you can completely control.

Constructive Anger Talk:

- *Experiment with setting a little boundary:* Start with some smaller issues that are easier to work through, and then work your way up to the tough ones. Focus on what would work best for *you*, not your family member, and decide what you would like to change. Does your dad insist on meddling in your personal finances? Does your sister constantly borrow your clothes, your car, your cash? Let your anger clue you in and help you to be clear and firm. Write a script if you need to, after reflecting on exactly what you want to say and what specific things you plan to do differently. You can request particular changes from the family member in question, but remember that you can't make them do anything. It's always more productive to work with what's in your control—you.
- *Talk about your relationship goals:* Tell your family about what you're trying to accomplish. Fill them in on the crucial information behind the changes you are making—clear boundaries bring

people closer; your anger doesn't negate your love for them—so they can understand where you are coming from and feel reassured. Clarify that your goal is connection, not criticism.

Listening:
- *Anticipate resistance:* Your family members may very well have strong reactions to the changes you're trying to make. It's normal for them to want to keep things the way they've always been, even if that creates problems for some. If they become angry when you set a boundary, remember to be accepting of their emotions, just as you would like them to accept and understand yours. Listen. Of course, if they are expressing that anger inappropriately, you'll want to let them know that while it's okay that they're mad, you'd like them to convey it respectfully.

For Triangulation

Anger Consciousness: Take the following quick test to identify triangulation in your own family. Triangles have three points, and you might be at any one of them. Ask yourself these three questions and fill in the blanks with the appropriate names:

Triangulation Mini-Quiz:
1. Do I ever find myself in the middle—carrying angry messages from one member of the family to another because the two people involved won't talk directly to each other?   Yes___ No___
   Write down: I carry anger messages between _____ and
   _____.

2. Do I ever ask others to carry an angry message for me, because I don't feel comfortable confronting the target of my anger directly?
                                              Yes___ No___
   Write down: I ask _____ to carry anger messages from me to
   _____.

3. Do I ever receive anger messages via a third party in my family?
                                              Yes___ No___
   Write down: I get anger messages from _____, but they are delivered by _____.

If you answered "Yes" to any of these questions, or had names to fill in the blanks, you are triangulated in your family. So your next step is to use good communication skills to get out of a triangle.

- *Constructive Anger Talk:* Rank your triangles from easiest to hardest to deal with. Next, pick your easiest triangle and decide exactly what you want to say, to whom, and when. We might suggest a narrative like this, with relatives X and Y:

1. X, I know you are angry with Y, but I'm tired of being your messenger. It makes me angry, and I'm not willing to do it anymore. Next time you're angry with Y, you'll have to talk to him/her on your own.
2. X, I know you think you're doing me a favor when you tell me Y is upset with me. But I'm annoyed that Y won't come to me directly and irritated that you go along with it. If you start to tell me again, I will ask you to stop.
3. If you're the one who asks a third party to carry messages for you, suck it up and next time you feel the urge, *don't do it.* Visit, call, or write to the person you are angry with directly. You might even ask the third party to refuse future messages, thereby helping you to achieve your goal.

Think Tanking/Positive Triangulation

Triangulation can be a good thing? Wait a minute! Didn't we just say triangulation was negative? Well, yes, so far, we've seen illustrations of its negative side, and triangulation *does* tend to be detrimental when it becomes a fixed pattern of interacting.

However, *triangulation can be beneficial when it is short term, used sparingly, or when there is a power difference that seriously threatens your safety or security.* For example, it would be better for a child to express her anger about an abusive dad to her sister than to confront him directly. If you are angry at your mom for forgetting to send you a thank-you card, but she's in the middle of a personal health crisis, it might be worthwhile to complain to a friend in the short run and address the issue with your mom when she's recovered. This kind of short-term triangulation is related to the adaptive anger skill of *think tanking*, setting your anger aside momentarily or consulting about it before taking more direct action. The critical aspects of positive triangulation are:

- The use of positive triangulation is conscious and purposeful: you are fully aware of what your reasons are for choosing to briefly suspend your direct expression of anger, while figuring out what you want to do.

- The use of positive triangulation is temporary in nature—you know you will not put off a decision about what to do with your anger indefinitely. You are not regularly using another person just to gripe about someone else; you are seeking advice or a quick reality check.

- The use of positive triangulation involves returning to the original source of your anger as soon as you can. You don't put off dealing with the person who made you angry and you don't make excuses for why this might not be the right time. As soon as you are clear on what you want to say and do, do it.

Listening: Be prepared for some feedback—and maybe even backlash—from the family system as you work to change your family geometry. Remember they're not in the same place you are with anger. Have your listening skills ready to hear and acknowledge the responses you are likely to get. Remember that listening isn't agreeing. Have empathy. It's hard for them too.

For Reworking Family Rules
Anger Consciousness:
- Whose rules are you playing by? Rather than succumbing to the temptation to neutralize your feelings and be nice to your family, practice hanging on to the emotional energy that's there, even if it makes you uncomfortable. Remember, you own this feeling.
- Ask yourself the following questions: How am I different from mother or grandmother? If my mother or grandmother knew my thoughts would she be shocked to know that I (fill in the blank)? In

what ways is it important for my life to be different from my mom's or grandmother's lives?

- Make a list of things you are angry about in your family, past and present. To help you make sure you remember important anger events, you might try putting these on a time line. Start with the first thing you can remember really being angry about in your family and go from there, recording all the major anger episodes. Note the *reasons* you feel the way you do. "I still resent the way my brother always put me down in front of the rest of the family because it was humiliating and made me scared to be myself later in my life." This will help you learn to validate your own experience, versus waiting for others to tell you it's okay to have your feelings.
- Sit in front of a mirror at home, when you have plenty of privacy. Talk to yourself about your gut feelings and your list of worst possible things that might happen if you express your anger to a particular family member (e.g., s/he will hate me; s/he will back away and never want to be around me again). Talk to yourself about the things you forfeit by being silent.
- Speculate wildly about the changes you will make as you unburden yourself of your family's opinions of you. Imagine what you'll find out about your family relationships if you express your anger directly (such as finding out you no longer want to live next door to your mother).
- Try this on as an affirmation, a mantra, a new guideline to live by: "Love means there will be anger between us. I love you enough to work past my discomfort and help you talk about your anger. When you get mad at me, I know you love me."

Constructive Anger Talk:

- Practice how you want to express your anger to the particular family member involved. You can do it in front of the mirror or use a tape recorder or just practice by yourself out loud. Imagine what the other person will say and how you will respond, continuing to hold your ground in the face of their response. "I will not tolerate your talking to me that way." When you feel ready, do it in real life. Go with your impulse to speak, because there will never be a perfect time. If you want to stay in connection, be sure to say so. If you feel as if it is too hard to do this verbally, face-to-face, write it in a letter. And send it. Or talk on a videotape. And deliver it.

Now that you've looked back at anger in your family-of-origin, let's look to the future. You may already be raising a member (or two or three) of the next generation, so you bear a huge responsibility for how you model anger. What practices do you still need to change? Even if you're not a parent, the information in this section can help you reform your unhelpful anger thinking—after all, you were once a child yourself.

Looking Forward:
Parenting with the Anger Advantage

Today's parents operate in all kinds of family configurations: traditional two parent, single parent, life partner parents, blended families with stepparents, and grandparents raising their grandchildren, just to name a few. While we recognize each of these situations carries its own particular flavor of family anger dynamics, it's beyond the scope of this book to address them all in individual detail. We've chosen to concentrate on the basic patterns and pointers that apply to every parent and child and invite you to personalize these to meet your own circumstances.

There's no way around it—if you're parenting, you are facing anger on a regular basis. Not only do you have to handle your own, but you have the responsibility for coaching your child into healthy anger habits as well. If you have been diverting anger, chances are that's what you are modeling for your children and teaching them to do as well. Learning to develop a healthy approach to anger as a family means coming at it from both sides—yours, as you deal with the daily frustrations of having your parental authority tested and questioned, and your kids', as they learn they must accept and follow the rules that keep them safe and help them grow.

As a parent, you have the opportunity to help your child develop an intelligent use of emotion. When parents *respond positively* to their children's expressions of frustration or distress, it creates connection and it helps them to learn ways to tolerate short-term discomfort in order to master an important situation, achieve a goal, and learn about their own internal experiences. The reverse is also true. Parents who repeatedly ignore children's emotions teach them to alter their experiences to fit someone else's need for comfort, to distract themselves away from their feelings, and ultimately to discard self-information that could help them solve problems, act creatively, and protect themselves from harm.

It's clear that helping our kids connect with anger is healthy for them, so how does it become such a family problem? For starters, much of the time that anger is directed at us parents! Along with the fun, laughter, pride, and sheer joy we experience as parents come frustration, contests of will, and lots of misunderstandings. Besides the wear and tear from all the conflict, we can be plagued by the nagging thought that somehow all this anger means we're doing something wrong. We may interpret our children's anger as some kind of parenting failure: "If only I was a decent parent my child wouldn't get so mad at me!"

However, stories that women tell about their own experiences point to a different truth. In fact, we can stop looking at family anger as a problem and appreciate it more for the fierce, strong bond it represents. Maybe anger is part of what's *right* about your family. Listen as Maggie, a 24-year-old education student, talks about what her anger toward her mother and other family members meant to her when she was younger:

> *I have most of my arguments with the people that are closest to me. I remember times with my mom when we would get into really bad arguments and later think, "Gosh, why did we say those things? I'm terrible!" and feel really bad about it, but at the same time we know each other and feel comfortable with each other more than I would ever feel with a friend or acquaintance. With my family I'm more apt to react right away than I would with others, because I'm safer. The ironic thing is that I'm the closest to my mom of any person in my*

life, and yet, we have had more arguments than I've ever had with anybody in my life. Love is such a strong feeling and anger is such a strong feeling. I feel more comfortable with her than I do anybody. I know that my mom and I could get into a fight and she'd love me no matter what.

Maggie finishes with a significant and telling statement. She has come to understand that it is within the context of love that anger can be an honest, vulnerable, sometimes painful, but ultimately valuable family experience. Did you grow up with a rule that went something like, "If you love me, you'll do as I say. If you don't follow my wishes, then you do not love me," in your family? If so, you may have come to believe and behave as though anger and love cannot coexist. But the truth is that we can love someone with all our hearts and still become very, very angry with him or her. When anger is expressed within a loving family environment, ties actually become strengthened as children learn how to navigate the ups and downs of relationships in ways that will benefit them throughout their lives.

How can we as parents help our children take advantage of all that anger can teach them? First, we can recognize how our goals and the goals of our children clash. Parents have as their primary charge to protect their children and keep them safe, so they can grow to healthy maturity. Children have as their ultimate goal to learn and grow, which must involve taking risks and trying out new behaviors. Because of this fundamental opposition, we can't help but come into conflict with our kids, and wherever there is conflict, anger is likely to be aroused. It's time to accept anger's natural place in our family dynamics and give up the idea that happy families are never angry. Second, we can move *toward* our children when they're mad, rather than away from them. Realizing our children's anger is a distress call, a signal of vulnerability, we can choose to lean *into* our relationships with them even when they declare they're angry with us. Listening with empathy sets the stage for working things out.

Finally, we can learn about the particulars of anger that come with each stage of a child's growth. As children move through their developmental phases, different challenges present themselves, as well as new opportunities for allowing anger to help each child grow up knowing who she is, what she wants, and how to keep herself safe.

Based on both our clinical work and interview research with women—many of them moms—we have learned an important fundamental truth; love and anger go together, for everybody. Women need to know this so that they can learn to allow anger to signal connection between themselves and their children.

Your Anger and Mine: The Growing-Up Years

Ages Three to Six

Young children who are preschool and early elementary school age are still learning about rules and focused on developing the skills to follow them. They are working on the self-control and cognitive understanding needed to follow parental direction. Parents begin to lay down the foundation for healthy anger expression at this age by giving youngsters ways to act out their anger that are safe and appropriate. Since their verbal capabilities are limited, young children typically need behavioral outlets, and parents can offer appropriate options instead of attempting to shut the anger down.

Let's say your four year old throws a tantrum because she is not allowed to continue watching television after her allotted hour. Telling your child to simply, "Stop right now!" without allowing her to express her rage leaves her with two unfortunate options:

1. to directly disobey her parents out of the need to do *something* with her anger and disappointment, or
2. to begin the process of negating her feelings.

Instead, you can allow her to let her anger be known in ways that are acceptable to the family. Perhaps it is alright for her to sit and cry in front of the TV until she's come to accept your direction. Or, perhaps she's too disruptive and needs to be taken to her room where she can get her anger out without disturbing the whole family. You're working to create a new family rule: everybody's feelings are important. The message is that while her behavior must follow family guidelines, her feelings are her own, and all of them, even anger, are accepted.

Ages Seven to Ten

Children of middle elementary age, say up to age ten or eleven, have by and large mastered the concept of family rules and have gone a long way toward developing the skills needed to obey them. In fact, they often become quite enamored of rules and delight in creating many of their own.

Ever notice how children at this age can spend more time arguing over the rules of a game than actually playing it? This arguing lets them test and retest to see if the rules are bendable, who is in control, and how much control *they* have. Children repeat the process with their parents and siblings, in search of answers to the same questions. When your responses indicate that the adults are in control and that there is some reasonable flexibility allowed in the rules that are for the most part set firm, then children feel secure and confident in their understanding of how their world works.

Holding firm in the face of repeated challenges provides the most effective parenting for kids this age. As much as they may fight it, your children gain security from learning they are not powerful enough to change the structure that keeps them safe and well. With all this testing, though, tempers are bound to flare—both theirs and yours. Whenever you feel your irritation rise, keep in mind that *your children are not trying to make you angry*, they simply *have* to find out if the walls of their structured lives will crumble—a little or a lot—if they push as hard as they can. If you can hold on to your emotions and not take your kids' outbursts personally, you will be teaching another new family rule: we can be mad at each other and still love each other.

And sometimes, especially as they move toward adolescence, the pushing goes too far. As important as it is to let your kids show their anger in appropriate ways, it's also crucial that they learn when enough is enough. Often some respectful anger expression on your part will convey to your child the message that he needs to back off. Focus on helping him to learn about boundaries and feelings by talking honestly about yours. For instance, "I get really angry when you sneak behind my back, and I feel disrespected. Maybe you're mad at me too because I said no. Let's find another way for you to show it."

Ages Eleven and Above

Anger is vital to your teenager. Developmentally, teens need to have more room for self-determination than middle elementary–aged kids. Parental direction that once felt firm and secure now feels rigid and oppressive to them, sparking more anger and conflict. Parents who continue to enforce rules and limits with the same control that worked so well when their child was eight or ten now find their parenting is suddenly missing the mark and has become an obstacle rather than a positive influence. The challenge is to adjust your parenting as your teen grows and matures. You want to match their pace as they become ready to take more control over their own lives and decisions. When your parenting falls behind their need for independence, teens can become agitated and panicky. Your teenager needs more input in how her life is lived, so finding a way to make room for this in your parenting style is a way to help her grow. Anger helps your adolescent learn that she has a voice in this world.

Anger between parents and teenagers has a reputation for reaching epic proportions in America. But it doesn't have to be that way. Teens who are invested in their families, who strongly identify and have a sense of belonging within the family, and who feel they are valued by their parents and siblings, have the highest motivation to follow parental rules and guidelines. One way to instill this family loyalty is to respect your teenager's feelings, no matter how much you disagree with him. As long as he is following the rules, he's doing his part, and his angry arguments are a helpful way for him to express the frustration of having to comply. If you make rules against the anger too, it feels to him like you are trying to control his mind as well as his behavior, a condition that would be hard for anyone to tolerate for long.

Keeping these developmental changes in mind will help you to understand where your child's anger and frustration is coming from at different times in his life. In addition, exploring the nature of your own anger as it arises in different disciplinary scenarios can help you sort out what's healthy for you and your kids and what is not. What's happening when your own anger at your child becomes mixed in with the discipline you are trying to carry out? When does it help and when does it begin to make things worse?

Anger Expression vs. Discipline

The nature of discipline involves taking action to correct our children's inappropriate choices. Often these choices have had negative consequences for us as well as the child involved, so it's to be expected that while in the act of disciplining we sometimes find our own anger rushing to the surface. It's healthy for our children to witness our anger as a natural result of the poor choice they have made—as long as we are expressing anger appropriately and maintaining respect for those around us, including the child involved.

However, if we are using punishment to vent our anger, we are not only putting our own needs before the child's, we are allowing ourselves to externalize anger in a way that is potentially harmful. It's important to use constructive anger expression when we choose to be honest with our kids about our anger, and it's especially crucial during discipline. Instead of using anger as a weapon during discipline, we can turn it into a helpful tool. Here Eliza tells how effective her anger can be when she expresses it respectfully and appropriately to her children:

> When I express anger then everybody starts working. Everybody kind of says, "Mommy, what can I help with?" or "What can I do?" When they see that I'm angry because nobody's helping to clean the house they must think, "Oh, she's mad, maybe we ought to clean."

Eliza differentiates between her anger and disciplinary actions. She refrains from punishing her children while she's angry and in this instance uses her anger expression *instead of* disciplinary action, in a way that helps the children understand how she feels about their lack of cooperation around the house. She doesn't use her anger to punish or play games, frighten or inflict pain. She simply shows anger on her face and in her voice, using words that give the children information they need about what happens to mom as a result of their actions.

If, however, you find yourself too caught up in your anger to discipline in a nondestructive way, it's vital that you take some time to work through it and cool down. Give yourself some space, let your kid know you are feeling angry and why, and make it clear you are too upset to discuss it further at that time. Then, once you've had a chance to process your anger (you may wish to revisit the anger expression tips in chapter Two), you can turn your attention to choosing an appropriate form of discipline and communicating your decision in a respectful way to your child. If you don't have the luxury of taking time for yourself, then use your think-tanking skills to keep your anger where it needs to be while you deal with your child.

Allowing a child to witness our anger in response to her actions differs radically from believing a child *deserves* to be disciplined when we feel anger toward her. In the example above, Eliza's kids decide to change their behavior and help their mom out when they come to understand her frustration and their part in engendering it. The repetition of these learning experiences over months and years helps children develop empathy, understand the consequences of their actions, and make more sensitive choices.

There are other ways to apply anger skills—anger consciousness, constructive anger talk, listening, and think tanking—within the context of parenting and family. How do we use each of these to establish new anger rules with our kids? We describe our favorites below.

MOVING AHEAD WITH ANGER IN PARENTING

Think Tanking Anger: A Time-out for Parents

1. Hold your anger in suspended animation for a moment and give your subconscious mind a green light to begin processing the feeling—working to figure it out, where it comes from, what its meaning is, what you need to do about it. Far from trying to get away from this emotion, you secure it

below consciousness for the moment so that you can recall it and think about it when the time is right. Remember, think tanking is not repressing or suppressing your anger. You feel it and know it, but are giving yourself a little bit of time to decide what to do with it. This helps you make the best decision you can, using both your emotion and your intellect together.

2. When you notice the first flickers of anger, irritation, annoyance, frustration, or rage, take a deep breath in through your nose. Exhale through your mouth. Focus on a part of your body or clothing. For instance, look down at your hand or a ring on your hand, a watch, a sleeve. Take this moment to mentally separate yourself from the situation and silently acknowledge that you are angry.

3. Deliberately change your focus from your feelings to your thoughts, as you plan how you want to speak and what you want to say. Remember the goal of your discipline is to provide concrete consequences for your child's poor choices. Don't try to lecture or teach while you are struggling to contain your anger.

4. Keep your disciplinary moment brief and to the point. If you feel unsure about a decision and need more time to think about it, tell your child he'll have to wait until you've had time to consider it carefully. Remove yourself from the situation as soon as you are certain your child is safe, and find a place where you can attend to your anger.

Establishing Your Own Family Anger Rules

One of the most helpful steps you can take is to work with your kids to develop anger rules for your family. The rules need to reflect a combination of what your kids find helpful in letting out their anger and what you find you can tolerate. There are many alternatives you can offer your children, but the most important consideration is safety. We suggest the following rules become part of every family's approach to anger expression:

- You may not do anything that will hurt yourself.
- You may not do anything that will hurt others.
- You may not do anything that will hurt anything in our home.

Clearly, a child must be *in control of her outward expression* in order to stay within this structure. Anger expression that is out of control or unmanageable is also unsafe and will not help your child. When he loses control of himself in anger, your child will most likely feel anxiety, guilt, or shame instead of empowerment, clarity, and strength. This is not part of the helpful model of anger we hope children will carry with them into adulthood.

With safety and control clearly established, your next step is to pick some concrete ways the kids can express their anger so they won't feel forced to divert it. Think about the adult anger expression exercises described in chapter Two. These are divided into verbal and physical categories. The younger your child, the more likely he will want and need physical release. Our experience has been that angry children will act out what they cannot talk about. But just like adults, most kids will engage in both physical and verbal anger expression when given the opportunity.

It might be a struggle initially to find ways to allow children to both hear their own anger and show it in front of others. Over time we've accumulated a collection of anger expression options that have worked for a variety of families. Since family values vary so much, those suggestions that are acceptable for some families may be considered inappropriate or disrespectful by others. Take a look at the list below, and choose an exercise that is closest to your comfort zone to start. Then you can add others from the list or create your own. Remember, you can customize these to fit your family's needs and values, just as long as you're promoting anger expression, not diversion.

Verbal Release:
- Talking, yelling, complaining, etc., alone in one's bedroom, outside in the backyard, sitting in the car, or wherever there is privacy
- Journaling in a private notebook that is not read by others
- Writing poetry (especially favored by teen girls)

- Tape recording thoughts and feelings on a tape not to be heard by others
- Listening to or playing loud music that matches one's feelings

Physical outlets:
- Kicking, hitting, or punching something soft such as a pillow, cushion, blanket-filled backpack, punching bag, stuffed animal, or mattress
- Throwing ice cubes, bean bags, or plastic balls at a fence or outside wall
- Hammering nails into a block of wood
- Tearing up newspapers or old phone books
- Slamming doors
- Sport activities—running, slamming a tennis ball against a wall, Rollerblading, etc.

Again, research shows it's important for children to learn to separate the physical release of anger (as in venting exercises) from the ways we show anger in our relationships (as in a conversation). They should be told that the point of throwing sticks at the back fence or pounding their mattress is to let out the angry energy in their bodies, so they can feel ready to talk about their anger afterward.

If you've lived under the assumption that an angry kid needs discipline, not freedom of expression, or if some of these physical activities seem a bit daunting, take a minute to explore your fears. A child (or an adult) could engage in any of the exercises above with all their strength for as long as their endurance holds out, without bringing a bit of harm to themselves or anyone else. That's a powerful experience, which is why it works so well in dealing with anger, one of our most powerful emotions.

In some situations, just having the option of letting out anger without causing damage, getting in trouble, or suffering retribution is enormously helpful for a child. However, research with adults demonstrates that we can maximize the usefulness of this kind of release in a couple of different ways.

The Connection Between Thoughts and Feelings

First, when a physical release activity is accompanied by some kind of cognitive processing, a more powerful benefit results. This means that whenever she can find words, written or spoken, to go along with her physical anger expression, your child's experience is more meaningful to her. Secondly, it's important to eventually have direct communication with the person who made you angry. If, along with expressing it in physical ways, your child has the opportunity to talk about her anger and the issues connected with it, she'll have a better chance of experiencing empowerment and success. You can guide your child to find this helpful connection between actions and words as part of the anger expression process.

- Whenever your child chooses a physical activity in order to release anger, monitor him to ensure his safety.
- After he finishes, see if he'll share with you his feelings and talk about the related issues.
- If his anger is directed at a sibling or playmate, coach your child to use respectful words in communicating feelings and negotiating a change.
- If another adult is the target of your child's frustrations, help him decide if it's safe and advisable to approach that person and, if so, how to go about it. He may want to call Grandma on the phone to let her know it hurt to be forgotten on his birthday, rather than tell her in person. Keep in mind that not all adults tolerate anger from children very well, even if it's expressed respectfully. He may need support in dealing with the social consequences of being frank.

Now that you have identified some overall strategies for using think tanking, anger rules, and the thought-feeling connection, you are well on your way to claiming the anger advantage for your family. If you find yourself getting stuck here and there as you progress toward making a healthy space for anger within your loving family, keep the following in mind.

Mom's Anger, Kid's Anger: Guidelines for Getting It—Together

Focus on what they do, not what they say.

Your goal is compliance, not mind control. We ask a lot when we require our children to do something they don't want to do. To insist that they also *agree* with us is asking too much. It should be your children's behavior, not their words or facial expression, which indicates their compliance. They need to express their frustration, but if they do so impertinently (e.g., by cursing or calling someone names), don't respond by demanding they keep quiet. Instead, teach them appropriate words to use when they strongly disagree with you.

It's not attitude, it's anger.

Be careful about labeling a child's anger as a "bad attitude." Adults often jump too quickly to reprimand and lecture about attitude when a child or teen makes it clear they don't want to conform. Comments like "Don't give me that look" and "Why do you have to spoil it with your attitude?" arrest kids' expressions of how they feel right at the point when they need some way to let off steam and communicate disagreement with us. Acknowledging anger and resistance with "It sounds like you really don't agree, but I'm glad you decided to come along anyway" or "I can tell you really don't want to do this, so thanks for keeping at it" is much more helpful. These statements tell your child you got their message and appreciate their compliance in spite of their inclination to refuse.

Remember—you're the adult.

That means you're not going to further an angry exchange by insisting you have the last word, shouting down, threatening, or getting even with your kid. These are the behaviors of someone looking to escalate a fight or crush a child. If you find yourself engaged in this kind of control struggle, ask yourself if you are using fights with your kids to express your own unresolved anger and be sure to seek other outlets if this is so. Sometimes older children and teens will bait parents, so guard against biting the hook. The best way to do this is by sticking to the issues you want to discuss and refusing to get pulled off course. Remember, if you feel confused or concerned about how your anger is coming out, you can always take a break to think tank your emotion. Then use negotiation to explain to your child what your concerns are while you listen and learn about theirs.

You don't have to change just because they're angry.

Sometimes the pressure to parent perfectly leads adults to feel obligated to change the rules when kids begin to express negative feelings. Don't let this get in the way of listening to your kids' anger. You need not agree with your children, and you certainly don't have to change your rules because they are unhappy. Just listening to your kids' anger lets them know you respect their feelings and are willing to give them some space in your relationship to work through the hard stuff. You may hear things that lead you to rethink some of your rules or expectations, but base any changes on the information you've gleaned and your kids' best interests, not on taking the path of least resistance.

Never use your anger to intimidate or frighten your child into obedience.

The threat of abandonment is the scariest thing in your child's inner world. Be careful not to imply you're leaving, either physically or emotionally. Ask yourself if you have used these words—or some variation of them—in your home: " . . . *and if I catch you sneaking out again, so help me, I'm sending you to live with your father (mother, grandparents, parole officer)."*

Each of us has run into someone who uses their anger like a baseball bat. They swing away with violent force, sweeping down everything in their path until nothing is left standing and the way is clear for them to do as they like. Direct anger expression is something very different, indeed. If we object to our children using tantrums to get their way, we must be careful to avoid using hurtful anger ourselves as a means of pressuring our children into submission. This abuse of the power behind anger only leads to more relationship problems in the future. Expressing anger is a way to make feelings useful, not a way to control others.

GROWING AND LOVING THROUGH FAMILY ANGER

With some new family anger rules in mind, do you find yourself noticing how different things are from the way you were raised? When you start to make lasting changes with your kids, this affects not only your parenting and current family life, it often causes you to reexamine anger patterns with your own parents and can lead to real emotional breakthroughs. What we see women doing differently with their anger in relation to their children ripples into feelings of increased confidence, not just at home, but across diverse areas of their lives.

So do the ideas and guidelines we've presented here work for real women in their families? We've seen it countless times. Here, Beth talks about important changes in how she sees anger consciousness, think tanking, constructive anger talk, and listening. You'll see clear boundaries. Beth has her own words for some of these things, but regardless of their names, the advantages they have brought to Beth in her family life ring loud and clear. She has learned to embrace the truth that love and anger can coexist in her relationships.

> *I've started consciously setting boundaries. I always try to think about the consequences of saying yes or no. I make different decisions now, and I think a lot more about everything I do. I try to keep more focus on the reasons why I'm doing things and what's good for me. I am a lot more able now to say that I need to think about something, and I'm not afraid to change my mind later. I used to feel forced into doing something I didn't want to do, but now if I accidentally say "Yeah, I'll do that," I don't feel so bad that I go back and change my mind when I realize I really don't want to do it. That makes the biggest difference, setting those boundaries.*
>
> *I can finally see it isn't the end of the world. We aren't going to get divorced just because I get really mad! And that is a really positive thing for me because with my mom, whenever she was really angry at me she would just leave me with my dad or grandmother and not come back. Now I can see that just because I'm mad or he's mad, no one has to leave the*

way she did. Even if one of us feels like we need to take off, it's just for a few hours and then we come back.

By hiding our anger, we would never solve problems, just cover them up. Because we wouldn't face it, we were never able to sit back and look at it to see what would really help.

Recognizing the signals of anger coming on before I get too angry really is important. That way I can be just a little angry instead of full-out angry, and do something about it before it's just too much to do anything about, or gets so big it makes me physically sick. I imagine that everything—what happened and how I feel about it—is in a drawer and I can open it and look at it when I want to, and then I can put it back in and shut the drawer when I don't want to look at it anymore. Internalizing that concept really helped me a lot because I could look at those things and examine them and see what I was feeling, one by one, without it overwhelming me.

Now I feel that I can be angry with any of my family when I want to. It's so much better because it's not nearly as tense for me as it used to be and I don't feel nearly as much pressure. It's so much more manageable now that I can know I'm angry. I can be angry, deal with it, deal with them, and then I get over it. I can enjoy them more and when I don't enjoy them, I can leave! I feel like I can be closer to them now.

FOUR

The Perfect Couple
Anger and Love Together

I *always have to get it off my chest, so I end up talking to
John about it. I know I can talk to him. I mean, I don't
plan on "Okay, let's have an argument," but I know it
will bring us closer together. He comes back to me, and he
sees things in a completely different light. I know that if I get
my anger out, we'll go to a different realm, a different level.
And I love that. Because then, the next day, I just see a whole
new John. It's made me realize there are so many levels of love
in this relationship, it's not just black and white. And I love
that, it's very freeing for me, it's very flexible for me.*

—Denise (31)

LOVE AND SEX IN THE REAL WORLD

In the traditional romance script, two young, beautiful, heterosexual
people find themselves attracted to each other, spend some amount of
time getting to know each other (courting), fall more and more deeply
in love, and then marry, have kids, and live happily ever after, their
respective relations harmonizing in one big happy family. We all know
this story. The romance novel and film industry have built multi-
million-dollar fortunes with this formula. Of course, some roadblocks
always give it spice, but in the end, the two lovers blissfully walk
arm-in-arm into the sunset. Does it fit your life? We didn't think so. It
doesn't fit most people's.

So, let's rework the traditional script. Two people at some point in their more-or-less adult lives find themselves attracted to each other. Lugging their suitcases and tote bags full of fears, insecurities, guilt, past diverted anger, and possible abuse from their families and previous relationships, they tentatively start to get to know each other. Both have conflicted ideas and feelings about sex. They may or may not ever live together, get married, or have children. Or maybe there are kids in the picture from a previous relationship. The relationship may last only as long as a one-night-stand or, if they get more involved and the chemistry between them works and there is some level of emotional commitment, the relationship continues to develop.

Then there are complicated relationships with each partner's friends, coworkers, and families that must be negotiated. Meaty issues about boundaries emerge. How do I want you to show your affection? How do I show mine? Should I change or not? Can I make you change? These are important questions because they're all issues that help the partners define who they are, both as a couple and as two separate individuals.

Sex, if it occurs, ranges from brutal to disappointing to mundane to pleasant to fabulous. Partners rarely completely agree about the meaning, value, timing, frequency, and techniques involved. If the relationship lasts past about 18 to 24 months, the chemistry begins to fade (this is a biological reality), and one or both partners may begin to wonder if it's time to move on. If they stay together, the couple has to adjust to these typical changes in desire.

And there's anger in this story. Lots of it. This is love and sex in the real world. Our lives may not be fairy tales, but they're also usually not bleak tragedies either. Love and sex in the real world is an honest story and often a story of courage and a testimony to our adaptability, resilience, resourcefulness, and need for authentic connection in our lives.

Yours, Mine, and Ours: The Nature of Anger Between Intimates

I'm angry at Todd because he's a slob. I don't see why he can't clean up his place a bit, it's a dump. He knows I don't like it, but refuses to do anything about it. At least he keeps himself and his clothes clean! I'm also pissed off because I'm bored. He never wants to try anything new. He's into basketball and country western music. And that's about it. If you'd ask him, he'd say he's angry because I nag too much and that I don't want to have sex enough. That's his idea of what's wrong with the relationship. How can he expect me to want to have sex in such a gross mess though? Hardly the setting for romance! He thinks I'm too picky and that none of that should matter.

—Becky (33)

Becky has one view of what there is to be angry about in her relationship with Todd. Todd has anger of his own, but sees the situation quite differently from Becky. An outside observer might have a third version of their dynamics—one probably neither Todd nor Becky can see without stopping to take a deeper look at the relationship cycle they've created. Becky's anger isn't the problem. Her anger is trying to tell her that relationship changes are needed.

To get a handle on how anger operates in close relationships, let's examine the progress of a hypothetical relationship over time to see when anger arises and how it functions at the different stages. Knowing when to expect anger over the course of a relationship and what that anger tends to be about can be a big reassurance. Gaining perspective on anger as a natural and valid part of two people learning to be themselves together is an essential part of anger consciousness.

There is a predictable patterning to most relationships. Our initial attraction usually has something to do with someone's looks and other outward signs that they are desirable and have a personality that complements ours. But once we interact, we determine if there is mutual interest and chemistry in a relatively short while.

If we start to spend time with someone, the relationship moves to a getting-to-know-you stage in which we usually try to find out what we have in common with the other person. We most often become attracted to those with similar backgrounds, attitudes, and values to our own (opposites may attract, but they make for rocky romances).

During this initial phase, we generally ignore signs that our potential new love is different from us or annoying in some way. We pay attention to the zingy feelings and marvel in the wonder of total fusion (this is normal). Little episodes of anger that occur when our partner surprises us somehow—doesn't call when he usually would, makes a sexist joke in front of his buddies—tend to get swept under the rug. Can you think of times when this has happened to you? Take a minute to reflect on a previous or current relationship. Are there things that really irritate you now that you chose to ignore at first? Even if you can think of only an example or two, you are already expanding your anger awareness.

During the madly in love stage, many women convince themselves that, "No one knows him the way I do," that they can change him, or, "He's different with me." It's hard to see completely clearly through the hormonal haze. Boundaries between partners at this point are fuzzy, and we have a difficult time determining who we are as separate people.

The desire to merge with our new love often takes sexual form, although the timing of this differs from couple to couple. But sex is not just sex. Physical intimacy has complicated meanings between two people forging *something new* between them. Sex is a symbol for unspoken patterns of closeness and distance between these two, so *anger about sex* usually signals deeper and older hurts or expectations about what each should do in relation to the other. Sex also symbolizes the togetherness and separateness of two people in a love relationship, both necessary parts of their connection.

Do you feel annoyed and hurt when your lover brushes you off? Are you mad when your lover chooses not to talk to you during or after sex? Do the two of you find yourselves suddenly bickering about something like household chores when sex between you has been less than ideal? Look back to your family and notice if your current feelings echo early patterns of ignoring, rerouting, or cutting off communication that you experienced in your family. Making connections between early anger dynamics and your current sex life can lead to real "Aha!" experiences; openly sharing this awareness deepens the true mutual understanding between you and your love partner.

When you make a long-term commitment to each other, you and

your loved one enter the next stage of relationship development, and new issues start to arise. You begin really to think about what *you* expect from this potential life partner, forcing you to notice your separate selfhoods. You think about what it will be like to be a part of each other's families. If you both want children, you think about what it will be like to be parents together. Arguments and heated feelings crop up in this stage, as well they should. Realize that a lot of conflict at this stage is normal. After all, you're determining how you'll be together and at the same time maintain distinct identities.

How do you know if you're having too much conflict at this point or if your disagreements are normal? The best guidelines we can offer here are to say that if you are fighting day in and day out without resolution or if you and/or your partner are getting verbally or physically abusive with each other (calling each other names, vicious insulting, throwing things, forcefully restraining, hitting) you should seriously reconsider continuing the relationship or seeking professional help. If you are having difficult discussions, but they result in *progress* (new learning about each other, solutions), that's great. Also, trust the little voice inside you—if in the quiet moments you have to yourself, perhaps before you drift off to sleep, you often find yourself wondering if he's right for you, if you find yourself making excuses for him and talking yourself into why you should stay in the relationship, these can be markers for real problems later on. When you feel bored, resigned, anxious, sad, or mad more than you feel excited and happy about your future partner, this an imbalance worth noting.

If you decide to commit to each other and settle down, life continues to throw you curves and new challenges as kids come into the picture, parents age, jobs come and go, sexual patterns change, and the vagaries of fate toss you accidents, illnesses, or lottery winnings. Each new event brings emotional reactions from you and your partner, and the opportunities for anger are almost limitless. This anger is important because it constantly reminds you both that you exist independently of your love, while being forever intertwined. Know that anger should be a regular experience for well-functioning stable couples. A good relationship isn't defined as anger free—a good relationship means couples use their anger as a cue to connect and engage with each other to strengthen their bond. When you ignore the powerful benefits of expressing your anger, you may end up like Clarice, who writes about how anger issues, left unattended, have affected her marital relationship:

> *I am so angry with my husband right now. We no longer have sex, and that is one of the reasons I am so angry! So it is really a double-edged sword, isn't it? I can't seem to feel sexual or want to have sex with all of this anger hanging over my head.*

Notice how sex is a metaphor for what's going on in this relationship. Clarice feels furious about her partner's ongoing avoidance of problems in their relationship, so she pulls away physically too. Clarice talks about her growing frustration with the inability to process anger with her husband:

> *It isn't resolved and even though I've tried to resolve frustrations for the last one and a half years, they haven't been resolved and it seems like I am just left with a huge pile of shit to be angry about. While I work to hash out my feelings and anger, as I want to resolve and relinquish it right away, his approach is to ignore and avoid. He thinks that by ignoring conflict or pacifying me with placating words, keeping the status quo, then things are great! Boy is he WRONG!*

When negativity reaches an intolerable point, one or both of you may become so dissatisfied in the relationship that you may begin to think about other options—getting out or finding another partner. Clarice's ongoing frustration with her husband's failure to deal with the anger in their relationship has brought her to this point:

> *All of the energy spent NOT dealing with our issues is going to go to waste as I fear our relationship will soon be over. I do know that my anger is telling me something though, and that I need to pay attention and take action.*

You may stay in a boring, dead relationship for the sake of the children or because you don't have the resources to leave or just out of habit. When relationships end, the partings are rarely mutual and involve a process all their own. Most often, one person gets dumped and another does the dumping. According to John Gottman, well-known couples' researcher and therapist at the Gottman Institute in Seattle, relationships that are highly dysfunctional and filled with intense negativity from the start usually end quickly (in about two years) whereas relationships ending after years of togetherness are more often characterized by lack of affection and positive emotion.

When a relationship breakup occurs, anger still has a positive role to play. Anger is a natural part of working through the loss of a partnership. Insights generated from exploring your anger after your lover is gone often provide critical information that you can carry into a new and improved relationship in the future; it tells you what needs your ex never met, what boundaries he crossed, and what you don't ever want to put up with again (you might even try writing these down as helpful reminders). Anger at this point may be intertwined with sadness, anxiety, guilt, or positive emotions, such as a sense of freedom. Such mixed emotions can be confusing and unsettling, but don't let your anger slip by unnoticed. If your ex isn't available to work through the emotional aspects of the breakup (most aren't), stay in regular contact with trusted friends and family or a good therapist. Talk about how mad you are, and use what your anger tells you to make different choices next time around.

It helps to look at romance through the lens of attachment. If your early family experiences led you to feel unlovable, you may tend to avoid intense, long-term relationships, or stay distant in them. If your early experiences were full of uncertainty—"sometimes I'm loved, sometimes I'm not—you probably feel more anxious in your adult love relationships. You may, in fact, find yourself wanting faster or deeper connections than your partners, with anger escalating in tandem with your sense of hunger and vulnerability. If you bring unresolved childhood trauma and loss into your romance relationships, you probably have bouts of intense fury at times, usually triggered by reminders of early hurt. Trauma survivors possess both deep needs for connection and gnawing fears of it. Anger can serve to signal either the darkness of disconnection or as a companion to fear—pushing a partner away to a safe distance. Researcher Sue Johnson of the University of Ottowa encourages partners to thoroughly explore their needs for connection, their places of vulnerability, and to understand how anger guides us to our most fundamental bonds.

One way for exploring these intricate patterns is to use the genogram. If your partner is reluctant to participate in this exercise, it can be reassuring to tell him or her that the genogram doesn't require anybody to change who they are or to commit to acting differently. The genogram is just a drawing of your family tree that may help the two of you understand each other better.

Joint Genogram

To gain awareness about your anger patterns and your partner's anger patterns, extend the genogram exercise you did in chapter Three. You already have yours done, so sit down with your partner (at a time when you're not angry with each other) to create a genogram for his or her family-of-origin, using the same instructions. Look at the two together to find your inheritance of anger dynamics and attitudes. Did you hook up with someone who repeats important anger styles that you learned in your family? Was he attracted to you because his family was always aggressively shoving anger out and he likes your quiet avoidance of conflict?

Each couple's joint genogram is completely individualized to their own relationship. This exercise builds understanding and a sense of shared responsibility for the health of your relationship. It can be helpful to look for patterns of diversion—for example, if you both avoid conflict, you run the risks of drifting apart as critical issues in your relationship go unaddressed. If your partner or yourself come from families that externalize anger, that should be a red flag for potential abuse. If you learned to use anger appropriately in your family, but your partner's family was passive-aggressive with their anger, you'll know to be on the lookout for some stubborn power struggles. Use your genogram to track problems with attachment too, paying special attention to disconnection, loneliness, fear, and shame.

You can also use your own growing set of adaptive anger skills to talk about issues noted in the joint genogram; he may also be able to learn from seeing you do things differently. So the joint genogram can be one important way of learning about the anger themes in your love relationships. A natural outgrowth of discovering the patterns of anger that each of you picked up in your families is a better awareness of what triggers your anger and that of your partner.

Sharing Your Anger Triggers

No matter where you are in the process of your love journey, it can be helpful to take a little bit of time to identify what trips your anger wires, both to develop your own anger consciousness and to be able to share these important hot buttons with your partner. Make a list of things that are likely to make you mad in any relationship and a list of what makes you mad in your current relationship. In their research, Beverley Fehr and her colleagues find that women's anger is triggered most often by their partner's betrayals of trust, personal criticism, lack of consideration, and forgetting important personal information. Consider having a conversation about your triggers with your lover at some point when you are both calm and receptive. Women often describe feeling closer than ever to their partners when they take this important risk. Your partner can do a list as well, to share with you. While you can do this exercise anytime, it can be particularly beneficial early on in a relationship, preventing miscommunication and lack of awareness before they become problems.

A Word about Affairs

Betrayals of trust are fundamentally anger-inducing events, and an affair is often considered to be at the top of the list of disloyalties. Infidelity may come up at any point during the relationship life cycle and involves anger on all sides. Rates of infidelity have long been thought to be higher for men, but women now seem to be catching up. In their recent (2001) summary of infidelity research, David Atkins and Neil Jacobson at the Center for Clinical Research in Seattle and their colleague Donald Baucom at the University of North Carolina note more recent studies show more equal rates of infidelity for both genders. In men and women under 40, rates of infidelity in the context of a marriage relationship are virtually identical and hover around the 25 percent mark. Likewise, while popular lore suggests that affairs always destroy relationships, research in this area shows otherwise. Affairs happen for lots of different reasons. Sometimes an affair calls attention to critical issues in a partnership that the couple has been unwilling to face, and they work it through, either to stay together or separate. But sometimes one or both partners have affairs in a revenge-distancing cycle so they don't have to come close and struggle out issues together, and yes, this generally means anger is being diverted.

Cheaters may be angry with their primary partners for a host of things (infrequent sex, lack of affection or appreciation) they believe contributed to their need for an outside relationship. The person who has been cheated on feels angry about the fundamental betrayal of trust. There is anger from a wounded sense of self as a desirable partner and from having the stability of one's relational world deeply shaken.

We now turn our lens to focus more pointedly on the relationships between anger and sex. It is the sexual nature of romantic relationships that critically distinguishes them from friendships or family relations and sex is a basic form for expressing adult attachment. Many women experience their sexuality, as well as their partners', as fundamentally tied to their anger.

ANGER, SEX, AND YOUR ROMANCE

What Women Learn about Sex and Anger

There are striking similarities between what society teaches women about anger and what it teaches women about sex. This comes as no surprise, considering that both anger and sex have been seen as negative, particularly for women, throughout the history of the dominant culture in this country. Many of these attitudes persist today. Consider the following parallels.

There are cultural taboos on both sex and anger, and women's gender role socialization generally tends to focus on suppressing both of these aspects of self. Women often fear both sexual and angry feelings, worrying that they will lose control or be rejected if they let even a little bit of either of those feelings into awareness. Women learn very early not to ask for what they want or to express what they feel too directly.

Women's anger and sexuality also tend to get suppressed in the service of maintaining relationship status quo. Women often divert their feelings of opposition to keep the peace between their partners and families; women often neglect their own preferences for sexual behaviors, timing, or frequency of sex in order to please their lovers.

Since sex and anger represent power, claiming them goes against traditional teachings that women should be passive, receptive, and prioritize attending to others over any form of self-expression. Women who *do* find ways to declare their anger and assert their sexuality find they feel more powerful and in touch with who they are in relation to others. Both anger expression and sexual assertion are acts of self-definition and freedom in a love relationship.

Sex and Anger for Real Women

We have come to understand the complex and varied connections between sex and anger for women through our own research, clinical experiences, and our in-depth study of the professional literature. Clinical psychologist Mary Kiely studied the narratives women tell about their sexual desires. Kiely's work did not focus on anger at all, but we were struck by the anger themes within the text of the 20 women that she interviewed. Our reanalysis of Kiely's data proved to be a gold mine of examples about anger in sexual relationships.

Some of the things about sex that made women angry were related to the families they grew up in. Women expressed anger at parents for not showing them positive ways of having intimate relationships or affirming their daughters' sexuality as they developed from children through adolescence and into adulthood. They also felt anger at being robbed of true intimacy by having to suppress their sexuality.

Women described anger at discovering their fathers', brothers', or partner's pornography and what that meant about these men's views of women (seeing them as objects to be bought, looked at, and used).

Pornography angered many women, contributing to negative feelings about their own sexuality. Some women felt angry at men for the ease that they appeared to have about their own sexuality and the positive attention they receive for it, while women's own sexuality is often put down.

A number of women belonging to minority groups felt incensed about prejudicial comments that linked their ethnicity and sexuality. We found similar reactions from some of the participants in our focus groups. Latina women were annoyed that they were routinely perceived as hot-blooded and African-American women were angry at being seen as loose. Arab-American women noted that others assumed they were sexually repressed because they were Muslims, a stereotype that felt insulting and demeaning to them.

Women were angry at each other and at themselves for being silent with each other about sex and for competing with each other over men and men's approval. They felt annoyed with themselves for just going along with what's expected of women instead of contesting stereotyped ideas about women's sexuality. Some of them expressed irritation and confusion about why they had such a hard time being assertive in their intimate relationships when they solidly stood up for their principles and needs at work.

In Kiely's study, a number of women mention their partner's infidelity and primarily talk about feeling sadness, disappointment, or self-blame in response to this betrayal. But in some of our own research on infidelity, women describe feeling anger in relation to a partner's unfaithfulness. Vanessa, one of the women we recently interviewed, speaks loud and clear to this issue:

> *The biggest thing to me is faithfulness. If someone is unfaithful to me, I go from Cinderella to Schizorella . . . no slipper for me! Tell me the truth, tell me you like someone else, okay. But don't let me catch you cheating on me or I'll kill ya!*

Although Vanessa tunes directly into her anger, many other women experience anger mixed with paralyzing questions about their own desirability, as well as the commonly asked question, "What did I do wrong and what could I have done differently to keep my partner from straying?" Again, we see women's traditional gender role training as they so often take responsibility for their partners' indiscretions or exits from the relationship.

Our research supports much of what we found in Kiely's interview data. For example, consider this powerful indictment of pornography by Marella, who responded to one of our Internet surveys:

> *I am 26 years old, married with a five year old. My anger is only about one thing! And it takes me over sometimes like a rage. I hate men's lustful thoughts, I hate the women in G strings on wrestling! I hate the* Man Show. *I yell at my brother if he sends my husband a picture of a naked girl over the Internet. I hate* Maxim *magazine, I forbid my husband to be involved with ANY of these things. I cry and get upset. The thing is, he's wonderful. Never cheated on me, great dad. Just wonderful! The thought of him having a guys' night out just sends me into distress, because of how the other guys are. This world seems to be all about men and their lust for women! Anyone else feel this way? Help!*

Ironically, as strong as Marella's feelings are on this issue, she apologizes for them. She says she hates her own anger, revealing her uncertainty about the legitimacy of her perceptions. Marella feels alone and unsure; is this an okay thing to be angry about? Can someone normalize this rage for her? Yes! Pornography makes many (but not all) women feel angry and hurt. While most feminists make the point that pornography fundamentally reduces us to objects of sexual consumption, at a less abstract level, women report that when the men in their lives use pornography, women lose that key sense of specialness in their relationships as a result. Is he just turned on by his *Playboy* bunnies or does he want to be with *me*? Me as a whole person who matters in his life, not just me as a convenient hole, as one woman noted. When we feel angry about pornography, this fierce emotion directs us to reclaim our dignity and to demand the respect we deserve as intimate partners. Being mad tells us we want to reconnect, but not if it means sacrificing the sense that we're uniquely valuable and desired in our partner's life.

Women's experiences with sexuality and anger are often rooted in important earlier experiences. A victim of date-rape in a prior relationship, Suzy now uses her anger to monitor the guys she is with; her anger acts as a radar for detecting possible coercion, thus keeping her safer in her current relationships.

> *A man can live in the ease of knowing his sexuality is his own unless he decides differently. A woman, on the other hand, lives in the constant knowledge that she is physically at the mercies and integrity of the man she is sexual with. If he feels forceful or dominant, she must be aware of to what extreme he'll take it, and decide what to do about it. I think a woman knows that she is always a potential victim. It's maddening if you are one who refuses to live like a victim.*

In our face-to-face interviews with women, anger and sexuality are not always linked together. Alimah, a young Muslim-American woman, says:

> *To me, sex and anger are like two separate entities. I can't imagine combining them for myself. I do have a boyfriend now and we get along well. It [sex and anger together] is not an experience I have had; sex is just pleasurable.*

Alimah does get angry about some societal attitudes about sex and plans on continuing to use her anger to guide her in the future:

> *Nowadays, you hear about sex all the time. Before it was sacred, now it's more like everyone's doing it. It makes me mad how people toy with it. It's not a toy, it's something very personal. I've learned a lot from my own experience. When I become a parent, I'll know what I want to do. Don't always go with everyone. People appreciate you more if you stand up for what you believe in.*

Sometimes women *use* sexuality as a tool to express anger indirectly, as when a woman indicates resentment by *not* showing her arousal or excitement with a partner as a means of punishment. Women also describe using their sexuality to express anger by publicly flirting with other people—to show anger about something or to make the partner jealous, often in retaliation for a partner's infidelity or lack of attention. Other women may withhold sex completely from a partner when angry. Finally, some women may *not feel* sexually aroused when angry (they consent to sex but do not experience any pleasure during the encounter). In a recent interview, Tracy talks about how sex and anger are connected for her:

> *If I am angry with my husband, I don't want him to be near me. I want him to leave me alone. Don't touch me. My former partner thought the ultimate way to make up after a fight was to have sex. My first husband would come home after work and accuse me of being unfaithful when I hadn't been. When I'm angry I won't have sex. The desire and behavior are gone.*

Tracy's example brings up two ways to achieve more intimacy through a better use of anger. First, she can process her strong feelings with her husband and thereby make it more likely that she will reconnect with him sexually, if she so chooses. Second, she has learned that sex doesn't decrease anger for her; lovemaking doesn't necessarily solve a problem between partners. Her anger consciousness has developed from these experiences.

In our most recent study, surveying women on anger and sex, we find a very strong relationship between the tendency to suppress anger and having a negative view of one's sexuality. On the flip side, women who express anger outwardly have higher sexual satisfaction scores. In our interviews for this study, while some women show wonderfully healthy views of themselves, their sexuality, and their anger, many divert their anger and feel tentative or ashamed about their sexuality. Anger diversion often plays a large role in keeping our romantic relationships from being their best.

ANGER DIVERSION IN LOVE RELATIONSHIPS

Do You Divert Anger with the One You Love?

You may recognize yourself, or some part of yourself, in some of the women who tell their stories in this part of the chapter. To check out your anger style within intimate relationships, imagine yourself in these scenarios and pick the responses that most closely fit how you react. Answer as honestly as you can.

1. You've had a lousy week at work and feel overwhelmed; you go over to your boyfriend's apartment on Friday night and you'd really like to be pampered a little bit. Your partner is on the couch, glued to the TV set. He asks you to sit with him, but doesn't seem interested in conversation. You

   a. Feel disappointed and ashamed for being so selfish. After all, at least he wants you to be with him; he's not out drinking like your past boyfriend.

   b. Start yelling at him, saying, "You're always watching that stupid TV! Can't you tear yourself away from that crap for two minutes to even kiss me hello, or is that just too much to ask?"

   c. Sit with him for eight minutes until there's a commercial, push the mute button on the remote, and tell your partner you're irritated with his focus on the TV. Let him know that you're feeling stressed from work and in need of his loving arms around you.

   d. Tell yourself to be patient and not bug him. The movie will be over in a couple of hours and then maybe he'll be more responsive. You decide to go upstairs and read instead, but find it hard to concentrate because you're annoyed and can still hear the TV, a grating little reminder that you're not getting what you need.

   e. You decline his invitation to sit with him. You decide his place really needs some tidying up and start vacuuming. You're glad you don't get mad easily.

2. You're walking down the street with your boyfriend of three months, on your way to a party at a friend's house. As a truly beautiful, fit woman walks by, he says, "Why can't you look more like her?" You

   a. Admit to yourself that you're really too fat, and always have been. He's right, you should look more like her, you want to look more like her. You feel depressed.

   b. Slap him across the face and say, "Screw you! You're the most insensitive asshole I've ever known, you sexist pig!" and walk away for good.

   c. Immediately touch his shoulder and stop walking. You tell him "That really hurt and I'm angry you said it. I'm going to ask you not to say things like that again."

   d. Tell yourself that you know you're angry but that this isn't the time or place for a conversation. You're in public and it would be embarrassing. You're on your way to a party together and this will just have to wait. You remind yourself that you don't want to alienate him by showing that you're irritated anyway. By the time the party is over, it just doesn't seem worth it to bring it up anymore.

   e. Say nothing. Women who get upset about things like this are just not secure enough in who they are.

   f. Once you're at the party, you find yourself on the other side of the room from your partner, flirting with one of his single business partners. Strangely enough, you've never really found him that exciting before, but tonight there seems to be some real chemistry between the two of you. You're having a great time.

3. You've been invited to go out with your girlfriends and you really want to go. Your husband says he doesn't want you to go out. He hates it when you're not around and says he needs to have you at home; you're his life, his love, his inspiration, his rock. He says he misses you every minute you're not together and just wants you to be with him. He lays the sweet talk on really thick. You also know from past experience, if you do go, he'll pout and punish you when

you get back home, saying you don't care about him and accusing you of caring more about your friends than you do about him. You

a. Decide that he's really more in need of you than your girl-friends are right now and the important thing to do is to focus on this relationship. After all, he's your husband—what were you thinking? You stay home and let him fuss over you.

b. Shout at him, "You're not going to control me, you manipulative jerk! Why don't you get a life of your own and stop trying to keep me at home all the time? I'm not your frigging mommy, you know?" You stomp out of the house, slinging your purse in the general direction of his head as you go.

c. Sit down with him on the couch and explain to him that you love him, care deeply for him, and intend to spend lots of time with him, but that you feel mad when you make a reasonable request to see friends and you feel unsupported. You reassure him, but make it clear that you intend to follow through with your plans.

d. You try to set aside your anger at his dependence on you and try to understand the reasons why he is the way he is. You remind yourself that his mother was cold and rejecting and that you're helping him to heal from that by being with him and being a warmer, more loving person in his life. Besides, he'll be such a pain in the butt if you do go, and the thought of the upcoming hassle will ruin your time with your friends anyway.

e. You agree to stay home with him. No sense in getting upset. He asks if you are mad and you say, cheerfully, "No. I'm glad you love me so much."

4. You are at your in-laws' for the winter holidays with your husband; his two sisters are also there with all their kids. You and your husband are in the guest bedroom, which is right next to the room where all eight kids are staying (two sets of bunk beds and sleeping bags on the floor). Your

husband is in the mood for sex; you feel nervous about it with all the kids on the other side of the wall, and besides, you're exhausted from all the family interaction, but he's really interested. You

a. Agree to have sex with him, because you know he's been tense and hassled all day with all the family goings-on. You know he'll feel a lot better, and in the long run, your irritation at his request will fade. You think about how important it is that he be happy and sexually fulfilled, and in the back of your mind admit you're worried he'll leave you or be dissatisfied with you if you don't cooperate.

b. You whisper to him in a biting hiss that he's out of his mind. You turn your back on him in bed and when he tries to touch you again you push him roughly aside, and get up, dragging the blanket with you, to sleep on the living room couch.

c. You explain to him that you feel annoyed with his request and give him the details about your discomfort. You let him know that you find him desirable, but that you want a rain-check.

d. You agree to have sex with him but decide to be as super quiet as you can about it. You don't really enjoy it and remain irritated during the whole thing, reminding yourself that it will only last about five or ten minutes anyway.

e. You agree to have sex with him and it's fine. Not great, not terrible. You feel proud of yourself for being able to go with the flow. The next day at the holiday brunch, you find yourself criticizing your husband at every turn; he didn't make the kids take their showers before the meal and it's an embarrassment, you laugh at his frustration in carving the ham, you tell him not to talk with his mouth full like a three year old, and you're too busy to help him find that present for his father he's misplaced.

Scoring:

All "a"—Internalization. You're not comfortable with your anger and tend to blame yourself and put other's needs ahead of your own. You take on guilty feelings instead of getting mad at your partner.

All "b"—Externalization. You bypass your relationship needs through aggression and disconnection.

All "c"—Adaptive. You're using a direct, respectful approach instead of diverting anger.

All "d"—Containment. You try to set your anger aside and hold it apart from your relationships. You know you're angry, but are not willing to act on it.

All "e"—Segmentation. You deny or don't recognize your anger at a conscious level. But since it's still there, it probably leaks out in other ways that seem unrelated to the initial event(s) in which your feelings are denied. Passive-aggressive behavior is likely. You may need an outlet because you habitually segment or contain anger.

Mixed. There may be situations in which you respond differently from others. Many women have mixed anger diversion styles. This exercise helps you see which ones you might use at various times; asking yourself why you chose different types of options for each scenario can help you learn more about your own anger profile. Which answers went with which questions? Are there patterns there? For example, some women might have different responses in private than in public. Or perhaps situations in which kids or family members are involved evoke different responses than ones that are only about you and your partner.

If it turns out that you are someone who diverts a lot of her anger in love relationships, you may be missing out on critical opportunities for connection. Although this may seem strange (the opposite of what your mother told you), diversion contributes to lackluster romance in the long run.

The Costs of Diversion in Love Relationships

"What *do* women want in their love relationships?" you ask. While individual women want different things, there are some fundamentals we all seem to want. In order to address this most fundamental question, we'll take a framework synthesized from a number of leading love researchers, including the feminist writers of the Stone Center at Wellesley College and Yale love expert Robert Sternberg.

Sternberg believes all good love relationships require three elements: passion, commitment, and intimacy. Passion is the chemistry between partners, the physical attraction and sexual excitement aspects of the relationship. Intimacy refers to the sharing of personal meanings and dreams, emotional closeness, and the respect and support of a partner. Commitment is the intention to stay in a relationship. It's important to note that the levels of these three dimensions vary over time within a particular relationship, and that is normal.

According to the Stone Center's Self-in-Relation model, women grow primarily within the context of their important relationships with family, friends, and romantic love interests, and the *level of mutuality* in these relationships either helps or hinders that growth. High mutuality means both partners feel emotionally connected to each other and are supportive of each other's individual growth as well as the health of the relationship. Mutuality means each knowing the other deeply enough that you are aware of vulnerabilities—but choosing not to exploit them—and both knowing and respecting each other's boundaries. This doesn't mean that every relationship looks 50-50 on all tasks; it means that each couple openly negotiates issues to both partners' satisfaction. So, mutuality means *talking and listening* about each other's emotions, as they arise.

Both of these two theories have something to do with the attachment between lovers. Secure attachment bonds lead to emotional closeness, commitment, and mutuality. Insecure ones lead to emotional distress and legitimate angry protest at the disconnection between partners.

Diverted anger keeps women from experiencing passion, intimacy, commitment, and mutuality. Regarding passion, effects of diverted anger pop up at any stage of the sexual response cycle (Donelson, 1999; Silverstein, 1989). Some women lose all interest in sex when they suppress their anger. Some women who suppress their anger about past abuse avoid sex altogether, as it constantly reminds them or even repeats earlier sexual coercion. At the arousal stage, women may not lubricate. Suppressed anger relates to a number of physical difficulties during the sex act itself, such as painful intercourse, uncontrollable vaginal spasms, or an inability to reach orgasm if it is desired. Or sex may just not be very interesting or fun.

Holding back frustration and rage keeps women's needs from being voiced and met. It allows their boundaries to be violated without complaint. This pattern often leads to depression. If you keep your anger to yourself, your partner never knows the real you, and part of your relationship will always be false. Suppressed anger often leads to a host of physical symptoms including headaches, gastrointestinal problems, and other medical problems that take valuable energy away from the *possibilities* that exist between you two. When you fail to communicate your anger to your partner, you say in effect, "You're more important than I am." If this pattern becomes entrenched, it is easier for your partner to take advantage of you; if you keep giving, your partner is tempted to keep taking.

The opposite pattern—hurling insults and accusations—also decreases intimacy and mutuality. Since such self-protective tactics make it dangerous to get close to you, your partner won't. Relationships are less likely to remain intact if they have to bear the weight of constant aggression, conflict, or incessant fault-finding.

Let's turn now to some real-life examples of how diversion dynamics manifest in women's love lives. As you read, ask yourself how diversion is keeping each woman from getting what she wants. Then ask yourself if diversion is keeping *you* from getting what *you* want.

Internalization

In romantic relationships, internalization involves turning anger at a partner back inward on the self, constantly blaming yourself for problems and believing that you are somehow deficient; that if you were just better somehow—smarter, sexier, more diligent around the house, whatever—then things would be better. In a classic case of this dynamic, hear Carla, a 40-year-old woman who was once engaged, as she describes her relationship with her former fiancé, who she calls "a master brainwasher."

> Anything that I did wrong such as forgetting to put the silverware on the table, he would say, "I cannot believe you did that. You can't do anything." He had me so brainwashed that when he rejected me, he said "I thought I loved you at one time but I was wrong. You're just not the best one for me." So my self-confidence was so destroyed by that time, by this periodic, subtle brainwashing, I blamed myself—"Carla, you can't do anything right. You forgot to put the silverware on the table. You served some lettuce that had some brown leaves on it. You did so many things wrong that you just killed his love for you." So I had so much anger directed toward myself that it literally was making me physically ill. I never was a person who coughed a lot when I was sick and I had a persistent cough for two years after this happened. It was making me physically sick. Finally, I stumbled on a book on psychologically abusive relationships and it explained what goes on and I could see myself in it.

Here we see all the signposts of internalization. Carla ends up believing that it is her fault that the relationship had problems. If only she could get fresh lettuce! Carla's anger turned inward also results in physical illness, as it takes its toll on her respiratory system.

Externalization

Externalization in romantic relationships means bypassing your feelings of vulnerability by lashing out aggressively. This tactic sends a message to your partner to watch out and back off. It says "I'm dangerous!" The problem with this diversion is that it leaves out the part of anger that says, "I have a connection with you that is important to me. I love you and need to work something out with you." Tracy, who talked earlier about how her angry feelings seem to completely turn off her sexual feelings, finds other, potentially destructive outlets for her anger in her relationships:

> Although my anger is not expressed sexually, I do feel the need to destroy something and have in the past thrown things

or kicked walls or slammed doors to release the physical welling up of rage inside of me.

If Tracy throws objects she has designated as "safe" anger tools (like hurling ice cubes at a brick wall), the action probably serves a purpose, helping her vent intense emotional energy. But if she kicks a hole in the drywall of her living room, she causes herself unnecessary grief instead. Similarly, Judy, an African-American woman in midlife, talks about externalizing anger in her relationship with her now ex-husband:

> *When I would get so angry as to be violent, it made me lose valuable things that if I hadn't gotten so violent, I wouldn't have lost . . . throwing plates, throwing things of value that I liked and he knew I liked. Instead of abstaining from that, I did it out of anger.*

Both these women describe destroying property when they are angry. It is unclear from their descriptions if they have also been physically hurt themselves (punching a door can break the bones in your hand) or if their partners have been hit by any of the ceramic missiles launched. In more violent relationships, both partners may engage in physical abuse, externalizing their anger though hitting, kicking, biting, pulling hair, shoving, and the like. In such cycles of violence, the tender and caring feelings that lovers have for each other become buried in hurt and pain, often never to be accessed again.

Below, Kate gives us an example of externalizing anger in both subtle and blatant ways; her anger is meant to be an aggressive assault on those closest to her. She wants to protect herself from vulnerability and hurt by being on the offensive first.

> *If you piss me off I will tell you and you will deserve it and it's your fault. When I tell you something, I mean what I say and I say what I mean. And I don't have to do it with yelling, because my directness will saw you in half.*

Kate also clearly does not like the idea of her partner being let off the hook. She wants him to suffer:

> *You've done this to me and you are not off the hook. I truly know what I'm doing. And sometimes I would not get engaged. I say, "Oh I'm busy. I have to go somewhere and do something." And let them live with it for a while, knowing that I might be pissed when I get home, them not knowing if the forgiveness is going to come.*

Kate feels herself more motivated by retaliation and control than by a wish to *relate honestly with* her romantic partners. Why? Before you reach the conclusion that Kate has some kind of twisted personality, recall her family-of-origin, discussed in chapter Three. Kate contends with memories of a physically, verbally, and emotionally abusive father and a mother who was, for the most part, emotionally unavailable because of her own mental illness.

Kate survives this arrangement, but not completely unscathed. She bears the scars from more than 30 years of diverted anger at parents who abandoned and exploited her. Now, she finds it almost impossible to cultivate a mutual love relationship.

Containment

Remember that containment involves knowing that you are angry, but intentionally putting your anger aside. Rosa, 21, is in a long-distance relationship with Rob, but they see each other almost every weekend and on holidays. While Rosa notices her anger, she tries to keep it in check for as long as possible:

> *I know when I'm angry with my boyfriend, I get real quiet. I won't say anything because I'll say something that will hurt his feelings. I'll try to be calm because he wants me to talk to him and I just don't feel like it. I just want to be away from him, find my own spot. I don't want to hurt his feelings, so I'll say, "Rob, just let me be, or let me be calm because I don't want to be angry." Sometimes I'll go swim or go for a walk. If*

I'm angry, sometimes I just want to sleep or kind of mope around. But it builds up.

Rosa knows she has anger at Rob, but rather than address her anger directly with him, she more often reverts to avoidance to protect his feelings. At a less conscious level, many women like Rosa contain their anger out of fear that direct anger expression will hurt their relationship.

Segmentation

Segmentation can be recognized as an indirect expression of anger or a complete denial of anger. Indirect expressions of anger in intimate relationships show up as passive-aggressive behavior; forgetting things important to your spouse, accidentally botching this or breaking that, or nagging about something other than the true source of your anger. Segmenting can involve leaking anger, sideways anger, sneaky anger. And in its most extreme form, segmentation can be total denial of anger. Some women have sealed off their anger so completely, they literally do not recognize it any longer.

Beverly, age 72, has come to a complete denial of her anger at this point in her life. She acknowledges there are some things that used to upset her, but feels that by eliminating her anger she has improved the situation with her husband:

I have a marvelous husband, but he reads and there are times that I need to talk to him and he's not a good listener and that really bothered me. I handle it a lot better now, and he is better. My not getting angry I think helped him a lot too. I was very vocal about it and I just wasn't nice to know and I didn't like that person [her angry self], so in time I taught myself patience and now I don't get angry.

Beverly describes repeatedly in her interview how, since age six, she has been working to eliminate anger in her life. She is pleased that she's been successful in sending it so completely underground that it is now totally invisible to her. But lingering questions remain. Who listens to Beverly? How do her needs get met? Will she go to her grave with her husband quietly reading and happily ignoring her?

In contrast, women who can identify their anger diversions make crucial movement toward claiming their anger advantage. Some of the women above have done exactly that.

From Self-defeat to Self-discovery: Anger Diversion Transformed

Remember Carla? Reading about emotionally abusive relationships triggered a re-evaluation of her life, eventually resulting in anger consciousness and then slowly, real changes in the way she feels about herself and in the way she acts:

> I gradually started to see the situation as it was, so I changed the anger—ceased to direct it at myself. I directed it at him. I finally reached the point where I could turn my anger from me, blaming myself for it and turn my anger toward him. It was constructive in that way because it freed me from false self-blame and let me get out of the relationship.

Carla's metamorphosis makes sense if you consider that anger helps women define themselves and that self-definition is a fundamental part of healthy romantic relationships. Carla's transformation came from two years of soul-searching and reading, gradually rediscovering who she was and making new sense out of what had happened to her in a love relationship in which she had lost herself. Like Carla, you can learn to embrace your anger and to use it more effectively in getting what you want in your romantic partnerships.

ANGER IN ACTION:
USING ANGER TO PRESERVE AND ENHANCE INTIMACY

> We've both done a lot of growing and a lot of growing together, and being able to talk about what makes us upset with each other is one of the things that has brought us closer. I think in

a way the anger helps. We don't like to see it, but it helps us to grow, to build that bond with each other. I think holding things in and not being able to talk about them will hurt both of us.

—*Trina (23)*

Anger is vital to the ongoing health of a relationship; without it, partners stagnate and stew in unresolved issues, losing both their sense of self and their connection to each other. Using your anger advantage with your intimate partner will make *you* happier, because your needs are more likely to be met, your boundaries are more likely to be respected, and you will be known and accepted for who you really are.

How can anger make your love relationships more satisfying? You have really already started—by identifying your anger diversions, genogram anger patterns, and anger triggers. The ideas and action steps below show you additional ways you can gain the advantages of anger in your romance, based on our model's four adaptive anger skills.

Raising Anger Consciousness: Understanding Your Anger in Love

- Motive matters: What are your goals in bringing up your anger? Keep a positive goal—like deepening your connection with your lover—in mind when you tell your loved one how you feel. If your goal is to hurt, punish, intimidate, degrade, or manipulate your partner, you risk sabotaging the bonds between you. Your emotional needs are unlikely to be met, as these styles only serve to escalate negative cycles in your relationship by inviting attacks.
- Mixed bag: If you know your anger is mixed with other strong feelings, be clear about all the parts of your distress (fear, shame, guilt, sadness, anxiety, embarrassment, etc.). Your partner may respond more empathically if s/he knows you have caring and loving feelings along with your irritation.
- Savor the memories: Remind your partner of times when the two of you have overcome other difficulties and handled other expressions of anger with positive results. Developing a history of shared

effectiveness in resolving conflicts is a good base to refer back to when anger is at hand.

Constructive Anger Talk: How to Dialogue about Your Emotions

Couples in conflict feel annoyed, and that's normal as they constantly negotiate and renegotiate their togetherness and separateness. But it's not anger per se that is the problem. In John Gottman's studies, he notes that both happy couples and unhappy couples fight about the same amount and often have arguments about the same thing over and over again. (Sound familiar?) So what makes the difference between these two types of couples is their ability to *process* their anger and conflict *after it is over.* "Processing" means the couple talks over the argument with the intention of deepening understanding, being supportive of each other's perspectives, and possibly making positive changes. They may even eventually laugh at their own fights.

To set the groundwork for constructive anger talk, examine your beliefs about anger expression in your close relationships. Expressing your anger *verbally, responsibly, and respectfully* leads to a number of positive outcomes in a love relationship: (1) Consciously expressing your distress demonstrates that you trust your partner and desire more intimacy; (2) *Constructive anger talk* allows your partner to get to know you better and helps you define who you are in relation to this important person; (3) *Constructive anger talk* also creates an expectation that your partner should reciprocate at a similar level and in a similar way. Thus, if you share frustration constructively, you are more likely to get a supportive response—and hear more about your partner's anger too. Here are some specifics:

- Small doses: Avoid storing up your anger. If you find yourself blowing up over minor things (he trips over your feet and you want to hurl obscenities at him), that probably indicates you're not dispensing your feelings regularly enough. A big reaction to a little event means you've been hoarding your anger over time—perhaps even old resentment of former loves or others who hurt you.

- Claim what's yours: When you speak about your wrath, use "I" statements and try not to blame your partner or make global judgments about his or her personality. Be very specific and detailed about things that anger you. Ask for what *you* need, not what your partner "should" change.
- If you feel safe enough, talk about feeling vulnerable along with your anger. Let your partner know it's *because* s/he matters to you that you fear your anger will drive a wedge between you. Be careful not to apologize for being mad.
- Balancing act: If you have some degree of culpability in a bad situation, own up to it . . . but be careful not to fall into the gender trap of taking on *too* much responsibility. Be particularly careful not to revert to containing or internalizing if you're used to pulling away in angry situations. The same holds true for offering compromises. Compromising helps partners come together, but use your anger to hold your ground on issues of key importance to you.

Think Tanking and Variations: Still Life with Love and Anger

- Time-out: If you feel like you are getting confused or so anxious that you can't get your points across, take a break. Ask your partner for ten minutes or even a day to regroup, alone. Use think-tanking strategies to help you dive down deep into the emotions you have and study them. Write down your experiences, thoughts, and feelings. Make a script for yourself to read aloud if you like. Return to the conversation when you are ready, but don't put it off for more than 24 hours.
- Seize the moment: As an alternative to break time, experiment with letting your loved one in on what is happening to you at the time. "I'm starting to get queasy and I feel like I'm tied in knots." This can slow down conflict escalation by giving your partner a way to gauge how intense you are feeling right now and respond accordingly. It may also give each of you that extra minute to get back to constructive conversation.

Listening:
Do You Hear What I Hear?

- Listen and hear: Tune in closely to what your partner has to say. Listen for the feelings and try to say things that indicate you're listening intently ("So it sounds like you feel unappreciated and sad when I complain about things you haven't done around the house.").
- Listen to your partner and try to see his/her point of view. *This is not the same as giving in or agreeing.* It just means soaking up enough to understand what is going on. Listening and understanding do not necessarily require you to change.
- Create an oasis: Let your love relationship serve as "base" when you and your partner need to vent the cares and frustrations of the day. Make it a rule that you won't judge each other or try to explain away the problem. Just listen.

When All Else Fails

- Go with it: If you do find yourself just getting in a yelling match with your partner, let it happen and worry about fixing it later. Keep yourself and your partner physically safe. If you find yourself at the brink of behavioral aggression or violence (versus just feeling extremely furious), walk out or away for awhile. Soothe yourself with something safe. Think tank what happened in the fight and revisit it using the skills and techniques of constructive anger talk and listening. Being able to work on repairing the hurt and confusion of a fight is one thing that separates couples that last from those that break up.

So, do real people actually use these skills in their real love lives? You bet. If you have doubts, check out Dee's story. Watch how she moves from anger diversion in one relationship, to anger consciousness, and then into adaptive anger skills with her most recent partner. Dee writes about a journey in which her internalized anger, appearing as self-doubt, self-hatred, and depression, eventually clamors to be heard. Dee first hears this message in her body, which won't calm down. Finally, in an attempt to settle her insides through exercise, Dee finds her suppressed anger spilling forth, illuminating a path for positive change in her future romances.

I had broken up with this guy I'd dated for about 18 months, and I was totally miserable. It was one of those real up-and-down relationships where I was in ecstasy when we were together and depressed and anxious when we were apart. He was slippery and made me feel crazy a lot of the time. I felt like it was my fault that we broke up; I wasn't attractive enough or traditional enough or I was too clingy or too something. I tried to ignore his drinking, his lies, the lack of sex with me, and the fact that he once cheated on me with his next-door neighbor. I tried to focus on the good stuff. But when he cheated on me a second time—that was the last straw. I was too hurt to put myself through it any longer. He was furious that I wouldn't see him anymore. I was depressed.

For four months, I was haunted by vivid nightmares of his new girlfriend, who took on giant proportions in my dreams, towering over me, laughing. I was thoroughly demoralized. This had been my first relationship in eight years, and I'd blown it.

Little by little, I began to feel angry. At first, I just noticed these little flashes of fantasy. Slashing her tires. Slashing his. Wishing she'd get hit by a truck. Wishing he'd get hit by a truck. I was uncomfortable with the violence of my own thoughts and tried to rework these fantasies into something more socially acceptable. So I decided maybe he'd cheat on her or get tired of how stupid she was and he'd leave her. But the angry visions kept on returning, and building. Soon, I began to feel an agitated, churning anger in my body, like a nervous energy and I couldn't calm down. It wasn't anxiety. But I was having trouble sleeping and working. I had a rowing machine that I had been using as a clothes rack—and I cleaned it off to see if the exercise would help me calm down. I started to work out on it with the idea that if I could just exhaust myself I would be okay. What happened was totally unexpected to me.

I would be on my machine, breathing hard. Gasping for air, I'd find I didn't have the energy to keep down my anger anymore. And I realized just how much energy I was using to squelch it. Then, I would be engulfed in a fierce, physical anger that pumped my legs and arms faster and faster. I'd start thinking, "Fuck that alcoholic, lying, cheating asshole! I don't deserve to be treated like that! I'm not crazy and screwed up. He is! I don't care what I look like, I don't deserve to be treated like that! Ever! Never again! I will NEVER, EVER LET ANYONE TREAT ME LiKE THAT AGAIN! I WILL NEVER EVER PUT UP WITH THAT AGAIN!" I found myself having bursts of insight, linking together past relationship patterns with this latest fiasco; how I'd repeatedly let others convince me that I wasn't up to par and so I got whatever I deserved and didn't have a right to complain. All of it finally flipped around in my brain and I realized that at some human level, I didn't deserve to be violated in that way. And I was angry. And that anger carried me through months of work-outs, months of feeling the rage over and over again, and solidifying my resolve in my heart and my head. The anger carried a light with it that helped me see how to treat myself better in the future.

Since then, I've been in two other relationships. One I terminated when it was clear that it was going nowhere; I was bored and he had started to mistreat me, and we were unable to really communicate. It was the first time I ended a relationship (versus the guy leaving me). That felt good. I am currently celebrating the fifth year of a really good relationship. When Eric and I first got together, I set some ground rules. No lies, no infidelity, no alcohol. One strike and you're out. I had never set ground rules in a relationship before. That also felt good. I have learned to listen to my body and to be aware of anger when it happens and I know it's a good guide. It means, "It's time for us to talk."

Dee's offended, outraged, incredulous, angry feelings allow her to access the kind of self-respect that cannot be learned any other way. To be heartily repulsed and angered by a lover's abuse puts a woman at eye level with a person she may be idolizing or tiptoeing around. Self-respect translates into more mutually satisfying relationships too. Dee and Eric have a much different kind of partnership, one in which each person expects the honest emotion of the other. Eric has the ability to hear Dee's irritation when she gives voice to it (e.g., "Okay, I get it! You're pissed."). Likewise, Dee takes in Eric's expressions of feeling (e.g., "You hate it when I walk away during a fight."). This kind of mutual exchange keeps them on the same playing field together, struggling out life's ups and downs with mutuality and respect. Magic happens for the two of them as they learn to be startlingly honest in a connected, caring way.

> *I guess I never thought it could be this way for me. No, we don't have some kind of utopian, perfect relationship. But it's pretty f-ing good. I've been amazed and delighted by the difficult things we can work through. I just look at him sometimes and think, "He's really great for me. This is what it's supposed to feel like." It's hard when he's mad at me. I hate thinking I've hurt him. I still get scared about being rejected when I get pissed off at him too. But somehow we manage to get it all out on the table. We'll stay up half the night if we have to. I'm learning to say, "What you said really hurt me and I'm angry" and, by the same token, "What I said really hurt you, didn't it? You're mad." He usually does that for me too, even though sometimes he gets defensive and scowls when I tell him I'm mad at him. We come back and talk about it until we can both stand to hear what's going on without blowing up, shutting down, or leaving the room. No, I can't say that I always want sex when he does, but still, I'm looking at this guy and feeling a lot of love for him. I'm feeling very confident in us.*

This is the kind of exhilaration and satisfaction that adaptive anger can bring you in your intimate relationships. If you can start to use these skills in your romantic partnerships, you can carry them on into other important domains of your life. We turn to one of those critical areas in the next chapter; how anger can benefit you in your friendships.

FIVE

Are We Still Best Friends?

Getting Mad, Getting Close, and Getting Clear

Truth and tears clear the way to a deep and lasting friendship.
—*Marquise de Sevigne*

When Nora's daughter got into a fight with the daughter of her close friend, April, she thought little of it at the time. She soon noticed that April did not feel the same way. They talked tentatively about the girls' fight but once their differing opinions became obvious, the two women quickly backed away from the issue. Nora let the conflict slip into the background, figuring it was more about her daughter than herself. But April's anger grew and began to show in the ways she avoided Nora, who in turn, withdrew from April. Both friends were part of a tightly knit group of women who had shared much of their lives over the past 14 years, and it wasn't long before others, such as their mutual friends, Nancy and Trudy, were caught up in the unresolved issue. Nora noticed she was being left out of some group get-togethers and shunned by others of the group. Her hurt grew to the point where she decided to end friendships with all involved. She talks about what happened next:

> *That's when Trudy said, "No way, we are not going there! I am not letting that happen," and she insisted we all get together to talk it out. It was frightening, but I was relieved that it would finally be out in the open after all those months. We met at Nancy's house, and I remember sitting there, going over it all. I wasn't angry by then, I was more hurt and sad. But April was still furious, and she talked about how she felt*

her daughter had not been treated right. I still think it was not a good thing to be so involved in the girls' relationship, but you know, it was really a big deal for April and she was hot. Nancy said she felt she had made it worse by letting April constantly confide in her about it, instead of pushing April to talk to me. Anyway, we did finally get it talked out, and things really changed after that. April and I made a big point out of calling each other to go to lunch and stuff, which was very awkward and hard at first. But then it just got better. We all got so much closer—you know, when you go through something like that you really know how much people care. And it's so much easier to be honest with each other now.

Just as in family and love relationships, friendships involve differences of opinions, needs, and desires. If we pretend these can be resolved without anger, we are fooling ourselves and buying into the anger myths so common in our culture. Once we embrace the idea that friendship and anger can go hand-in-hand, we are on our way to a more honest, and even a more fulfilling relationship.

Most of us are surprised from time to time by a flash of rage or hot resentment toward a cherished friend. Ever caught yourself playing out an argument with a friend inside your head because you just couldn't imagine having it happen out loud? We're taught not to expect anger within the context of friendships, so we tend to doubt our feelings, our friendship—or both.

FRIENDSHIP FUNDAMENTALS

What makes friendships so special and supportive? In some ways they don't seem that different from our other ties, since we are often close friends with our family members, our lovers, and our coworkers. But friendships typically have more space and flexibility since there are usually fewer demands placed on them. For example, friends expect less of each other than romantic partners in terms of commitment—after all, there is no formal "to have and to hold, through sickness and health, till death do you part" ritual for friends. And of course, a defining feature of a friendship is that friends are not required to meet each other's needs in the areas of sexuality and romance.

Friendships also tend to be based more on mutuality, meaning there is less unequal power to complicate the skirmishes that sometimes flare up. Friends also usually share far fewer responsibilities, such as house maintenance and child rearing, so there is less opportunity for disagreement about who is going to take care of which chore. And because the emotional intensity in a friendship is typically less than that in a romantic relationship, friends tend to be far less preoccupied with each other on a day-to-day basis, which reduces the number of disappointments and misunderstandings that can take place. It's no wonder that friendship can sometimes seem like a safe haven compared to our marriages and love relationships.

We begin to sort out these factors as we grow up and learn about the social and cultural expectations for friendships. Nancy Rumbaugh Whitesell and Susan Harter, in their 1996 study of adolescents, report that girls are especially sensitive to differences between classmate and best friend relationships. The girls' responses indicate a perceived injury brings on stronger and longer-lasting negative emotions when it comes from a best friend as opposed to a classmate, and girls make this differentiation more than boys. So when conflict arises, the anger and hurt we feel toward close friends often becomes magnified due to the importance of the relationship.

As women, we are particularly sensitive to how the degree of closeness in a friendship can impact our expectations, responses, and need to maintain the relationship. In fact, researchers Sara Arber and Jay Ginn found in their study on women and aging that we rely on our friendships more for support than do men. They also documented how, as women go through life, our friendships act as buffers against tragedy and changing life circumstances.

As women become bold enough to bring our anger to the table in a friendship, we can expect substantial rewards. We find our friendships not only survive but improve as a result of honest emotional expression and—most important—we are able to deal with and resolve the issues that create conflict between friends. In fact, the act of revealing ourselves to each other *deepens* a relationship. Research by Patricia Rind on female friendships has led her to conclude that *being known* by another is the "defining characteristic" of relationships that develop into best friendships. The trust and understanding that result from allowing a friend to know who we truly are, including our anger, hurt, and pain, increases the intensity or closeness of the friendship. There's nothing quite like the knowledge that we are accepted and loved for who we are—warts, anger, and all. How can we know this acceptance unless we are willing to show the totality of who we are? There is also nothing that can substitute for clear communication about what's bothering us when it comes to working things out with those we love. The freedom to talk about what makes us angry gives us the opportunity to ask for and work toward change.

In making a new friend, we first explore, and then settle into, a pattern of give-and-take that most suits our personalities and needs. There are almost inevitably some bumps in the road on the way to becoming friends, which in the beginning we may overlook in the interest of establishing a strong bond. Eventually we come to know and trust each other well enough to pay more attention to our differences as well as those things we have in common. And even the best of friends can travel down a rough path through angry territory from time to time.

Our ability to steer our way safely depends a lot on the information we bring with us on the journey. We have all our previous experiences with anger at our disposal, guiding us on which words and actions to use and which ones to avoid; which emotions can be expressed and how much intensity is acceptable; when to reveal ourselves and when to stay private. We make our decisions based on what has happened during past conflicts with other friends, the lessons we were taught on our culture's expectations for women friends and how they treat each other, and the beliefs about anger we absorbed at a young age from our families-of-origin.

ANGER DIVERSIONS IN FRIENDSHIP

When we divert anger, we block the growth of the relationship. Why, then, do we feel compelled to hide our feelings? Is it because of our own preconceived ideas about the acceptability of anger in friend-ships? Is it because we believe our friend will not tolerate constructive anger talk? June, age 25, expresses her anxiety in an interview:

> *With my friends, if I were mad I would be more apt to keep it inside and not exactly say things right then. You know, with a friend you think, "Did I mess up our friendship? Are we going to speak again?"*

Jacqueline Weinstock and Lynn Bond, two University of Vermont researchers, have found college-aged women have many mixed emo-tions about conflict in their relationships. While many women in their study recognized the positive potential conflict brings to friendships, they also defended their choices to avoid conflict in order to prevent threatening the relationship, which was seen as vulnerable since friendship is a totally voluntary commitment.

When anger is perceived as a threat to relationships, it's natural for women, in learning and absorbing this message, to be inclined to divert. We act on the belief that the best thing we can do for our friendships is minimize and hide our anger, so that it doesn't spoil our friendship, or get in the way, or turn our friend against us.

We hear many stories about the ways in which women experience anger that are not helpful to themselves or their relationships. An initial analysis of some of our most recent focus group dialogue led to the compilation of the following ways in which women experience anger diversion within the context of their friendships:

1. Tell someone else first. Don't ever go right to the person with whom you're angry. You don't want to hurt their feel-ings, and of course, you probably imagined whatever made you mad.

2. If asked, never admit you're angry, especially if the one who's asking is the one you're mad at. Instead, say, "I'm confused," "I'm a little upset," or "It's no big deal."
3. Never use the word "anger" or "angry" when you talk with the person who has raised your ire.
4. Hide for a while. Avoid the person with whom you're peeved and let it blow over.
5. Since being mad at your friend means something is gravely wrong in your relationship, be sure to get rid of the nasty feeling as soon as possible. Do whatever it takes (except of course, discuss it with them—don't do that). Try to forgive or do something incompatible with being mad. Invite the person over for dinner; give them a present; tell them how wonderful they are.
6. Pretend you feel fine. Go on as if nothing has happened. Or, at the other end of the spectrum, be as dramatic as you can. Act as though you have been mortally offended or that your friend's betrayal has made you ill with grief. Do something that will force her to prove her loyalty or give in to your needs.

This list gives us a broad overview of what kinds of diversionary ideas and actions are operating in women's friendships.

However, avoiding and submerging anger as we do through diversion is neither effective in ridding ourselves of the feeling nor helpful to our friendships, as we've heard time and again from study participants and clients. As much as we'd like to pretend we're solving the problem by ignoring it, we can't really wish or think away our anger. And, since the issues that initially created angry feelings continue unresolved, they will trigger our frustration and rage again and again until we address them. When our anger business is unfinished, we're left with the chronic physical and emotional strain of tense, distant relationships. Diversion pacifies little else beyond our need to conform.

Rerouting Anger with Friends

Use the anger stories you've read so far, as well as your own knowledge about yourself, to consider how anger diversion affects your friendships. What diversion styles are you most likely to use? Maybe you have different styles with different friends. Make a list of the friends you see most often. Does the way you handle anger differ with each one? Can you be straightforward with Sue, but find yourself internalizing with Brenda and lashing out at Julia? What is different about each of these friends? See if you can identify why and how they are different. For example, if you blame yourself for feeling angry with Brenda, what buttons is she pushing? Is there something in the way the two of you interact that triggers an older hurt or fear (probably from your family)? Each of us carries what researcher John Gottman calls "enduring vulnerabilities"—our tender spots that others can trigger without even knowing it.

MY FIVE BEST FRIENDS			
How I show my anger (or not)	(circle #)	Where did I learn this?	
		Never/Always	(check one or more)
1. Name:	Contain	1 2 3 4 5	Old family pattern ___
_____	Internalize	1 2 3 4 5	Former friendship ___
	Segment	1 2 3 4 5	Former lover _____
	Externalize	1 2 3 4 5	Other_____
	Express Adaptively	1 2 3 4 5	
2. Name:	Contain	1 2 3 4 5	Old family pattern ___
_____	Internalize	1 2 3 4 5	Former friendship ___
	Segment	1 2 3 4 5	Former lover _____
	Externalize	1 2 3 4 5	Other_____
	Express Adaptively	1 2 3 4 5	

3. Name:	Contain	1 2 3 4 5	Old family pattern ___
_____	Internalize	1 2 3 4 5	Former friendship ___
	Segment	1 2 3 4 5	Former lover _____
	Externalize	1 2 3 4 5	Other_____
	Express Adaptively	1 2 3 4 5	
4. Name:	Contain	1 2 3 4 5	Old family pattern ___
_____	Internalize	1 2 3 4 5	Former friendship ___
	Segment	1 2 3 4 5	Former lover _____
	Externalize	1 2 3 4 5	Other_____
	Express Adaptively	1 2 3 4 5	
5. Name:	Contain	1 2 3 4 5	Old family pattern ___
_____	Internalize	1 2 3 4 5	Former friendship ___
	Segment	1 2 3 4 5	Former lover _____
	Externalize	1 2 3 4 5	Other_____
	Express Adaptively	1 2 3 4 5	

TO SCORE: Total your points, and check the category below that applies to you.

25–50: Doing well; you divert only occasionally.

51–75: You alternate between diverting and using anger advantageously.

76–100: You mostly divert; you only occasionally use adaptive anger skills.

101–125: You almost always divert your anger.

If you've scored on the lower end of the scale, congratulations to you and your friends—you're already taking advantage of your anger energy! If your score shows you to be diverting anger fairly consistently, once again, don't be hard on yourself. Diversion is what you've been trained to do, and a high score here just means you are very good at following social cues to act in a culturally accepted manner. You can use this opportunity to take a good look at the messages you've received about anger so far to see where they have led you. Now let's turn to examining a few of the major diversion experiences in more detail.

Anger Detours: Can't Talk about It!

Women tell us that sometimes getting mad at their friends can be threatening enough to make them run for cover. They want to work things out, but feel like it's hazardous to bring up conflicts. As a result, these women typically choose to divert their anger and end up communicating their fury without using words. They may distance themselves, act coldly, or use passive-aggressive actions to show their anger.

During a focus group discussion in one of our recent studies, Muriel, age 40, and her best friend Leigh, 41, give an example of this kind of diversion:

> Leigh: *I remember a time we kept you up late at night.*
> Muriel: *Their talking kept me awake when I was trying to sleep. So the next morning, while they were sleeping . . .*
> Leigh: *You were storming around, stomping all over the place. We didn't know until the next morning that we had been keeping you awake.*
> Muriel: *That's true.*
> Leigh: *It's sort of indirect, but we got the point.*

"Sort of indirect" is an understatement, to be sure! Instead of letting her friends know up front what she felt (annoyed, exasperated) and what she needed (a little more quiet), Muriel tried to let her stomping feet speak her anger for her, long after the fact. But the message was anything but clear and had to be interpreted by friends who luckily cared enough to take on the job. In the end, her actions resulted in neither mutual understanding and sensitivity nor a good night's sleep for any of the women involved. Ever find yourself dropping hints with friends this way? Think about whether you are making things easier or harder for them by withholding a clear explanation of your feelings. Did your actions move your friendship forward or become an obstacle to getting closer?

Ultimately, Muriel's tit-for-tat method of dealing with the conflict had as much, if not more, potential for distancing her friends as an angry but honest verbal declaration of her feelings. And while there is virtually no possibility of improving a friendship by stomping our feet, a willingness to express angry feelings in a respectful way will open a door to a better relationship. Whether or not one's friends walk through that door depends a lot on their own willingness to overcome their overlearned anger avoidance, but the opportunity exists nonetheless.

Another example of the refusal to discuss angry feelings comes from a graduate student who was part of one of our first research projects on anger and dissociation (numbing out when things get too painful). She tells how a friend's refusal to speak about her anger actually led to the demise of their friendship.

One day when we were having lunch together, Shelley shared a story about a recent intense and painful experience. I responded from the heart, and somehow it must not have been the right thing to say. Something in her face froze, and she stopped talking. Although I asked her what was wrong, invited her to tell me what she felt, and apologized for somehow hurting her, Shelley insisted everything was fine. Obviously, it wasn't—she was quiet and began to look around the restaurant, everywhere but at me. I tried to continue the conversation because I could tell she was upset, but she refused to talk about it. When I phoned her a few days later, she took another call from her second line after a few minutes, and never came back on. For me, this was enough, and I chose not to pursue the relationship any further. But I was sad that my friend would cut me off totally rather than share her feelings, no matter how upsetting they might be.

—Jackie (35)

Does Shelley so badly need to avoid her anger and hurt that she can't talk about it out loud, even if her silence means losing a friendship? Or is she unwilling to face her own intolerance of Jackie's honest mistake? Many different scenarios are possible, but the point is that following the rules to silence anger did not help this relationship in any way. Instead, diverting anger effectively ended it. Perhaps in making her decision Shelley was following a conviction heard from other women we've interviewed or counseled, that anger and friendship can't coexist.

Loud, but Not Clear: When Aggression Replaces Anger

Dani, a social worker in her mid-20s, tells the story of a friendship changed forever by unspoken anger that eventually spilled over into aggression between herself and her childhood friend Abbie. They had been buddies since junior high, where they met in Spanish class at their small-town school. The two spent their tumultuous teens together and at first they were inseparable. Each was so glad to have found a friend who understood how different they were from all the other girls in their school. They kept each other company and talked about the pettiness of the very popular girls. The two attended the same university, where they spent a lot of time hanging out together, talking about guys, doing homework, and shopping for clothes.

Later, when Dani became engaged to her college sweetheart, the two friends began to experience some rough times. Abbie acted jealous of the time Dani spent with David and often harassed Dani with her complaints. One evening when Dani forgot about dinner plans with Abbie, she came home to find Abbie waiting for her by the front door, furious and in tears. Abbie began to swear loudly at Dani, causing the neighbors to open their doors and look outside. "We both started yelling at each other and calling each other 'bitch' and saying how we hated each other. It was awful," Dani recalls. The two escalated their argument into an all-out fistfight, right in the breezeway of Dani's apartment building. "I'm not the sort of person who does things like that," says Dani of the experience. "I just hate thinking about that."

Now Dani still struggles to come to terms with what happened. She says that no real apologies were ever exchanged over the incident and that Abbie seemed to think of the incident as a mutual screwup, laughing it off in her usual style ("Yeah, we got kind of out of control the other night."). Dani finds herself wondering what happened to each of them as their newly uncomfortable friendship limps forward. How could she feel such burning rage toward a person she cared for so deeply? How could Abbie continue to pressure her for time and attention, in spite of the fact they had actually come to blows? Would they lash out at each other again at some point in the future? She could not answer these questions partly because she and Abbie had used aggression to *avoid* communicating about anger in a meaningful, constructive way. While some women choose violent words or actions as ways to evade dealing with the emotions they don't want to feel, others avoid processing their anger by shutting down the relationship.

Leaving Anger—and Friendship—Behind

When women believe that a certain level of anger in a relationship means they can no longer be friends, they are faced with a choice between diverting their anger to continue the relationship or giving up their friend so they may acknowledge their feelings. Often this stems from early family messages that say "If you're angry at me, you can't love me." It's important to realize that in friendship, as in other relationships, it's possible to become very angry with someone while still caring for them deeply. However, when we're taught to believe that anger does not mix with love, we can feel compelled to break off a friendship once our anger has reached a particular intensity.

> *I think when I'm really, really, really angry at somebody, I discount their importance in my life. If I've gotten to the Big Boom and that happens several times over—I'll cut you off. I'll cut you off and ice you out . . . I will if you keep pissing me off. And you might not see it coming either because I'm not going to get into it. I'm not living my life in turmoil. I guess that's where it hurts me, because I don't put up with it, the constant back and forth.*
>
> —Kate (42)

Kate may see herself as cutting off a person who is causing her pain, but in fact it's her anger she is trying to escape. Later in her interview with us, she confesses she often misses the relationship she had with the person she has cut off, and regrets to some extent that there is no longer any contact. In spite of this insight, she maintains her pattern of breaking off friendships in response to intense anger, perhaps because she doesn't feel she has a viable alternative.

The ironic truth is that *it is the diversion of anger, not anger itself, that can damage a friendship*. When we decide to swallow our frustration with a friend rather than talk with her about it, we put ourselves in the position of having to avoid our feelings, avoid our friend, or avoid both. Any of these choices will work against increasing the closeness of the friendship, as we have seen in both Shelley and Kate's stories.

In addition, cutting off a friend while anger diversion dominates the relationship does not necessarily get rid of the anger. Remember, diverted anger is still present, even though it's not acknowledged or spoken. In this state, feelings of rage and resentment can remain long after a once-treasured friend is no longer part of our life. How many times have you cut off a relationship in the middle of an angry disagreement in order to end all the strife, only to find yourself stewing long after you decided to part ways? And the very same problems may just come back around. Any issues that were left unresolved as a result of refusing to deal with the anger, and any wounds left unhealed, usually resurface from time to time in other friendships where similar interpersonal dynamics take hold.

On the other hand, when anger is brought out into the open between two friends, the anger advantage is brought into play. We can release our anger respectfully and honestly with the purpose of bringing about a fairer, more responsive balance in the relationship. When we put words on our anger, the issues and emotions don't feel so insurmountable anymore. This kind of anger doesn't alienate and isolate the way diverted anger does. Instead, it becomes a vehicle for bringing about welcome change in the relationship by allowing friends to address those very issues that, once resolved, will increase the experience of closeness and improve the relationship.

Telling Someone Else

In chapter Three we touched on a specific type of family dynamic called triangulation. This pattern of diffusing tension between two people by drawing in a third person goes on in friendships as well. Women we interview or counsel who seek out a friend or family member in order to vent their feelings of anger toward another individual typically feel some relief in sharing their angry feelings this way. Although this brings temporary emotional relief, a woman will likely continue to experience anger on an ongoing basis, since triangulation prevents addressing the relevant issues with the person who triggers it. Muriel, age 40, talks about how this works for her:

> *I often do not show my anger to the person I'm angry with. I think about it and stew about it, and usually I tell my other friends about it. The person never even knows I'm angry. They may know I'm a little bit upset. Except when I'm playing racquetball with Liz. But see, that's safe because I can smash the heck out of that ball. But to confront a person is a lot more intimidating.*

While some may see this avoidance as a means of keeping a friendship alive, it's hardly an effective solution, since there is no way to address and resolve the issue behind the anger. In addition, Muriel cannot be herself with her friends as long as she refuses to reveal her anger. She won't know if they accept and care for *all* of who she is until she finds the courage to face up to the intimidation she feels.

Triangulation is most helpful in dealing with anger that occurs in relationships where someone is in a position of authority over us. While this is not usually the case in friendships, since both parties typically have equal power, there are times when venting to a third person can give us needed space and time to work on a healthy approach to the situation. We'll cover these circumstances later in this chapter, as well as discussing the more positive aspects of triangulation in chapter Six, where workplace dynamics require creative solutions to power differential problems.

Now that we have a clear image of what some major anger diversions look like in the context of friendships, it's time to explore the ways in which anger provides an advantage in these relationships. The first step is to take a good look at ourselves as friends who can sometimes feel angry.

Making Anger Work for Friendship

When we're not really sure how to handle our anger in friendships, it's difficult to resolve problems and process through anger effectively so our friendships can continue to grow. The more detailed sense we have of our feelings and our actions when we're angry, the easier it is to see where a friendship might become derailed during a disagreement. The trick is making sure we have an accurate picture of who we are when we're mad at a friend.

Sometimes there is a big gap between how we see our anger in our friendships and what is really happening. For example, in our research, even women who insist they are anger wimps tell stories that contain courageous acts of self-advocacy and forthright expression of feelings. Others criticize themselves as acting inappropriately when furious but, after exploring further, admit they feel shame over mere dirty looks and long silences, not name-calling, foul language, or aggressive assaults.

Friendship stories come up over and over again in our focus groups and are often a hot subject to process in therapy sessions. To explore the topic further, we dug deeply into the current psychological writings for research and theory to inform the synthesis of these women's stories into our model for healthy anger. We found a parallel between the factors that strengthen ties between friends and the use of all the tools we call adaptive anger skills. Think tanking, anger consciousness, constructive anger talk, and listening are the skills you bring on your journey. By putting them to use with your friends, you will be taking concrete action to move yourself away from diverting anger and toward a helpful approach to working through conflict in your friendships.

But first, let's check out where you're at with these skills at the moment. Use information from your answers to the questions below to check your friendship anger skill inventory.

Your Anger Abilities with Friends

THE RUBBER MEETS THE ROAD: FRIENDSHIP CONFLICTS

Below you'll find six possible friendship scenarios that might make you angry. Answer the following questions about each one of them, in turn.

a. What will you say? (What words will you use to convey your sentiments?)
b. To whom will you say it? (If your answer is someone besides your friend, what makes it easier to tell this other person?)
c. How do you feel when you imagine going directly to your friend to talk?
d. When you think about your friend's possible reactions, what are the best- and worst-case scenarios you can imagine?

1. You realize your friend owes you money—from when she borrowed $200 a year ago—and you decide to say something about it.
2. Your friend agrees, two months in advance, to dog-sit for you while you're away on vacation. At the last minute, she tells you she can't keep your dog because she's afraid he will leave too much hair on her furniture.
3. Your friend comes to you, realizing that you owe her money—from when you borrowed $200 a year ago—and she would like to be repaid.
4. Your friend cancels out on going out dancing with you and your other women friends to have dinner with a guy she's recently met.
5. Your friend comes over for afternoon tea having failed to mention that she's getting the flu and brings her already sick and very whiny three year old with her unannounced.
6. Your friend forgets your birthday.

This exercise offers a detailed perspective on where you are with friendship anger. Now you can take a look at where you want to be and the route you will choose to get there. If you didn't end up at exactly the destination you intended to, the next few sections should help. Let's take a closer look at the unique ways anger consciousness, constructive anger talk, listening, and think tanking work to improve your relationships with friends.

You Can Control Where Your Anger Takes You

It helps to keep in mind just what you want to happen in your friendship when you disclose your anger to a friend. As you become familiar and comfortable with maintaining your anger consciousness, you can begin to ask yourself, "Where do I want my anger to take me in this relationship?" Below we've outlined our suggestions for using the power of your anger to accomplish a variety of different goals. Anger can help you strengthen your friendship, acquire more information about your friend, set some limits with your friend, and finally, extricate yourself from an unhealthy relationship with a friend who refuses to change. Whatever your objective, tapping into your anger energy will enable you to recognize and move in a positive direction.

Strengthening Friendships

There are tremendous opportunities for connection when two people who care about each other find the courage to explore the more difficult areas of their friendship. As scholars we've learned from our readings, our research participants, and our clients that *people connect through their vulnerabilities, as well as through their strengths.* Disclosing anger through constructive anger talk is an extremely vulnerable act for any individual. It involves issues packed with intense emotion and requires one to reveal a need or desire that is not being met and may never be met. We lay open the very part of us that feels the most raw and sensitive. Along with our anger we confess hurt, disappointment, and speak of what we hope for, what we feel we need and want but do not have. Are you willing to allow yourself to become this vulnerable with your friends? If so, your willingness to engage in this kind of communication will result in a level of trust, selflessness, love, and commitment unattainable for those who don't dare to expose their angry feelings.

Researchers at the Stone Center at Wellesley College, pioneers in exploring how women's identity develops within the context of their relationships, note that in relationships among equals (as in friendships) angry feelings are often mixed with feelings of love and caring. They recommend that women communicate anger to friends in direct and genuine exchanges, in which the angry woman's needs, rights, and boundaries are jointly considered with the needs, rights, and boundaries of her friend.

You can accomplish this in your friendships by holding on to both your anger consciousness *and* your sense of connection to your friend during a conflict. Choosing to acknowledge only one of these makes it hard to fight fair. For instance, if you become so angry that you lose touch with any feelings of connectedness, you run the risk of turning your anger into an attack against your friend. Here's where think tanking can really make a difference. It allows you to back off from the emotional intensity that could push you into externalizing and attacking, without losing track of your anger or denying it altogether. In addition, remembering how much you care about your friend can keep you from externalizing your anger and dumping it in a hurtful way.

On the other hand, if you lose track of the intensity of your anger, you may be hiding, diminishing, or camouflaging your anger to the extent you can no longer feel it. In this state, you may be appropriately sensitive to your friend's feelings and needs, but you won't get to express your true self, honestly communicate your feelings, and stand up for your needs. Over time, this produces a friendship based on an unreal version of yourself, which means you only bring what you believe are the acceptable parts of yourself to the friendship and keep the rest hidden. Therefore, it's crucial that you learn how to track both your anger and your love for your friend while working through a conflict.

Talk, Listen, and Learn

Constructive anger talk involves both talking honestly about your feelings and listening intently to what your friend is saying. In this way it creates space for both your feelings and hers, while providing each of you with important information about the other. You can each then choose what kinds of change, if any, you want to bring about based on what you've stated and heard. When friends choose not to talk about anger, but instead use non-verbal signals to express annoyance, no one has access to the important information words have the power to provide. These friends must do without the details that would help them decide how to resolve their disagreement, and thus they miss out on a significant anger advantage.

As we've mentioned, women who don't speak their angry feelings tell us they favor withdrawing or acting passive-aggressively when they feel mad toward a friend. Do you ever find yourself choosing to use the silent treatment on a friend in order to avoid talking about how angry you feel with her? This means that instead of admitting to yourself and your friend how you feel, you're taking action that's geared toward making her angry as well. Maybe you decide to cancel lunch together at the last minute as a punishment for her criticism of you in front of mutual acquaintances last week. Your friend may recognize that you are angry (or not, depending on the reason you give her for not showing up), but she has no information at all about your feelings and what is behind them. Instead of exploring your anger and telling your friend about it, your behavior invites your friend to become angry with you.

Perhaps you feel, when you no-show for lunch, that you've done enough to let your friend know about your unhappiness, and you decide to wait for her to make some kind of apology for her previous actions. How difficult will it be for your friend to recognize it's her turn to act and figure out what might help, if you've provided no specifics about your experience, feelings, or expectations? Your friend may guess accurately or she may err wildly. But without direct communication from you about the anger you feel, any attempts to make things right will be much more difficult.

Suppose instead of backing out of your lunch date at the last minute, you choose to meet your friend at the restaurant instead, with the goal of letting her know how steamed you are sometime during the meal. You feel apprehensive about her reaction and decide to spend some time thinking about what words you want to use. When you greet her, you don't pretend more enthusiasm than you really feel, but at the same time you don't dump on her as soon as she walks in. When you feel the time is right to broach the subject, you use "I" messages, statements that begin with "I feel . . ." so that your words do not attack her character, but instead offer information about what happened to you when your friend spoke the way she did a few days before. You honestly express your anger, but maintain respect for your friend's feelings all the while. You say something like:

> *I felt so betrayed when you talked about me that way in front of everyone. You've never done that before, and I still can't understand how it happened. I feel angry all over again every time I think about it, and I don't want it to change our friendship.*

Important and helpful information about your experience now becomes available to your friend. If she can tolerate hearing your anger, she'll be able to use that information to respond to your feelings, join you in resolving the problem, and protect your relationship from such incidents in the future. In the same way, you've had the opportunity to learn much about your friend in her account of why she acted the way she did when you found yourself feeling criticized and hurt. You gain valuable insight into her good intentions and her lack of awareness that her words had stung. Your new knowledge may even diminish the anger you feel the next time your friend's words feel critical (If not, that's okay too—anger happens!).

This is how constructive anger talk contributes to the way in which you and your friend know each other, which in turn adds to the health and well-being of the relationship. Talking about and listening to anger is a powerful way to learn how to be better friends.

Of course, some friends will have a harder time listening to anger, no matter how respectfully it's stated. They are afraid and critical of anger, as we've all been taught to be, and may respond negatively to your expressions of irritation even when you are careful to use constructive anger talk. In such a case, it becomes your turn to listen as your friend lets you know her hurt, outrage, or defensiveness. You need neither change your position nor her perspective on anger, but try instead to remain clear on the reality that it is possible to be both very angry with each other and very connected as friends.

And this behavior becomes especially vital if you find your friend is encroaching on personal territory or doing things that threaten you. In these cases, you can use your angry energy to set appropriate limits with your friend—a strategy that will do more to preserve and improve your friendship than any amount of holding your tongue or counting to ten.

Letting Anger Help You Say No

Pauline, 19, tells of her fury with a college suitemate, Lynn, who became so drunk she attacked Pauline physically and vomited all over the suite bathroom. After Lynn sobered up, she didn't remember what had happened. Pauline filled her in and also made clear how the event had altered their friendship. While she would continue to care for and support Lynn, Pauline stated she could not trust her any longer and would not continue the friendship unless Lynn got help for her alcohol problem. When Lynn agreed she had a problem and eventually left school for a rehab program, Pauline felt gratified she was able to help her friend while still protecting herself from ever being put in such a frightening position again.

Could you take a stand with a friend the way Pauline did? What if your physical safety weren't at risk? Ask yourself how high the stakes have to be for you to enter into open conflict with a friend. A common response we hear from women is, "I just hate confrontation! I'd put up with just about anything rather than having to confront someone!" But the effects of putting up with a situation can be devastating to a friendship. You don't have to avoid speaking your mind once you leave behind the notion that it's unfeminine to do so and go on to discover how getting clear with your friends about your personal preferences can enhance your friendships.

We've heard countless stories of how frightening it can be for women to face angry conversations. Even when they have gained some measure of anger consciousness and they know what they want or need in a friendship, it feels like too great a risk to take the next step of bringing their anger from the inside—the heart, the mind—to the outside where others can hear and see it. Whether it's their own anger or a friend's they dread, their aversion keeps them from talking about what they need in order for their friendship to flourish instead of founder.

On the other hand, women who have figured out a way to handle confrontation tell us how it works to keep their friendships satisfying. Those who step forward and take a position describe the experience as empowering. Alison and Shelby have reaped the rewards of speaking up. In a family interview they share their perspectives:

> *Alison: I guess you don't let people get to you as much if people know you'll get angry and not have to sit there and take it.*
>
> *Shelby: Yeah, if I've been too laid back about a situation I think it [anger] prompts me to action. Not necessarily to get up in someone's face. But sometimes it's a good thing, it gets you started.*

Sandy, a client, offers a quintessential example of a struggle between friends that involves anger over differing expectations.

> *I have a friend who isn't allowing me my space, and she's a fairly new friend. We've been friends for about six months. And she wants to call me two or three times a day! I'm not used to being called two or three times a day, and quite frankly, I don't have something to say to her three times a day! (laughter) And I certainly don't have anything I want to listen to two or three times a day! She's really resisting me trying to set limits about that, and it's making me angry and frustrated and I do not know how to express that with her to help us improve our friendship.*
>
> *I'd rather do it calmly and friendly, "This is what I need*

from you," than to have it turn into something unpleasant like, "Don't call me anymore! You're bugging the heck out of me!" where I'm really blunt about it, where I really might hurt her feelings. I'm sure this is something she's not cognizant she's doing.

—*Sandy (43)*

Sandy has been working hard on her constructive anger talk. She recognizes precisely the issue behind her anger and the limits she feels need to be in place concerning her friend's phone calls. She can foresee that diverting her anger will eventually lead to ending the friendship, so she works out how to be honest and direct with her new friend without appearing insensitive. After a few rebuffed attempts to offer information about her feelings, Sandy is now ready to move on to setting some concrete boundaries.

Rather than suffer in silence, all the while feeling used, annoyed, and maybe even guilty, Sandy is going to empower herself and enrich her relationship by letting her anger speak. How do such women go about using constructive anger talk to transform friendships? Here are some tips.

How to Set and Enforce Boundaries with a Friend

- Form a specific picture of what you would like to change. Do you know what you're asking of your friend and where you want to draw the line? In Sandy's previous example, she pinpoints those three phone calls a day as the problem and takes the time to identify her comfort level at somewhere closer to three calls a week. She'll ask her friend to come to some kind of agreement about what will work for both of them.
- Approach this process with the goal of improving your relationship, and the belief that handling your anger directly can accomplish this. Make sure you communicate your good intentions to your friend—it will make a difference in how she hears your anger. Sandy links her request for change directly with improving her friendship.

- Are you convinced your friend is trying to make you angry, out to win at any cost, looking for revenge? It's much more helpful to begin by assuming your friend has only the best intentions and wants to resolve the issue at hand. On the rare occasion that you are proven wrong in this, you will find out as soon as you begin to dialogue. But most likely, your friend just needs more information on what feels comfortable to you in order to make better choices in the way she relates to you. Sandy takes the view that her friend is probably unaware of the effects of her multiple calls. This belief helps her listen carefully to her friend when she responds to the confrontation.

- Be aware of how much emotional intensity you wish to reveal. This varies from friend to friend and circumstance to circumstance. In some cases a friend may not be able to tolerate hearing much anger, and an intense interaction does more harm than good. Dani and Abbie might have avoided a physical fight if they had noticed that the intensity of their feelings was taking them in a dangerous direction and taken things down a notch. It helps to engage in the verbal or physical anger exercises like the ones we describe in chapter Two so you can take care of your own need to freely express your feelings before talking to your friend about setting boundaries. At other times, when you anticipate the self-disclosure will deepen your friendship, choose to risk becoming vulnerable with a more passionate and emotional discussion.

- Hear the feelings behind your friend's spoken words. Focus on being true to yourself and honest about your needs, but don't forget to really listen and open yourself to your friend when she tells you what is triggering her anger. You will learn how your words and actions affect your friend and perhaps others also. Can you take this feedback in the spirit in which it's given? Are you open to changing in order to grow both in yourself and in your friendship? Sandy will need to be ready to hear her friend spell out how and why she would like Sandy to be more available in the relationship. Will she be willing to compromise, to change her own behavior in some ways?

If at some point in the process of boundary setting you find yourself unable to talk clearly about your needs or feelings or if your language becomes hazy and evasive, perhaps you are losing touch with your anger. Take a minute to refocus, and let yourself connect with your angry feelings so you can draw on the natural energy of your anger again. It will empower you to stand up for what you know you need in order for the friendship to develop and grow.

On the other hand, if you find your anger intensifying to the point of not being able to listen to your friend or wanting to cause her pain, you need a moment of reflection on the loving feelings you have for your friend. It will help to remind yourself of the reasons why you decided to have this conversation and how they are related to the over-all good of the friendship.

Remember, you each have the option of maintaining your own separate viewpoints, and your opinions don't have to match perfectly in order to restore peace and harmony to the friendship. Your goal is to make your position clear and in so doing, create an opportunity for changing the friendship into something that works well for both of you.

While working on setting boundaries with a friend, it's also impor-tant to keep in mind there are limits to the amount of control we can exercise over others. It's not hard to slide from doing our own anger work to working on someone else in anger—a move in the wrong direction. Clarifying the purpose of expressing anger helps our expec-tations stay in line with reality and minimizes the chances we will use our anger to try to control another.

Anger and Control

It's kind of like, if somebody does something to annoy you, you can either choose to accept that it might annoy you but that it's their habit, or you can say "Listen, this annoys me." And maybe that makes the situation better or worse, but you do have a decision.

—Maggie (24)

Note that Maggie does not say you have the option of changing the other person's annoying habit. Most women in our research express a great deal of confusion over this issue. How many of us have given up an argument before we ever started, thinking, "Why bother? She's never going to change."? Or decided that a little well-timed outburst should be just the thing to convince a friend she needs to cave in and see things our way, once and for all? The urge to control, to force our own agenda, often gets mixed up with anger expression. We forget that our goal is to let the other person know what we are feeling and where our own boundaries fall, *not to change the person we are angry with.* This is a tough distinction both because it's a subtle one and because it's not an easy one to live with. What's the point of arguing if not to try to get our own way? Certainly we'd all like to be able to dictate how our friend behaves whenever we're at odds with a choice she's making. That way we could ensure our needs and desires are met to the fullest. But the reality is that no one has such power, and if we act as if we can take control over another simply because we feel angry and we're willing to show it, we're denying the reality of our friend's power to determine her own actions.

If we decide our goal is to force our friend to change, we base our success on something that lies outside our control and therefore set ourselves up for likely failure. A much healthier approach is to focus only on those things that we can control—our own actions—and set our goals accordingly. With anger, expressing ourselves clearly and directly is a goal we can achieve. Because we can't control our friend's subsequent decision to change, we end up feeling less powerful if that is our goal.

In addition, we are used to thinking of anger as intimidating or threatening, and it's natural for us to expect that when we do let others know how mad we are, we are going to get our way. Think carefully about what you want your anger to do for you. Do you see anger as a means to manipulate others? Is it a way for you to insist others change in order to suit your own needs? In order for anger to become an advantage, it's important to envision using it to make decisions about your *own* behavior during a conflict, not your friend's. When should you speak up, what will you say, and what will you do if your friend's behavior continues unchanged in the future? It's not up to you to dictate how, how much, and how soon your friend should change. She's in charge of making those decisions, just as you're in charge of deciding how you will let her know about her hurtful or aggravating behavior.

Perhaps one of the biggest challenges in expressing anger directly and listening to our friends' anger is tolerating our own and others' displeasure. Women describe feeling both worried about how their anger will be received ("Please don't be mad at me for saying this, but . . .") and shocked and defensive when hearing a friend's anger come their way ("I can't believe she would talk to me like that!"). While these intense reactions are natural in our anger-avoidant culture, once we begin to think of anger in a new way it becomes a lot easier to listen to it, both in ourselves and others. It's not necessary to become defensive if, instead of assuming an angry outburst is intended to manipulate, punish, or bully, we view these emotions as an offering of information and an invitation to connect through new actions.

When two friends can process anger in this way, the result is positive and the relationship grows stronger. But what happens when the answer is "no," when your friend refuses to listen, hear, negotiate, or change no matter how honest or careful you are with your expression? If you get to this point with a friend when you're trying to make use of your anger advantage, decide how you want to participate in the friendship at this point. Do you want to stay friends, back off somewhat, or totally walk away?

If there is some way to carefully pick and choose your interactions so that the anger-provoking situation doesn't arise, then you may be able to continue to be connected, albeit on a more limited basis. If the friendship is more important than the issue at stake, you may decide to continue at the same level of closeness. It's critical, however, to avoid diverting anger in this situation. You can choose to go forward with the friendship, but you might have to say to yourself, "This person just always makes me angry when she runs late, and that's the way it's going to be. Yes, I'm angry." And you will have to continue to let your friend know how angry you feel when she's late. It's just that you have come to accept the fact that she does not choose to change, and you value her friendship too much to end the relationship over this issue. What you are then doing is continuing to *experience and express* your anger without denial or minimization and without insisting that your friend change when she's made it clear she doesn't wish to. If you divert your anger so that it becomes silent at this point, you run the risk of becoming resentful or quietly manipulative with her as time goes on. And she loses track of the consequences of her tardiness, one of which is it's endlessly maddening to you, her good friend.

You may be wondering how all this actually plays out in a conversation between two friends. Let's suppose Mary and Cathy, good friends for the past five years, meet for dinner a couple of times a month. Mary finds herself growing increasingly impatient with Cathy's excessive cell phone use during these dinners and decides to let Cathy know. One evening she tells Cathy exactly how she feels, and while Cathy acknowledges the calls are intrusive, she protests they are necessary because she must be able to respond to her children's needs while she is out. They discuss this for a few minutes, but Cathy isn't open to imposing any limits on her calls. How should Mary respond at this point?

She's likely to feel an even stronger swell of anger and hurt, since she took the risk of revealing her feelings to her friend and has been denied her request. Mary could decide to communicate her heightened feelings and push even harder for Cathy to make changes. This will obviously lead to a showdown over the issue—how much is Mary willing to risk over the cell phone situation? She could decide to cross over the line between communication and manipulation, using her angry energy to criticize or wound Cathy and insisting that her anger entitles her to better treatment from her friend. Although she may get her way, it's obvious there will be damaging consequences to the friendship.

On the other hand, Mary could become hurt and confused by Cathy's refusal to compromise and decide to hide her feelings. Mary may divert her anger at this point, saying "All right, fine, whatever," but then pull back from Cathy and remain distant for the rest of the evening or even for the next month. Again, the relationship does not realize any benefit from the disclosure of Mary's anger.

But suppose Mary decides to neither escalate nor withdraw, but simply stay true to her emotional experience while maintaining respect for her friend. She doesn't use her anger as a weapon to force her own agenda, but she doesn't back down from advocating for herself either. And because she can acknowledge her positive feelings for Cathy and the great relationship they've had in the past *even while she is angry*, Mary doesn't choose to end the relationship by giving up and walking out—either literally or emotionally. The key is Mary's ability to tolerate the presence of anger in the friendship—both her own and probably Cathy's at some point.

What does this look like in the real life give-and-take of a friendship? Typically, thoughtful conversations carried out over a period of time eventually lead to a resolution that works on some level for each friend. Compromise means no one gets exactly what she wants but everyone gets something she needs. When Mary tells Cathy she understands about needing to keep in touch with the kids and wonders if there's a less disruptive way to accomplish this, she succeeds in balancing her empathy and caring for Cathy with her own need to experience less frustration in their relationship. Perhaps if Cathy finds herself angry at Mary's apparent lack of concern for her children. When she makes that known, Mary has a couple of options. She can acknowledge Cathy's perception as accurate and offer more information about how she (Mary) came to feel this way: "Well, for just a few hours I'd like our conversation to take priority. I think you are too protective of your kids anyway, now that they're older." Or if Cathy's anger is stemming from a misperception, Mary can correct it: "No, I don't feel that way at all! I'm crazy about your kids and I know they have to come first. But can't we find another way to make sure they're okay while you and I are talking?"

Their ability to tolerate each other's anger throughout the process allows these friends the freedom to talk about and listen to feelings and concerns most relevant to the issue. In addition, the process itself provides invaluable information to each of them about both their needs and wants. If anger is off limits, the whole truth about what each finds frustrating remains undeclared and both are left hanging, twisting uncomfortably in their denial. But if they each give and receive this kind of emotional information, their relationship moves forward more fully informed and more satisfying.

Triangulation:
When Gossip Is Good for You (and When It's Not)

Although research supports the idea (Kennedy-Moore & Watson, 1999) that it is most helpful in resolving irritating situations to express your anger directly to the target of your anger, there are times when you may find it helpful to express your anger to another trusted source. This kind of conversation is very different from the harsh blaming and criticizing of another that is really just another version of externalizing anger diversion. There's an important distinction between harmful gossip and the kind of triangulating gossip that's helpful in keeping you on track with adaptive anger. The difference between the two involves our *intent to resolve.*

When we talk about ourselves and our feelings using "I" statements (e.g., "I'm having such a hard time with this." "I feel so torn apart and angry when I think of having to sit by and watch this happen." "I just hate it when he treats me that way. I want to reach over and slap him."), we claim the feelings and aggressive impulses as our own. This lets us work them out with another human being, make sense of them, get another view, receive validation and help from a friend. On the other hand, getting together with a friend to talk about how awful someone is (e.g., "What a bitch." "She is really out of bounds this time.") deprives us of the opportunity to talk about ourselves and how we feel. This latter kind of gossip constitutes externalized anger in that we focus on the negative traits or behaviors of someone else, without the intent to get resolution on our own feelings and needs. In externalizing gossip, we talk to get even. We talk to damage that other person's reputation or create a team of enemies for them. "I" statements, in contrast, empower us and help promote both impulse control and insight.

People stand to get hurt by irresponsible conversations. Therefore, it's important to clarify what we're doing when we vent to others. Ask yourself the following questions before you talk about your grievances to someone besides the friend who triggered them: (1) Can I tell this story using "I" statements only? (2) What do I hope to gain from telling my story to this person? (3) What would it cost me to tell my story to the friend I'm mad at? When you feel betrayed or let down, particularly by someone who is your peer, weigh the potential costs and benefits of having your disagreement with them, instead of without them.

Sometimes our fear of direct confrontation stems from real or imagined danger. For example, Dani describes feeling bullied and manipulated by Abbie's vaguely threatening and clearly demanding attitude that arose whenever the issue of Dani's boyfriend came up. She puzzles over why she repeatedly avoided the very topics she needed to talk about in order for the friendship to survive. Could it be she was responding to very real and powerful messages from Abbie whose best interests were served by evading the real issues? Perhaps her fear of Abbie started long before their physical fight occurred. Still, the only way for Dani to accommodate her friend this way was to swallow her own feelings and needs and stay silent, an untenable position in the long run.

Anger advantage skills can bring significant positive changes to a friendship when both parties are well intended and open to change. However, most of us have had the experience of somehow finding ourselves in a friendship on the decline. We've found ourselves suffering through a one-sided and only minimally rewarding relationship, which for whatever reasons has come to offer little hope for improvement. What started out as so much fun turns quite ugly, depressing, or chronically infuriating, and the respect and affection we once felt is no longer there. In cases like these, constructive anger talk can help you bring the relationship to a much needed close.

When Enough Is Enough:
Anger Can Help You Say Good-bye

> . . . It's about, "I don't like you," . . . "I don't like who you are right now, and I'm just not going to be in a relationship with you right now." So it's a coldness.
>
> —Kate (42)

Here Kate talks about what happens when she realizes she's not just angry at someone, she feels dislike and a need to separate from them as well. There seems to be a line that is crossed, either suddenly and dramatically, or slowly and gradually. A troubled but still viable relationship in which friends continue to grapple with the issues and push up against each other, at some point turns a corner and the two friends who are pushing against each other begin to push away instead. Or perhaps one friend eventually admits to herself she can no longer find even an ounce of compatibility or comfort in the relationship.

Just as in abusive or unequal love relationships, friendships become overly burdensome or one-sided, and ending them brings more peace than pain. At this point, anger expression offers a respectful and honest way to say good-bye.

Timing is the crucial element. If friends give up and walk away before they've even begun to try, they forfeit a friendship unnecessarily. Only after making an investment in direct anger expression and exploring the options opened to them by straightforward dialogue can they be certain they haven't given up too soon. If the decision to end a friendship comes while both friends are still diverting anger, they haven't given each other a chance to be real, act genuinely, and make things right between themselves.

Diverted anger cannot help or save a troubled friendship. But sometimes neither can direct anger. Perhaps the frank discussions stemming from direct emotional expression uncover significant personal disparities that have been avoided and skimmed over; or maybe the flexibility required to meet the needs and honor the boundaries of one friend is just not present in the relationship. When anger is not off limits and honesty is allowed fuller reign, most friends discover a deeper affection. However, a small number find their differences irreconcilable.

Kendra relates how acknowledging and expressing her anger led her to recognize long-term inequities in a troubled friendship. She decides the relationship cannot continue and takes steps to end it:

In my late 20s, I used to be friends with Tina. We had a lot in common; we both loved alternative music, reading, playing board games, going out to hear bands, poetry, art movies. She was super dramatic and beautiful (and well off, by the way), constantly in demand by guys and always invited to parties. I was a poor college student at the time and nothing special to look at. But we were both really introverts at heart and often would rather just hang out together at my house or her house and talk, have a drink or coffee, or listen to music at home. When we did go out, I was very much in her shadow, which was fine with me most of the time.

Tina had a lot of problems though, and we often spent time discussing these. Her relationships with guys never seemed to work out; a lot of times she'd end up with someone for a while who was really a jerk—alcoholic or abusive or both. Her dad had been abusive while she was growing up and her mom never really stood up to him and protected her. And she said her mom was critical, like a perfectionist about everything. I learned this stuff about Tina over about three years, little by little. Lots of times it would come out in her poetry or songs she wrote; she played guitar and sometimes performed in local clubs. And when she'd talk about her guy problems, she was totally entertaining. She talked just like she wrote poetry. I was always sucked in to being the confidential ear for her wild Bad Boy tales.

But I slowly realized it was all about her. I didn't have much going on in my life at the time, so after a quick update on my life, our visits usually consisted of extended monologues from Tina about her tragedy of the day. It took me a while, but I finally caught on. And the more I saw it, the worse it felt. No matter what story I had, she had to top it. Her problems were always bigger, more serious, more important than anyone else's. But I didn't say a word about it. Sometimes I found excuses not to get together. Then, one spring, I had a family crisis of my own. My parents were in a serious car wreck. I was 1,000 miles away and scared out of my wits. I called Tina to talk. "Wow, that's too bad!" she said. And then she started in on her latest guy story. I was on the other end of the line with my mouth hanging open.

A couple of days later, I called her and told her exactly how angry I was with her and why and ended the friendship. My anger finally did for me what I hadn't been able to do for years . . . it motivated me to dump her. Being pissed was reassurance that I wasn't just making it up—that she was selfish, needy, and really unable to be a friend. Feeling all of that sort of gave me a vision of what it would be like to stay friends with her—an endless series of long, involved, one-sided stories. And God forbid that anyone one up her with a problem of their own. It was going to be all give-give-give on my part and take-take-take on hers. I understood there were reasons for the way she was. But I wanted to be a friend, not her shrink. She'd probably never be able to see anything but her side of it and I finally could see that.

Terminating a friendship is always a last resort, and a rare necessity. Far more prevalent are struggles surrounding the preservation and building up of valued friendships. Are you ready to work on deepening and enriching a cherished friendship? Would you like to expand the scope of a wonderful companionship or hold on to an important friend when conflict threatens to alienate her? The following tips offer ways to harness your anger energy for all these friendship needs.

Guidelines for Friendship and Fury

1. Don't try to fix an intense fight in the middle of it. Most people can't do this; let the fight happen and then work on repairing the friendship after the fight. In their summary of studies on anger expression and interpersonal relationships, writers Ellen Kennedy-Moore and Jeanne C. Watson note that even people with good intentions who communicate well don't want to use these skills and have a harder time doing so when extremely angry.

2. Think tank your emotions if you feel confused or cautious about expressing them. Give yourself some time (but no more than a few days) to dive into the depths of your annoyance; talk with someone you trust if you need a reality check. Write down what you'd like to say to your friend.

3. Don't let yourself ignore anger when it's there. If you don't attend to it quickly, it will fester and taint your interactions with your friend on an ongoing basis. Based on our studies, diverting your anger, in the long run, will not help your friendship. (Remember Myth 4: Anger ruins relationships?) Even if you are think tanking, make sure you take care of your strong feelings sooner, rather than later.

4. At some time when you are *not* feeling angry with your friend, talk about the things that can make you angry in a friendship. Talk about how each of you would prefer to handle an anger situation before it arises. Make sure the conversation is personal and not abstract. For example, let your friend know what your pet peeves are and what you would consider a major violation in any friendship.

5. Listen to her concerns and boundaries with sensitivity and respect. You can't possibly anticipate every little thing that would ever arise, but you and your friend *can* exchange information about likely hot topics and about your own styles for dealing with anger. How will you make it clear that you want to have a two-way discussion in order to benefit and maintain your friendship?

6. Listen carefully to your friend's emotions and invite her to be frank with you about them. Hear her so well that you can repeat what she's just said back to her. "So, I'm getting it that you felt let down when I decided not to go on that trip to Cancun." "It sounds like you want me to back off when you're really having a hard time sticking to your workout schedule." "I hear you saying that you were furious with me because I wasn't taking you seriously." And check to see if you got it right.

THE ROAD LESS TRAVELED

The skills we've covered offer a multitude of options for the next time you find yourself at odds with a friend. As Donna, a professional woman in her 40s, reminisces about a lifetime friend, she reveals how they have been able to work with their anger to keep and enhance an important friendship.

Jeannie and I had a lot of the same interests and did a lot of fun stuff together. Jeannie could really listen to me when I was upset and vice versa. We've been friends now for over 15 years. In that time, I've had my problems and she's had hers; all the usual stuff—guys, family, work . . . just life. Sometimes we've lived in the same town or city, sometimes not. Sometimes we have worked together and sometimes not. But no matter what, we both have always agreed that it was really important to be honest and up front with each other.

So when she makes me mad or I make her mad, we talk about it. You can't have a friend for 15 years and never get cross with each other once in a while! In fact, we know each other so well now, that we can usually tell right away when one of us is mad. I know just the way Jeannie's voice changes, how her face changes, when I've done something to piss her off, and she can tell the same with me, because she comes and asks me about it.

I don't really like these talks—they aren't easy or fun. I almost always cry. At this point in our friendship, we usually don't go more than a day before talking about it. So far, we've always been able to either find a way to fix the problem or at least to understand it enough that we can let it go. Or one or the other of us apologizes and that's the end of it.

We have both said to each other that one of the things that keeps our friendship strong is that we can talk about anger with each other. Jeannie says, "I feel like I can always talk to you about it and we'll work it out, no matter what it is."

Maybe someday we'll run into something that stumps us, but so far, so good. It's not that we don't ever fight—it's that we can talk about it afterward and understand each other and be okay with each other. However awkward the conversation is, it still feels better in the end to have it. So in a weird way, our anger actually drives us toward each other, to fix whatever it is, because we want to stay friends.

I've learned a lot about Jeannie this way. For example, Jeannie hates to be interrupted; it feels disrespectful and rude to her. I was used to talking over people, since this was the way my family was and nobody ever took offense. I didn't even know I was doing it. When Jeannie kept getting mad about it, I felt so pissed at first, but I heard her through and said I'd try to watch it. I have gotten better at this I think. Another example is a time when I thought Jeannie was talking down to me, which made me angry. I told her and she apologized and told me it wasn't what she meant. Again, the anger worked to keep us on an even keel, and even to make us closer.

Like Donna, once you've made the leap from seeing anger as a threat to understanding its potential benefits within the context of friendship, you're on your way to discovering an empowered way of handling conflicts and disputes with friends.

SIX

Taking Care of Business
Anger Goes to Work

I was really mad at one point, working for the [non-profit organization]. We had an executive director who was incompetent and no one on the board understood what a real board member was supposed to do. But no one was admitting it. We're all just going to show up and we're not really going to bring up that we're not liking it, not getting it. And so I'm viewing myself as the factory girl who's just now jumped into business and I'm looking at myself as less than everybody else. And one day I just thought, "Okay, I may never be that sharp—maybe I'll never get it, but I just need to let this out." So at the next board meeting, I said, "I just need to bring something up. I need to step back. I'm not enjoying this. It's not fun. I don't get it. I'm voting on things I don't understand. And I perhaps don't have the business experience to be a valuable board member for you. I'm showing up but that's all I'm doing."

When I said that, the floodgates opened. I was asked to be the vice president. I jumped in and I started putting some systems together. So I used that energy. I pulled together a book that would be given to every board member. It told what we're all about. And then I created a system that would let us keep tabs on everything we do, financials, everything. There are no more excuses. I've stepped up to the plate. And from that, I created a program to help non-profits get organized. I got rid of dead wood. My anger came from the fact that no *one else would admit it, dadgummit. My anger came from "Good God, you're all calling yourselves businesspeople and this is the best you can do? Come on!" I just felt so empowered by that and so righteous. It's like if I can do this as a former factory worker with no training, my God, the confidence that I got from that!*

Now, I have a program that I can take to other non-profits to help them get started too!

—Jana (43)

Does Jana's story frighten you—or does it make you feel inspired? Jana has really hit her stride. By discovering a voice in her irritation, she strengthens her confidence to tackle a new set of responsibilities and urges on a new creativity she never knew she had. Speaking up makes her *more* of who she is, intellectually, socially, emotionally, and professionally. But all of her forward movement involves people. And people mean relationships.

Whatever your job, you should think of your workplace as another type of *family*. And family is where you learn to define who you are. Particularly for a woman, defining self depends on a relationship context in which she finds herself selling, teaching, creating, caring for others, writing, managing, planting, studying, or answering the phone. Work mirrors family in that it involves another *system* of people with whom we must interact on a regular basis, with whom we share a common workplace culture. Because of our relationships with them, the setting for our work becomes either a place in which we invest pride or where we stagnate.

What good does anger do for us at work? The intellectually clarifying process of exploring your anger can help you get a handle on things you'd like to change there. As you become more certain about feeling antagonism, and for what reasons, you gradually develop a *defining outer edge*. Anger helps you see boundaries, the places where your job ends and you begin; where your coworkers stop and you start. You see yourself as separate from your job—a distinct entity with priorities and ideas all your own.

What good does it do to view yourself in this light? How does being angry and *separate from work* help you at your career? Women tell us that when they have boundaries, they become much less vulnerable to the forces that urge us all to abandon our personal concerns and give the best parts of ourselves to an organization or to the almighty dollar. We begin imagining how life could be if we used our time as we want to, used our creative energy in ways meaningful to us.

Since relationship is central to work, many of the anger risks you face there have to do with *relationship change*. In Jana's empowerment story at the beginning of this chapter, she uses her anger to define herself in a new way. We hear her revolutionize not only an organization, but her thinking as well. She comes onto the scene feeling timid about her abilities in comparison with the other board members. But through anger consciousness, she comes to learn her strength and tap into some of her greatest talents—leading people in an effective, non-judgmental way. To do all of this, she has to become familiar with the meaning behind her irritation and ride the waves of her emotion into a new management role. Her power comes, in part, from her ability to use her anger advantage: that is, to pinpoint the source of discontent, give it a name, and bring it out into the light.

What makes us mad at work? We'll share women's stories and insights on this critical issue next.

BITTER PILLS

> *When I get mad in work situations usually it's because I feel strongly about a situation and either I feel like it's being ignored or not being followed or somebody isn't understanding my perspective.*
>
> —Melanie (24)

What Gets to You at Work?

From our interviews with women, it seems that the same basic relational elements that make us angry in our love relationships, families, and friendships—betrayal, inattention, lack of acknowledgment, abuse, and certain kinds of stress—make us angry in work and professional relationships too.

Melanie's quote (above) sums up a lot of what gets to us on the job. She works as a key advisor for the Greek fraternity and sorority system in a large university. At 24, she already holds quite a bit of responsibility and has to oversee the decisions of several hundred students. So Melanie, from whom we will hear often in this chapter, gets many opportunities to experience anger at students as well as other staff members whose agendas conflict with her keenly felt responsibilities to protect these student groups. Like Melanie, the other women in our interviews and focus groups tell us about experiencing workplace anger mainly in the following five situations:

1. gender-related discrimination
2. being taken for granted or used
3. feeling work strain on other life roles (or the reverse)
4. when others don't come through: apathy, incompetence, underperformance, or dishonesty
5. feeling compromised, demeaned, or abused

Notice that each item on this list of workplace anger triggers has something to do with relationships. Some research demonstrates that women not only express a wider range of emotions, both at home and at work, but also try to minimize the gaps between our work and personal lives. Therefore, we expect that women become angry at work for *personalized* reasons, blurring the lines between professional and private relationships. This means that emotional injuries at work have similar meaning in our lives that emotional injuries at home or in dating relationships have. In the next section, we explore women's anger at these common workplace situations. And since most women tend to divert lots of anger on the job, we look at what happens to them when they deny or muffle their true feelings.

The Boys' Club:
Gender Discrimination and Inequity

In meetings with him, I can say one thing and he totally

dismisses it, but if an older gentleman says it, "You're right. Yes, sir."

—*Melanie (24)*

Gender bias is a *relationship* issue. Connie Gersick and her colleagues report on a study of college business professors from around the United States. This group describes their relationships with colleagues as extremely important for helping build careers. However, where men experience their careers as games to be played tactically, women often experience theirs as a test of their abilities. In our own research, women say they often feel like the test is whether or not they can keep a lid on their strong feelings and only express them in masculine ways, through logic only with the passion removed.

Money and authority are part of the picture too. Women in some occupations have to work twice as hard to prove themselves or to be accepted at the same levels at which men are accepted and promoted in their positions. Often, these women get paid significantly less then their male peers. In fact, surveys show that women are primarily employed in woman-dominated occupations, which tend to pay lower wages, and that as the percentage of women increases in a given job, the salaries in that area decrease. Even when women break through the glass ceiling, they still often feel like they must outwork their male counterparts by a wide margin in order to simply be on par with them, accepted, treated as equals, or given equivalent raises and promotions, according to David Maume and Paula Houston at the University of Cincinnati. This kind of inequality makes lots of women furious, but few of us really know what to do about it.

Sexual harassment falls into the same category, and researchers estimate that about half of all women in the workforce experience some form of this abuse, according to Louise Fitzgerald of the University of Illinois at Champagne-Urbana. You may not think you've ever been sexually harassed at work because your boss never demanded sexual favors or threatened to fire you if you didn't put out. But if you've heard sexist jokes or seen girlie calendars or been on the receiving end of sexual comments about your appearance, these are all a part of sexual harassment as well. Typically, the reason sexual harassment can occur is that it comes from a person of relatively greater power or status in the organization and is perpetrated against someone of relatively less power or status.

Summer (22) is a bright, energetic student who works bartending and waiting tables at a country club to put herself through college. She lives independently and takes care of her own car, her own apartment, and her own financial business. She takes a lot of pride in being able to support herself, but struggles with her rights to express outrage when she is treated as a sex object by patrons and her employer at the club. Summer contains and internalizes her feelings by convincing herself they're not real.

> *I haven't thought of it as harassment, but just that he wanted to come by and touch me whenever we were at the cash register. I was rude to him one time and said "I'd appreciate it if you wouldn't do that." So later he fired me when I was 15 minutes late to work. I had called him and told him I was getting my car fixed, but he said I didn't call.*

Summer considers her limit-setting anger rude because it comes out in a very direct way. She also resists seeing her boss's behavior as sexual harassment, in part because she feels flattered to have this kind of attention at times.

> *But he does that to all the girls. You know, comes up and says how pretty they are and touches them and says "babe" to them. His wife didn't like it because I told her I wouldn't split tips with her if she just sat on the stool and smoked her cigarettes. So, at that point, he started not to like me anyway.*

When we talk about Summer's feelings about getting fired, she looks away and seems embarrassed. She avoids telling her parents about losing the job because she doesn't want them to worry or think she can't take care of herself on her own. She also seems to feel some shame about being direct with her boss and refusing to let him grope her at the cash register. As women, we often downplay our own injuries and discomfort in an effort to squelch the anger we would have to contend with if we were more honest about our experiences. In fact, we receive all kinds of subtle and not-so-subtle encouragement to dull our senses to what is happening to us at others' hands in the workplace. "He didn't mean anything." "That kind of thing goes on everywhere."

Think for a moment about your own workplace and the ways in which women are treated there. Do you notice discrepancies in wages, promotions, or authority? Do you find that women are treated as objects or equals? Many women say, "It's always been that way, so why bother getting mad about it?" Does this sound familiar? If so, we suspect you've had to learn some ways of numbing your resentment to cope with an unfair or abusive system, a system that hurts you in its sexism.

Overworked and Underpaid: Being Taken for Granted or Used

Being taken for granted involves the feeling that you're not considered as a whole person—that you have a life outside of work, that you have a family or a loved one or friends or other interests. The boss acts as though you can stay late with no prior notice, work all weekend, show up for a surprise meeting without time to get a baby-sitter, or do your job without the resources to do it. Your peers assume you will just fill in where they leave off or fail to acknowledge when you do. You get little thanks or recognition for the extra effort you put forth and you see yourself doing 12 times as much work as those around you, but you feel invisible and unappreciated. Mandy (27) talks about her situation as she juggles her work role as a teacher, her family roles, and her pursuit of a graduate degree.

> *I was asked to be on a committee that I wasn't real excited about in the first place. And I told them, "I have classes in June so I can't do anything in June." The third week in June, they called and said, "This is due at the end of the week." So, I had to rush to do it and I had to give up two of my ten days*

*of vacation to redo something that should've had better guid-
ance in the first place. That really bugged me and wore on me
for the whole time.*

Mandy feels disgusted not only because her time off is being
invaded, but also because she's being asked to take up someone else's
slack. In the end, she gives up part of her vacation to fix the problem.
She sucks it up and contains her feelings—and those feelings wear on
her as she plods through the project.

Other women in this kind of situation bicker endlessly with
coworkers or feel they just can't get along with people around them.
Do you find yourself constantly battling people or walking around feeling uptight, like a powder keg ready to explode? It may surprise you,
but this could actually signal that you're trying to hide too much of
your annoyance on the job. In a study of New York City traffic agents,
Elizabeth Brondolo of St. John's University and her colleagues find
that holding anger inside comes with *more* conflict, not less, and also
comes with job burnout. Jana, whose success story we heard at the
start of this chapter, says before she became conscious of anger, she
used to lash out in frustrating situations and go for the jugular as a
way to divert her true feelings. She also recalls this kept her from
being as effective as she knew she could be. Externalizing on impulse
kept her from reflecting on issues she really needed to think about and
created artificial barriers between her and the people she needed to
work with.

Pulled in All Directions:
The Strain of Work on Other Life Roles (or Vice Versa)

In a related vein, women also talk about feeling anger when work
dominates their lives to the extent that they must sacrifice alone time
with significant others, family, and friends—or when they feel *as if
they should do so*. For many women, the decision to have a child or
family life brings enormous career-related anxiety as they face being
blocked from advancement or discriminated against in obvious or hidden ways. For lots of women, having a family or even a significant rela-

tionship never seems to happen as mounting demands in the workplace crowd out other aspects of life.

Sound familiar? In our clinical practice, corporate and other professional women tell us about their attempts to forge relationships outside work and the difficulties they have in simply finding time to date. They often feel dominated by the travel and other time demands of work, yet tied financially to the rewards of this kind of career situation. Here, Haley (35), a corporate attorney, remarks about her professional life and the conflict she feels between it and her family life.

> *It's that I just seem to be pulled in too many directions at one time and it's just—I'd like to be able to say, "Okay, I'm going home to spend some time with my family, with my daughter and my husband," but then of course I'm either having to cancel something or I'm just not there as late as I ought to be. If I left my office when I got all my work done, well, I'd never leave of course (laughing) but if I left when I should leave, there'd be hell to pay for sure—somebody would have a crisis and it would be my fault or something would not be done.*

Haley convinces herself that her personal needs come last and that if she were to take care of herself, something terrible would happen. As she internalizes anger at her work system for pressuring people into complete devotion to the office, she finds herself caught in the cycle of guilt and overwork. This cycle leaves her feeling inadequate in all areas of her life: she's not working hard enough and she's not giving her family the time they deserve. Haley finds herself in a lose/lose situation.

Based on our interview research, when women say they're stressed out or in a bad mood, they often feel angry but find it more socially acceptable to say, "I'm just fried." This seems especially true when women work too much, when we feel the burden of responsibility for child care and domestic duties, and/or when we feel separated from our primary relationships by a job that demands workers to leave our family roles behind every day. This makes sense if you consider that women invest considerably more time in managing a household than do men. According to Dwenda Gjerdingen and her coresearchers at the University of Minnesota, even when both partners in a heterosexual marriage work outside the home, women outwork men by several hours each week, the average workweek for a woman being around 80 hours, a man's around 68. Also, since women spend more time working at home and family tasks, we devote less time to our careers, and the resulting picture is a more spread-out workload for women, spanning multiple roles and responsibilities. And let's face it: this can make us mad.

When Others Let Us Down: Apathy, Incompetence, Underperformance, or Dishonesty

Feeling taken advantage of happens in a variety of ways and is one area in which our participants report lots of workplace frustration. "Doing one's share" means lots of things to the women we've interviewed. It means using common courtesy, communicating clearly about issues of relevance in a work system, following through with responsibilities (especially in team project situations), and being available when needed. When coworkers or bosses let these things slide, we wind up feeling duped. Here, Claudia (53) remarks about some of her coworkers.

> I was very annoyed with these people. I was bumping on some deadlines and I had to get something ordered, and this person hadn't provided me with the information to do this. And there were two people involved—I e-mailed them both. One of them never even opened the e-mail—and the other one opened it but didn't respond. I was feeling very pressured to get this done—but I couldn't do it, because I couldn't get other people to do their part or give me the courtesy of saying, 'I am so swamped today, I'm not going to get back to you.' And when I found out that one of the people had left and gone shopping for an hour and a half, I was really steamed.

Relationship issues abound. When your officemate leaves you in the lurch, you wind up feeling obligated or unable to finish the job.

Whether your peer is sick at home with the flu or simply avoiding you, anger flares because their behavior, no matter how well intentioned or unavoidable, causes the whole department to experience the hassle of missing a deadline or losing a contract. This irritation comes from your *caring* and the sacrifices you make to do your part of the job. When you see the contrast between your own dependability and another person's inconsistency, it makes you question your motivation to work so hard. When that same person who lets you down gets paid just as much as you do (or more), you may be really irked.

But diverting your true feelings about this can make matters worse. Do you find yourself making lots of sarcastic remarks? "Yeah, right." Edie (46) was written up by her boss at the hospital where she works. Although she felt wrongly reprimanded, all she could think to say at the time was "Insubordinate? What's that?" Her sarcasm seemed to fuel the head nurse's ire, resulting in a big lecture that Edie didn't want to hear—in addition to compounded strain between them. Lots of our interviewees use sarcasm to help them feel momentarily better about work inequities. But while it may be entertaining, sarcasm keeps us from seriously considering the issues at stake and communicating them to our colleagues. We stop short of saying, in essence, "Here is where I stand." If you make cynical jokes rather than saying how you really feel, you divert attention away from your real self and your real ideas, sending a mixed signal about what you want and what you believe.

Sarcasm comes from diverted anger, often through segmentation. Segmentation causes all sorts of problems on the job—and even results in the very behavior that most irritates other workers there. Remember Jane from chapter Two? As a leasing agent, Jane needs continually updated policy information, availability lists, and pricing forms for her clientele. But she's repeatedly left out of the information loop: e-mails don't reach her, calls aren't received, and Jane is never invited to attend management meetings. So she winds up giving incomplete or inaccurate data to the people her company serves. Ask Jane if she's angry about the thoughtless behavior of her immediate supervisor forgetting to include her in vital company exchanges and she'll tell you, "No, I'm not angry. I'm just stressed out." "I don't get mad about this stuff. I enjoy lying to our clients (she laughs)!" And yet

Jane *behaves* as if she's seething on the inside. She calls in sick every other week, takes vacations at critically busy times, and seems oblivious to the impact this has on her coworkers. Notice the vicious cycle of passive-aggression Jane finds herself in. Although she fails to realize it, Jane has become locked in a continuous, invisible struggle with her bosses and coworkers; a struggle that would not have to occur if any of them confronted each other's behaviors directly.

Dumped On:
Feeling Compromised, Demeaned, or Abused

The story you just read about Edie's wisecrack also illustrates another workplace anger trigger. Getting called on the carpet, being asked to violate your ethics, taking the blame for a problem you didn't create, being humiliated in front of your peers—these are all examples of things that make us the angriest at work. We often feel deep loathing for the people who hurt us in these ways because we feel immobilized and unable to turn the tables to reclaim our dignities. According to Julie Fitness's research conducted at Macquarie University in Sydney, Australia, people who have less power in an organization seem to feel more *hate* in response to being humiliated at work than those with more power. This makes sense if you think of hate as a form of intense anger coupled with the sense of helplessness that can result from being one down in your workplace.

How do women divert this kind of helpless rage? Often by using food or alcohol as a buffer against the harshness of work strain or overwork, labels typically given to the kind of powerlessness that comes with these experiences. A lot of what women call stress seems to actually be anger, and much of women's dependence on certain kinds of foods (e.g., chocolate) or binge eating and drinking can be traced to our habits of swallowing anger about work. In fact, one study shows that women who try to avoid facing difficult situations at work are more likely to abuse alcohol, according to research conducted by Kenneth Nowack and Annette Pentkowski, of Organizational Performance Dimensions in Woodland Hills, California. In our interview research, when women talk about feeling stressed out, burned out, or frustrated with work, they often have stories about true anger to tell. When we query them about their stress, they frequently tell us about being used, demeaned, sexualized, overworked, underpaid, or discouraged from having a life outside of work. They tell stories about having to pull more than their fair share of the load, and they sometimes deal with their mounting resentments by comforting themselves with high-calorie food, nicotine, or too much alcohol—all signs that anger's being diverted. Michal (36) thinks her permanent frown lines are a result of bottling up anger, much of it work related. This former administrative assistant, now real-estate agent, used to smoke cigarettes as a way of dealing with anger she didn't know how to handle constructively and thinks her smoking has contributed to premature wrinkles. Work situations that felt hopeless drained her energy reserves and made her less likely to take care of herself because she was so tired of being mad.

Do you up and quit jobs when you become upset? According to research conducted by James Tucker at the University of New Hampshire, people who get mad on the job usually express themselves *indirectly*, rather than confront the targets of their anger. He finds that many people *quit* their jobs (which may be an attempt to get even with their bosses), they tolerate the situation (and probably contain their anger about it), and sometimes they steal or destroy company property (externalization) when they find themselves upset without a better vehicle for resolving the situation. We stand to gain little from stealing at work, quietly skulking away to find another job, or hanging in there while inwardly hating the situation. Sometimes leaving a job is the most liberating move you can make. But question yourself if you realize you change jobs every year. In a focus group conversation, Edie, a nurse, confesses that she tends to leave jobs when things don't go her way ("Well, you can just *have* this job."). Part of the problem, she speculates, is that she absolutely hates taking orders from people. But instead of using her angry energy to improve these systems or get into business for herself, she moves from job to job, hoping to find a place where things feel right, but always winding up disappointed.

How do you deal with anger at work? Try out the exercise below to see how you're doing in this department.

Anger at Work Test

Part I. Read each of the following scenarios and circle the response that is most like you, or most like what you would tend to do in a similar situation.

Scenario 1: The manager of your department wants you to improve your sales performance. She tells you that if you can't raise your averages by the end of the month, you will be demoted and receive a cut in pay. Do you?

    a. Feel embarrassed and think it's because you're not good at sales.

    b. Feel nauseated and sweaty.

    c. Try to keep a positive attitude. Getting angry will only make things worse.

    d. Tell the boss she's rude and insensitive.

    e. Tell the boss you feel worried and angry having this kind of pressure and deadline.

    f. Look for your friend and tell her/him about it.

    g. More than one of the above.

    h. None of the above. I do this instead:

_____

Scenario 2: Your boss discovers you've made a mistake in a recent report. He comes into your office but leaves the door open so all those around can hear him loudly tell you that you messed up and that it better not happen again. Do you?

    a. Bite your tongue or swallow your tears.

    b. Feel guilty and apologize.

    c. Shrug it off. Think about something else.

    d. Throw an ashtray at him.

    e. Pick a time to go to your boss's office and privately tell him that, while you are sorry about the mistake in the report, you felt embarrassed and angry when he announced your mistake as he did.

    f. Call your best friend and talk about it.

    g. More than one of the above.

    h. None of the above. I do this instead:

_____

Scenario 3: Someone in your office takes credit for an idea that was yours. This person is given an award, based on an idea that you developed but for which you were never acknowledged. This is the same person who comes in late every day and for whom you have done several work-related favors. Do you?

a. Keep quiet, all the while feeling sick.
b. Decide that you should have done something differently here. After all, you could have stepped in and told your boss it was originally your idea.
c. Think about how little it would benefit you to harbor a grudge; try to forget about it.
d. Wait until after dark and slash this person's tires.
e. Go right in and tell the person you expect her/him to make this right, or you'll do it yourself.
f. Try to talk about the situation with your sympathetic office-mate.
g. More than one of the above.
h. None of the above. I do this instead:

_____

Scenario 4: Most of the people in your department don't take their work seriously. You know this because they leave early most days, fail to answer calls, and miss their appointments. Meanwhile, you take up the slack. You handle the complaints made by people your coworkers leave stranded. You take the extra phone calls. You go the extra mile. But after a year, it's starting to wear on you. Do you?

a. Keep it to yourself and move on.
b. Think about how you're not handling the situation very well. You should be more assertive.
c. Feel pretty good about being able to always do more than other people.
d. Tell your peers they are lazy and unproductive.
e. Start redirecting customers to your coworkers' voice mail. Let your coworkers know that you won't be handling their appointments anymore.

f. Vent about the situation with the person across the hall, who works as hard as you do.

g. More than one of the above.

h. None of the above. I do this instead:

_____

Scenario 5: You're responsible for putting together a major project at work. To do this by the deadline, you must get information from several people who work with you. Despite repeated phone calls, e-mails, and memos, two of these people never respond to your request. With the deadline looming ahead, there's no other way to procure this needed information except to get it from these two people. Do you?

a. Feel yourself getting a headache?

b. Feel like you must be doing something wrong. Why won't they take your requests seriously?

c. Laugh it off—no point in getting upset. Just do your job as best you can.

d. Make a public announcement that the two individuals are not cooperating.

e. Go to your boss privately and explain the situation. Let her know that you're trying to give these individuals every opportunity to come through. Send a memo to the two coworkers explaining the situation. Ask them to please cooperate with the project and let them know you are unwilling to take responsibility for their lack of cooperation. If this fails, report back to your boss that you are unable to include these individuals' information in your project.

f. Tell your friend about it.

g. More than one of the above.

h. None of the above. I do this instead:

_____

SCORING: Add up your "a" responses, your "b" responses, your "c" responses, and so on. Having two or more responses of the same letter suggests a pattern in the way you handle anger at work. As you probably guessed:

- *"a" responses suggest that you tend to contain anger at work.*
- *"b" responses suggest that you tend to internalize workplace anger.*
- *"c" responses suggest that you segment anger in work situations.*
- *"d" responses suggest that you tend to externalize your workplace anger.*
- *"e" choices suggest a more assertive style of handling anger at work.*
- *"f" choices reflect the tendency to use gossip as a means for handling conflict or anger.*

If you chose two or more "g" responses, make a note of which responses you tend to combine. If you chose two or more "h" responses, write out your probable behaviors in each scenario and see what they share in common. It may be that different people provoke different kinds of responses in you, based on their authority and your relationship with them.

How Can I Stop Diverting and Start Developing?

The truth is that many people never become conscious enough of irritation to benefit from it professionally. Many women assume their anger is useless to them on the job and wind up diverting it into unconscious behavior that cuts them out of any real professional or personal growth. Instead of becoming actively engaged, they back off and become bored, listless, and unenthusiastic. When we see no options for investing creatively (and emotionally) in work, we preserve our energy by building barriers between us and the people we deal with, opting to put emotional reserves into our own survival rather than playing on a team. This leads to forgetfulness, nonresponsiveness, and a dulling of our abilities to build connections at work. We remove ourselves from active relationship life and envelop our minds in a protective fog (recall Jana's board of directors at the start of the chapter). On the flip side, if we bring more of ourselves (including our emotions) into our work in a well-thought-out way, we increase the chances for engaging people and ideas there. We become more fully present to think, collaborate, and enjoy.

If you find yourself giving away personal effectiveness through sarcasm, abuse of your body, unproductive outbursts, or submerged feelings—all signs of diverted anger—you need a different approach to the maddening situations you're bound to face in your job. Highly effective working women tell us that the real gains come from: (1) focusing energy on what makes us mad, and (2) doing something active about the antagonism we feel. How do you start the process? Let's first take a look at phase one.

Phase I: Focusing Energy on Your Work-Related Anger

Now that you have a sense of what makes you mad about your employment situation, you stand to gain clearer, more creative thoughts, deeper insight, and increased motivational energy to address those situations by giving them some serious concentration. Here are the strategies women find useful.

Think Tank Your Feelings

Has anyone ever told you, "It does no good to dwell on being angry"? If so, that person probably never experienced the liberation of letting strong emotions nourish professional growth. Dwelling on anger by giving it productive focus highlights your strengths in the situation, makes you more aware of your realistic limits, and helps you build momentum for doing something to change things.

Dive into the depths of the anger you feel and examine what's there. Allow yourself the privacy and time to experience *all* of the emotion that you find inside—avoid diverting any of it, even if you think it's too extreme for the circumstances. You may find old anger there, resentment at people who aren't directly involved in your work life at all (e.g., your high school science teacher, for telling you that girls should not want to be doctors). Jana says that when she first started in business, people would take advantage of her good nature and willingness to spend time getting to know them as customers.

*I would very blindly go and meet someone for a consulta-
tion lunch and then find out they're selling Amway and want
me to join their down line. There's anger there. And I have a
right to feel angry—it's like, "Well, I'm hungry, I need to eat."
So now my anger makes me know when I need to have a
boundary in business consulting. It's a call to action. A place
where I need to take charge. It was a decision to learn to use
anger as a positive tool.*

But when she first started think tanking anger about these situations, she found more there than she expected, including unresolved
anger at her dad.

*He was very critical, looking for any flaw. And I wanted
approval. I learned to smile when I was angry and say yes
when I really meant no. But now I recognize choices. You're a
victim when you don't have choices.*

You do have choices. Get clear: decide with whom you feel angry,
what they've done to trigger your emotion, and what you want to have
happen instead. Decide whether the risks you face warrant going
directly to the source (i.e., your supervisor; your employee) or if you
need to go to your best friend instead. Make a list of all the things you
would say if you were able to go directly to the person who's triggered
your anger. Use a physical outlet if the emotion is fierce. Do kickbox-
ing exercises and use the active time to imagine outcomes to your situation that make you feel empowered and strong. Videotape yourself
saying exactly what you want to say to the person you're most mad at.
Watch the tape until you feel comfortable with what you see. Imagine
yourself as capable and energized—ready to protect your interests.

Industrious use of anger counters helplessness. Anger defines you
as a separate, thinking, feeling being, with an agenda. But in the
depths of your anger think tank you may find that you've *learned* to
perceive yourself as helpless, confused, or lacking a purpose.

As you change anger assumptions you learned in your family-of-origin, you have the opportunity to transform your work patterns too. Challenge the ideas you received about what is proper (e.g., don't question authority, expect people to let you down). Step outside the lines on the sidewalk and imagine doing something fundamentally different from anything your mother or grandmother would do. Here's an exercise to get you started.

- Imagine the worst possible scenario: what would happen? Women in our research tend to say the *worst* thing would be to lose control and say things they later regret. What are some of those things for you (e.g., telling your boss you hate her; throwing a tantrum complete with screaming and flailing limbs)?
- What would happen if you made a scene? What kind of scene would you like to make? Women's fantasy anger scenes often take place right on the spot. They see themselves losing it in one giant string of obscenities. They also mention things like (1) not worrying about who thinks they are being a bitch, (2) saying things they have been thinking for years (e.g., "You cannot treat me this way any longer. I refuse to accept this."), and (3) letting go of the pressure to be attractive (in other words, letting their faces show their indignation without worrying that they appear ugly or mean).
- Allow yourself to see it all happening before your eyes. What would you wear? What would you say? How would that feel? See yourself as you want to see yourself, with as much bravado as you'd like to have. Picture yourself saying absolutely everything you'd like to say—no holds barred.
- Play out the potential consequences in your inner theater. Keep breathing deeply while you watch the show. What happens next? Are you left without a job? Are you without friends and a future? What's left for you after you've made yourself perfectly clear?
- Now, imagine all the possibilities *in between* sucking it up and making a scene. What are the options?

Listen as Lydia (65) describes her well-learned generational lessons about women making a scene. Although she eventually let them go, these unfortunate lessons taught her to think of her emotions in extreme terms—either you turn them into muffled, ladylike hurt or you go into complete hysterics. While she was once trained to transform anger into hurt, she instinctively knows her feelings should be valid. There *should* be a place between the extremes. "I should be able to voice this because it's a part of me."

> *We weren't allowed to get angry. It wasn't ladylike to show anger. So therefore we couldn't stomp, we couldn't scream . . . And so I went into the hurt and then I could express myself because it was coming from hurt and not anger. Very confusing. People probably misread me.*
>
> *I think there's appropriate anger. But it's how we do it, how we respond, how we speak that will improve the situation, rather than make it worse. And if something triggers us, we need to find out why.*

Lydia's conclusions are important. Just because she lets go of the gender rules about voicing opposition, she doesn't automatically become a raging monster, unable to get along with people. She finds her own balance.

Jana, who is now president of a respected non-profit organization and owner/manager of a personal coaching firm, says that in her business experience once women begin to find their voices (express opinions they once kept to themselves) an anger emerges. Sometimes this anger feels out of control at first, but we need this energy to get us mobilized for action. Eventually through constructive anger talk, this sense of raging anger becomes more manageable and less frightening, but not until we make friends with it. Jana describes that hearing herself say things aloud—speak about controversial issues at home and at work—helped her gain the angry momentum to make enormous changes in her work life. Gradually she became more and more comfortable with these feelings and what they meant to her. She transformed her life from quiet victim to outspoken and successful businessperson.

Through think tanking, you may actually discover the hard reality that you have few choices about what goes on at work, few opportunities to contribute and be heard. Your supervisor and peers may fear and avoid people's real feelings, silently encouraging each other to divert anger so that it goes home to others or inside their bodies, or to treat work as short-term employment, a place to meet immediate needs but not to invest energy for the future. You see people being punished for showing honesty, rejected for having feelings that differ. You may also be living from paycheck to paycheck, relying miserably on a system that makes you uncomfortable and lonely. For you, think tanking may force a realization that you need intensive self-care (in order to survive) and new ways to protect your passion and ideas while you tolerate a bad situation or the energy to find a new job. Or, you may find through think tanking that you have some room to grow at work. Your job may not be perfect, but you want to try using more of yourself to make things happen there. For you, this thoughtful time is about making deliberate plans for speaking your mind. Here are some important issues to consider.

Consider the Power

Where we sit on the workplace totem pole makes a difference in how we need to approach anger. When we're one up, we have relatively more power and we're much more able to use strategies to confront directly; there is often follow-through on our suggestions and we are usually treated with respect. When we're with peers, people who have the same level of power, we need to negotiate, explain, and share constructive anger talk—but we can feel more at ease to speak honestly. But when we're one down, we really do have to be more careful. Here, positive triangulation, think tanking, alliance-building to gain power in numbers, and using diplomatic language are most critical.

What do you do if you find yourself in the one down position? When you feel dumped on, what do you risk in sharing your feelings with the person(s) responsible for triggering them? What do you chance in holding them back? Here's a sample list of anger scenarios.

1. I will say something that gets me fired.
2. I will lose all control.

3. I will say something that causes my boss/coworker to feel uncomfortable or defensive.

4. The discomfort s/he feels will result in my being treated badly at work (maybe given even more assignments or unreasonable expectations).

5. I will *not* say something and then feel like an incinerator inside.

6. I will *not* say something and then lose my creative edge because I'm working so hard trying to hide my anger (perhaps even from myself).

7. I will successfully hide my anger, but then get sick or depressed or anxious because I'm storing the stress of so much unresolved conflict.

8. I will successfully hide my anger, but lose interest in this job.

9. I will realize my anger, speak it to safe others in my social circle, and realize I cannot tolerate this job any longer.

10. I will realize my anger, speak it to safe others, alter my behavior with the person who's triggered my feelings, and elicit a negative reaction in this person (e.g., s/he will resent that I no longer volunteer to do everything myself).

Look closely at the risks you face in being direct. Look at those you face in choosing *not* to be direct. Think seriously about the change you need and how you might get it. What if the risks in talking about it are too high? Becoming fully conscious you're peeved about the workload, feeling taken for granted, and in need of something different gives you an important edge. Even if you choose not to tell the target person how you feel, you *should* tell *someone*. Our interview research suggests that women often devise creative solutions when they begin to voice their opposition to being used or overworked. Just hearing ourselves speak emphatically about our desire for change heightens our awareness of the possibilities we never knew existed.

Consider the Outcome

Think carefully about what you want to happen as a result of sharing your side of things. The outcome you seek helps determine your approach.

Since, as adults, we have to face the consequences of our actions, we have to realize the negative possibilities that exist when we voice anger at issues like the boys' club or being dumped on (e.g., loss of a job, further discrimination on the job). On the flip side, when we hold it back, we forfeit chances to create change for ourselves and for the women around us. Here's Deidre's (30) story about challenging the status quo. A few years ago, she worked with a man (Jerry) who, although friendly and kind, constantly remarked about her appearance, saying her husband was a lucky guy, and so forth. While at first, she felt flattered and said, "Thank you," she began to get the sense that Jerry was not just being kind. So, while she gave it some days of thought, one afternoon she had had enough of the awful feeling—and decided she needed to use her anger *in the moment* to set Jerry straight.

> *I had talked with my boss, who thankfully was a woman. She seemed to understand and, even though she wanted to protect our working relationship with Jerry, she knew I couldn't continue to be hit on and not put a stop to it. So that week when I had to see him and he started in with his remarks, I came back at him with, "You know, Jerry, when you say that, I get really uncomfortable; I wish you wouldn't do that anymore." He immediately got defensive and tried to say I was making a big deal out of nothing, but I just knew I needed to react quickly that particular day. It pissed me off because I felt him encroaching on my space and I needed to back him off, right now.*

Jerry never harassed her again. From that moment on, he was all business. Was their relationship strained? Deidre says yes, but that things ultimately worked out. They continued to work for the same company, but Jerry kept his distance and Deidre protected herself. Bottom line:

sometimes you have to act, *now*; sometimes it helps to hold back while you investigate the situation; sometimes you need to do both. Never hide from yourself, but be prepared to deal with the consequences of your honesty. Deidre feels satisfied with herself for speaking up.

But now consider a different example. Are you in a management role at work? Leaders and bosses contend with unique situations. Their anger is incredibly vital to the insight of an organization, but also must be expressed in ways that protect their authority and leadership while respecting the needs and contributions of their employees. Research findings are mixed when it comes to the social consequences of expressing anger at work. According to some studies, supervisors sometimes *lose* effectiveness among their supervisees when they openly express their feelings. This unfortunate phenomenon has an even more regrettable gender twist. Kristi Lewis of the California School of Professional Psychology reports that in her study of emotional expressions at work, male leaders receive lower effectiveness ratings when they express sadness while female leaders receive lower ratings when they express either sadness or anger. This type of gender bias means that we as women sometimes have to find ways to knowingly give our sharp feelings a mental space they can occupy until we find ourselves in a place of emotional safety.

But in a study conducted by Larissa Tiedens at Stanford University people view leaders who express anger as being higher in status than those who express sadness. What does this mean? Tiedens concludes that people see leaders as more competent when they're angry versus sad. Leaders' anger, when expressed responsibly, lets people know where the boundaries are. Our disagreeable emotions (versus our more wounded ones) promote understanding of what's going on between the people that make it happen at work; therefore we need the anger to help us comprehend our surroundings. But we also have to walk the tightrope between uncensored open expression and the adverse impact of diverting our feelings. Here are some tips.

1. **Do the two-step. Keep in mind that your professional emotion-consciousness happens in at least two stages. First, becoming very aware of how you feel *before* you do anything about it gives you the upper hand you need. Only by sitting**

in stage one for a short time can you *deliberately* choose a means of anger expression that protects the larger interest of your organization. You're the boss, so your expressions of disappointment and frustration have a huge emotional impact in the group. You may in fact decide that your best move (stage two) is to talk to your mentor, therapist, partner, or best friend *instead* of discussing anger with the employee or supervisee who's triggered it. This person's emotional maturity and personality style play a role in determining what happens when you speak candidly about being peeved. Think tank your feelings and consider the outcome that will best take care of the organization—and you.

2. Speak—don't spew. Leaders bear the responsibility of making themselves very clear without hurting or demeaning those working under their charge. Avoid name-calling, derogatory remarks, and reactionary displays of retribution. Remember, you're the person who sets the emotional tone for the rest of the group. Use constructive anger talk strategies, just like you would with your friends or family.

3. Lend an ear. Although you may have the last word when it comes to your organization, your supervisees need a voice as well. Listen closely to their grievances but keep your internal boundaries intact. That means empathizing with their discomfort, letting them know you hear them, but realizing it's probably not about you. The fact that you're in charge makes you the target for employee resistance and resentment. So, expect people to push *against* you once in a while. This actually helps the organization grow.

4. Treat yourself well. Take care of yourself by having someone outside the group to whom you can vent confidentially. After a stressful, angry encounter with someone at work, debrief with a person who has more authority than you— and mentally leave supervisees' anger at work. Imagine yourself dropping the negative exchange in a particular bin on your desk or bookshelf as you leave the office. Go get a massage or soak in a hot tub. Reward yourself for listening.

Use Gossip as Resistance: Share Your Voice with a Friend

Women in our research, at all levels of employment, tell us they need to tell *someone* when they are angry at work. Telling someone helps us focus critical emotional and intellectual energy on the issue making us mad. We want an ally to share our feelings and help us feel normal again. This seems to be even more the case at work than at home, partly because when we're at work, we're in more unsafe relationship territory.

> *Melanie: So I hung up the phone and I'm like, "Ahhh! I can't believe this!" And then I walked up here and said, "Nina, oh my God, that man drives me crazy!" I run to her, because she's heard me talk about it before.*

> *Mandy: At work, I walk away if somebody upsets me and I go find my one person that I complain about everything to and I complain about it and I feel better and it's over with.*

> *Kate: So if a coworker is consistently rude, I just shake my head and maybe let somebody else in on it by making eye contact or something.*

Kate finds a momentary partner through eye contact. She looks up and finds someone who *gets it* in that moment and suddenly she's not alone. Kate uses positive triangulation (as discussed in chapter Three) to gain an ally in her feelings. The main thing to remember here is that positive triangulation—which usually takes the form of helpful gossip—helps us get a handle on our emotion, learn about it, and practice voicing it, when it's not allowable or advisable to express it directly to the person irritating us.

Were Kate to contain her anger alone, she would be more at risk for internalizing it, promoting feelings of aloneness, inferiority, and shame. In workplace anger, it's very important for us to share our feelings with a sympathetic other in order to defend ourselves and safeguard our morale. In fact, lots of employees who have grievances against their employers choose gossip as their first step in solving the problem, according to a study of workers conducted by James Tucker at the University of New Hampshire. Individuals talk to each other, pass judgment, determine who's at fault, and assign blame.

How does this help the situation? It depends on the powers that be. When your supervisors and authorities value individual feelings, invite your feedback, and provide venues for emotional expression, anger works more to your benefit as you use it *directly* with the person who's triggered it. On the other hand, when authorities at work punish those of us with different feelings from their own and when the job is relied upon for economic sustenance, the rewards of anger must be acquired in alternate ways.

Again, take care to avoid *unhelpful* gossip. That kind of triangulation is less productive for you and risks hurting others needlessly. Maggie sums up her attitude about this kind of chitchat.

If I'm having lunch with fellow teachers and they start discussing other fellow teachers that aren't around . . . it definitely doesn't promote a positive workplace and I wouldn't want someone saying things about me that I didn't know. So that makes me angry. When people say things behind people's back—really if they have a problem they should go to that person and right it.

People seem to lose respect for coworkers whose gossip is unhelpful and habitual. Make sure you're choosing carefully the person to whom you vent and make sure you talk privately, with the explicit purposes of working on your own feelings, of getting a reality check, or of seeking advice for you, not ruining the reputation of the person who's triggered your feelings.

Get the Upper Hand

Over and over, women tell us they want to stay in control at work. As researchers and therapists, we've wondered about what this means and how useful it is for women to focus on control. What does control really mean? Do we as women need to worry about staying in control? Staying in control means lots of things for the women we've interviewed.

> *Claudia: I really feel like I maintain control very well most of the time. I am unfortunately susceptible to the time of the month—and when I overload with emotion, whether it's hurt or it's anger or whatever, I get emotional, and that makes me mad (laughing).*
>
> *Interviewer: What do you mean when you say you get emotional?*
>
> *Claudia: Well if I have a tense feeling I'm trying to express to you, I may not be able to do it without breaking up—and you know, and, and . . .*
>
> *Mandy: Crying?*
>
> *Claudia: . . . crying or showing the emotion in my voice.*
>
> *Charlene: Instead of being calm and . . .*
>
> *Claudia: . . . right and that makes me mad because I think particularly men discount what you're saying then—"Huh, just one of those women"—so frequently I will say, "It upsets me that I can't express this without the depth of my emotion showing, but the thoughts are real and the fact that I'm cracking up as I'm trying to tell you this only expresses how strongly I feel" because my husband, ex-husband, would say, "you must be PMSing." I'm a CPA and came through accounting when that was not common for women, and so I feel like I've always kind of had that pressure of "an emotional woman."*

What is *control* anyway? In Sandra Thomas's research, women feel out of control and powerless when they lose it and let their anger out explosively *or* when they tuck it inside and try to hide it there. Either extreme proves frustrating and ineffective. Nobody wants to be thought of as a foolish or mentally unstable person. But diversion in any direction costs us opportunities to develop ourselves. In our participants' stories, there seem to be at least two sides to the control issue. The unhelpful side of control happens when we overemphasize control and shame ourselves into rigid ways of interacting with people. But the helpful side of control means:

1. believing in the credibility of our emotions (even if they make our eyes water)
2. consciously using our ability to *wait* and use discretion
3. opting for *deliberate* anger strategies
4. revealing those things we *choose* to reveal to *whom* we choose to reveal them—when we think it's a good time
5. protecting ourselves from retaliation when we're at risk

This helpful side of control can be labeled the upper hand. The upper hand does not require us to buy into mistaken notions like "If I cry at work, I will cease to be authoritative." The upper hand does not require us to try to control other people. The upper hand is an internal phenomenon. It's a place of emotional strength that comes from a basic trust in what you feel, even if it causes you to tremble and perspire.

Claudia sits on the verge of self-discovery. She has all the information she needs to start claiming her upper hand, if only she can let herself turn loose some myths. She wishes for an opportunity to place appropriate blame where it belongs and begin letting herself off the hook for showing her true colors at work. Claudia wants very much to give credit to those feelings, but has been taught to discredit herself any time her emotions occupy the foreground, instead of staying neatly tucked away behind her more logical experiences. Claudia also wants to go ahead and believe in her anger, even though it happens to be burgeoning at *that time of the month*. She would very much like to let go of the idea that tears and hormones disable her and make her words meaningless. Claudia is ready for change.

Do Claudia's angry tears sound familiar to you? Anger is most likely to make us cry when we feel alone, unsponsored, or unsupported in our moments of indignation. Also, we often assume that our anger and sadness are going to get in the way of our work agenda instead of helping us figure things out and giving us emotional assistance to look critically and uniquely at a problem or creative project. What can Claudia do to get the upper hand? First, sharing regularly with a trusted friend or mentor can help with this acute aloneness in angry situations and make her feel stronger when she's mad at work—so over time, she may have fewer tears when she gets really mad. Hashing these issues out with someone trusted helps us stand taller, breathe a little more deeply, and perceive the value in getting mad, which in turn promotes our using emotion to solve problems on the spot. *"Because I feel so strongly about this, I hope you'll hear how much I value this project."*

Yet another reason for frustrated tears is that we sometimes feel embarrassed by our emotions, especially our anger. To help with this problem, remind yourself that you're in charge of deciding what a legitimate feeling is. Again, having a friend or mentor in your field of work can be critical in helping you receive validation for your griev-ances as well as your ideas about what needs to change. As your collaborator empathizes with the pain of your fury, you begin to empathize with yourself.

Deliberate work anger strategies also help us get the upper hand because they can be planned in advance and practiced when we're alone. These include:

1. **Being able to walk away and regroup.** "I'm really irritated by what just happened in here, and I want you to know that. I'm going to think about what I want to do about it for a while, but right now, I just need for you to know how I feel."
2. **Keeping a treasured token** (e.g., a small stone, a picture of a loved one) at work to comfort ourselves when we're feeling alone or embarrassed about our strong feelings. Holding or looking at an object like this can help us reconnect with other, more affirming parts of our lives at moments when we feel the whole world is against us.
3. **Practicing body awareness and breathing exercises.** Even when we feel the most livid, in the midst of a board meet-ing, during a confrontation with a boss or client, while being lectured or criticized, we can always center our con-

sciousness on breathing, taking care to inhale (through the nose) and exhale slowly. This helps to relax us and focus our attention on what is happening inside us—and focusing inside helps restore the equanimity we need in order to befriend ourselves in these moments and continue feeling strong.

4. Giving up sarcasm. Begin to imagine what would happen if you started taking yourself seriously and giving other people the chance to do the same. "No, I really don't agree with that." Even if you give up the wisecracks for just a week or a day and replace them with a moment of silent meditation, you might discover the meaningfulness of your own thoughts.

5. Perhaps most important, allow insights to emerge from the fierceness of your pain. The chaos inside you signals the need for critical thought. At work, sharp feelings generally mean at least one of the following things.

- You value the products of your labor and feel they're being threatened or undermined.
- Your personal dignity is being compromised or disrespected.
- You value your working relationships and sense they're in jeopardy.
- You perceive that your place in a system is being invaded or threatened.
- Rewards for your effort do not seem to match your investment of time or energy.
- You perceive your creativity and contribution are not received, considered, appreciated, or rewarded.

Which of these best fits your situation? Knowing exactly what's being invaded or unacknowledged helps you decide what to do next.

The Synergy of Good Mentoring

Melanie comments on the value of mentoring in her developing professional life.

It's always been important to me to have a strong supervisor. Someone I can release things to and s/he can say, "This is what I'm thinking." And when I took this job, the person who was my direct supervisor was awesome. She had been in different advising positions. She had so much experience that I thought this was going to be a great experience for me. And it had been, but she left in March. So I don't have that sounding board or somebody to give me that perspective on how they would handle it.

I could have walked in her office after the meeting and said, "Guess what they did." And she would have been just as mad as I was and that would have made it easier for me to get over it. But also give that constructive criticism and challenge me. Because my initial reaction is to say, "Look, you really pissed me off." But that's not always the best way.

Through her mentoring relationships, Melanie learns to maintain her awareness of others and attention to her own feelings at the same time. In talking with a supervisor who understands the emotional issues in her work setting, Melanie receives validation and encouragement to act on her passion while keeping the upper hand.

What exactly is a mentor? A mentor can be anybody who is a good listener and has some understanding about your line of work. Ideally a mentor is someone in your field who can offer advice in addition to personal support. But a mentor can simply be a good friend who knows you well and is willing to be very honest with you. How do you find such a person? Ask yourself: (1) Who do I admire and trust? (2) Can I approach this person for advice? (3) Would I feel comfortable telling them about my strong feelings? Developing a true, professional mentoring relationship is complicated, but it often happens spontaneously, over time, between people who are drawn to work together because of common interests and approaches to the world.

Must you have a formal mentoring relationship to get this kind of synergy? Not always. Sometimes strong working friendships offer the same thing. In fact, we often suggest to our clients that they have an anger buddy or two; people they can call during difficult anger moments at work. Do you know other women working in your field who could team up with you to support each other's emotional work life? You could meet regularly for lunch to talk about what angers you and what you want to do about it. You may find that these relationships energize and inspire you. This happens because honest relationships tend to validate our feeling experiences as well as our more logical thought processes. To be highly effective and creative, you need both. A formal or informal mentoring team brings out your most creative inspirations because they invite you to use all parts of yourself in the process of solving a problem. Rather than shutting you down by denying the passionate, angry, sad, or elated parts of you, a mentoring group *really hears* you because they take both your opinions and your feelings (even the ones you think are totally unreasonable) seriously. But take note; this kind of emotional support often catapults women into dramatic life changes.

PHASE II: DOING SOMETHING ACTIVE

Leaning into Anger at Work

What does it mean to lean into your anger? It means being proactive with anger at work; being knowingly visible and audible. It means basing your actions upon insights you glean from focusing carefully on your emotion and sharing it with certain others. It means using constructive anger talk and listening skills. In the next example, Melanie uses anger to help clarify her position and make it known. She tests the waters with some of the students, to see how they respond to her directness. Melanie uses her anger well because she keeps sight of both being angry *and being in relation to others*. This lets her go with the flow of her anger or *lean into it*, instead of shrink away from it, because she knows the relationships will remain standing after the anger is done. Melanie feels little shame in being angry. She becomes very familiar with her dissent in the moment and lets people know about it, in ways that signal, "Step onto the playing field with me. I'm not afraid."

I did share with them that it is important to me and I

think they almost respect me more than if I had come in there and not mentioned their grades. They respect me because I did show them that I was really angry with them—but at the same time I can respect them. Most of the time people know that if I'm really mad about something then I'm going to explain to you what it is and hopefully hear your side of it, and then let's move on.

Students and peers at work never have to play guessing games with Melanie because she has no need to hide out or manipulate them. She sends the message that just because she's peeved, there is no reason to run away. Melanie has little need to get over it either. She takes all the time she needs with her emotions and avoids rushing herself into some kind of emotional foreclosure. Instead of feeling embarrassed or guilty about being perturbed, Melanie dives down into the whole point of her frustration and uses constructive anger talk to deal with the thing that ticks her off. She also takes time to hear the other side of things, a skill that helps bolster her credibility with students and peers.

Use Your Passion to Promote Excellence

In this case, one of Melanie's student groups wants to elect an officer whose grades aren't up to par. Notice how she cares fervently about the issue at hand and uses that zeal in promoting academic achievement.

I do have high expectations. If people aren't meeting them, I'm so angry. It's sometimes hard for me to see their perspective. Like the grades in the [AHCP] group. They know what they're supposed to do, and they choose not to do it, and it drives me crazy.

I don't know if I would show it to them, but I'm still mad. And part of that comes from not having a chance to talk to any of them yet about being frustrated. It's really hard for me not to share it.

Do I want to say, "I respect that you guys made this

decision, but I don't really agree with it?" Or do I want to say, "I just think this is ridiculous." Or maybe I don't want to say anything at all. Do I want to say something to the president? I could probably go in and say "No" just based on the university policy. But that's not really my way because I want them to make decisions and learn from them. But I don't want them to think that I support this.

Melanie wrestles with herself about how she will show this group her anger, but she has no intention of rushing herself through it or pretending she's not angry. At the same time, she adopts a balanced view of the situation. She knows the limits of her power to influence this group. She also knows that she is there to provide guidance and that *her gut feelings matter* to the situation. Her opinion is about bettering things and the group benefits from having to hear her opinion, whether they agree with it or not.

If I haven't had a chance to release it and I go into that meeting about the grades, I still may be mad. I may have the non-verbals that say, "I really don't care right now because I'm still mad at you." And I don't want to be that way. Most of the time I'm not, because I do share it. That's where I'm struggling—do I share it and keep harping on it even though they already know, or do I not share it, but in my actions say I'm still angry?

I go through in my head what it is that made me angry. Over time I start to see the other side of the situation. Then I go back to my point, even though I can see the other side.

There have been plenty of times when I've gone to a student and said, "Look, I totally freaked out about that situation, but the more I've thought about it I understand where you guys are coming from." So I'll admit to them when I realize I've overlooked their side. But I'm still not at that point. There's still that dissonance in me that says, "I don't understand their viewpoint."

Notice how much Melanie cares about this issue. Do people benefit from one worker's angry passion, even if she represents a minority viewpoint? You bet. Melanie has enormous positive influence, even if her students don't adopt her philosophy about academic standards. She demonstrates that even though one person cannot control an entire group, one person can voice a powerful opinion and stand out in the crowd.

Melanie *listens*: she demonstrates a willingness to take another's point of view, try it on for size, evaluate the worth of it, and maybe even learn something new. Melanie has little need for defensiveness because she's not ashamed of her anger in the first place. She has a reaction. She deals with it openly because it's valid. Her reaction is about wanting the best for her student groups and her university. The confidence that she has a legitimate concern allows her to listen carefully to views that are different.

What work issues do you care very deeply about? What aspects of your job give you feelings of pride? These are areas in which your angry passion can lead you, and others, to excel.

Use Your Passion to Find Your Path

Mandy, a 27-year-old teacher feels intense anger at her husband's ex-wife because she feels this woman is vindictively draining the couple's financial resources. So, she makes a plan. Listen to Mandy describe her situation and how it's motivated her to take charge of her financial and career future.

> She (my husband's ex-wife) makes more than the two of us combined, but keeps calling, telling us that she needs more money. Part of the reason that I'm getting my master's right now—and I'm planning on getting my doctorate—is so that I have something that she can't touch. She can take his salary as much as she wants to, but she can't do that to me. And so that's why it's really important to me to have this. I obviously don't make much as a teacher, but as a principal, I can make quite a bit more. That's something that I can do to keep control of my situation.

Other women describe similar situations. Vivian (46) says being passionately angry about the state of one marketplace propelled her into another.

I had worked for four years on this degree in rehab psychology and then found out I couldn't get a job in the field! Boy was I pissed. I had to figure out another plan, so here I am. I'm training to be a massage therapist and I feel really good about it. I think this is a way for me to make a real difference in people's lives. Anger at the situation helped me figure out what to do next.

Dani (24), a social worker who we met in chapter Five, struggles with a job she likes, but which overworks and underpays her. She loves to play guitar, and through talking to friends and family about her situation, she's become motivated to turn her hobby into a full-time job, perhaps by setting up a studio and teaching guitar. Pay attention to how Dani's anger gives her a metaphor that points to a different sort of life.

I just don't think anybody should have to work like this. It's not natural. I think we should have other things in our lives. But our jobs dominate our lives, and that's not good for us. The anger—it's like I'm in a barrel and I can't dig my way out and I work my ass off and don't get paid half of what I'm worth. I have been so mad about working late every day and spending weekends doing my paperwork that I have started to think about getting out of the barrel. I want to be my own boss, schedule my own appointments, make my own hours. I'd really like to get to a point where I work about five hours a day and then take the rest of the day to do other things.

Some women say passionate anger at the people who teased or overlooked them in high school gives them intense energy to achieve their career goals. Some say passionate anger at a former partner, lover, or boss propels them forward into creative ventures (like helping other women protect their personal financial interests by forming a local women's business league). For other women we know, anger at social injustice calls them to work as attorneys, teachers, writers, social workers, and ministers to change poverty, inequity, violence, intolerance, or environmental abuse.

Thanks for the Anger

If you find yourself in any of these passionate situations, you may find *thankfulness* a refreshing way to help you clarify your thoughts and ideas. Yes, it's true: crediting the target of your wrath, even if this person was truly mean or abusive to you, seems to foster women's use of emotion in decision-making and career change. Clear, unfettered emotion helps us achieve by focusing our energy where we need it most. Here's how it works.

1. Buy or make a thank-you card. Address it to the person who has triggered a lot of fury in your life, particularly if that feeling has anything to do with your work.
2. In the card, begin a list of all the things you've gained from being totally furious with this person. It might sound something like this:

   "Dear Jim. I'm writing to thank you for being unfair to me when I was your employee. Thank you for cheating me out of my raise and for always making me work the late shift. Your behavior has taught me to respect myself enough that I'll never, ever work in a store like yours again. Through my experiences with you, I have learned that when I am an employer, I need to watch out for the welfare of those working for me. I also have learned that I am smarter than you—and that I can run my own business if I decide to do that. Being furious with you has taught me the value of surrounding myself with people I trust, who want me to succeed and care about me sticking around. Sincerely, Ann."
3. Continue brainstorming all the benefits you reap from being unambiguously angry at this person: I got out of a dead end job. I started to recognize sexism everywhere else too. I

decided I want to work for myself. I enrolled in classes to start learning about horticulture (so I can run my own business).

4. Now, this is a card you may never want to send. This is a card to keep tucked inside your favorite book or sitting on your desk . . . someplace where it can remind you of how far you've come and how useful it was to get mad and get clear.

Sometimes angry passion leads women to correct their existing work situations, sink deeper roots there, and excel by being stable, long-term contributors to their organizations, communities, or networks. Here, J. C. (36) talks about working through tough issues and seeing some light on the other side.

I've been surprised by how well he [my boss] has responded to my telling him when I'm angry. I always sort of take my time and plan exactly what I want to say, but I think he and I are on more equal footing now. He still does things that annoy the crap out of me, but I sense that he takes my views into account. It makes me feel some hope that this is going to work out after all. I'm glad because I have the feeling I can be most productive in a place like this.

You too may decide you want to stay with your current job, go to the source, and work your conflict out directly. But whatever move you decide to make, passionate, conscious anger almost always invites you to take some risks. When you're ready to act, remember the pieces of these women's stories that ring true for you. Use constructive anger talk that refers to your feelings and to the concrete behaviors that trigger them ("I'm angry that you _____."). Breathe deeply and talk about what changes you want ("I'd really like to see _____."). Listen to the person who's triggered your anger. Try to take their perspective, but hang on to your reality ("I see what you mean, even though I still feel angry about it."). Remind yourself that you have your emotional responses for good reasons. Use healthy gossip and mentoring to get a reality check. Keep a clear image of yourself as strong, capable, and possessing integrity. Imagine your mentor and your best friend standing beside you. Ask yourself: what am I willing to risk to fight for something new and better in my life?

————

In conclusion, women's voices teach us important things about anger at work. First and foremost, conscious anger is your friend. Instead of fighting against it or diverting it into unproductive behavior, grabbing the insights in your anger lets you learn about yourself as a working person. It gives you borders and passion for doing things splendidly. Anger at work doesn't have to result in burned bridges, unless the bridges need to be burned. And when it's time to terminate a working relationship, anger helps us see the way. As Jana so aptly describes:

It's not about judgment. It's not that we're trying to say anybody is a bad person. Let's take judgment out of it and get to the real issue. I'm angry and this is why. I'm ready to step up to the plate and take responsibility for myself and for my work. Are you?

SEVEN

Success Stories
Anger in the Transformation of Women's Lives

R eal women use anger to their advantage every day. Ordinary
women and extraordinary women make their dreams come
true by accessing the power and clarity of their hottest feelings
of opposition and their long-standing resentments. How do they do it?
When we look across the stories told by all the women in our interview research, we find an essential common thread. Women who are
very successful at channeling their anger into passion and creativity
and helping others do the same with theirs, these women develop *their
own philosophy about their emotional life.*

Rather than assuming the rules and conventions of their mothers
or their therapists, these leaders come to their *own* understandings of
their anger. They explain themselves in their own words. Sometimes
they see their indignation and annoyance as a signal they've been hurt
and have experienced a loss. Sometimes they view their attempts to
repair that hurt as moving toward the other person, an attempt to get
inside that other person's psyche, to understand what has happened so
that they can make some meaning out of a bad experience. Some
women say they make friends with their anger and come to know it
like the back of their hand. Regardless of the words they use to portray
their anger life, these exemplary women show us that it's up to each of
us to consciously, deliberately write our own emotion rules and meanings and to live by them.

You've Come a Long Way

If you're saying to yourself "I'm not a leader" or "I'm not exemplary"—think again. If you've come as far as this chapter, you're already mentally reworking your old ideas about anger. If you're reading these words today, you've knocked out a huge hole in the brick wall that society builds to keep women from examining their anger up close and personal. Maybe you've already started taking action on your new emotional understandings. When it comes to women's anger, if you're doing *any* of these things, consider yourself on the cutting edge.

Who's Savvy Now?

Take a few minutes to size up the things you've learned and appreciate how far you've come. You're informed about whether your anger is a catch in your throat, a knot in your stomach, an impending headache, or heat in your face. You know how to tell when your anger is mixed with fear or sadness or guilt, and which is which. You know when you're just a bit irritated and when you're absolutely fuming.

Once you were a little girl and you learned to control your hostile actions. You learned not to hit or throw rocks at people who ticked you off. You learned to avoid name-calling and derogatory remarks. You learned what was legal and illegal, ethical and unethical, right and wrong. These remain important, but now that you're a grown woman, you are ready to mature past these early lessons with the realization that anger and aggression aren't the same thing. You are ready to embrace and use your anger for your own good and the good of other people too. Dana Jack, a psychologist and professor at Western Washington University, once said, "A woman's development begins with an act of disobedience." For women, *growth and disobedience often go hand in hand*. Sometimes, disobedience means allowing your angry voice to be heard.

Do you notice yourself feeling less and less unsettled about being pissed off? If so, you may be well on your way to wholeheartedly embracing your anger. You move past your dread of anger, past the idea that you might become engulfed by your anger, past feeling vulnerable because of your anger or humiliated by your anger. You realize that even if your anger was prohibited or penalized earlier in your life, you can be okay with it now. You have little need for anger myths in your life. *This is anger consciousness at its best*; you understand where your ideas and reactions about anger developed, you can identify your own anger patterns, you aren't trying to divert your anger in any way. You welcome your anger as the adaptive and natural response that it is and feel good about it!

In addition, you have a real working toolkit of skills at your disposal when you choose to express your anger. You know you have choices about when, where, how, and how much. Does this mean you get madder than the rest of us or stay madder longer than the rest of us? Probably not. But you have less need to pretend you're delighted when you're really irritated, more tolerance for the honesty of your natural response, and more tolerance for others' too.

If you're like most of us, you've put up with some true discomfort learning about your anger. That takes courage. Even if you haven't mastered it all (this is an ongoing process that can take some time), you're already on your way. This means that you can use your anger advantage right here and right now. What is it you've been wanting to do? Hoping to do but not sure that you dare to do? With the focused energy of your frustrations, irritations, and outrage as a guide, what are you waiting for?

But You Can't Just Walk in Here and . . . !

Maybe you're still experiencing some hints of hesitation in your anger action plan. Being a woman and claiming the authority of your anger may still feel risky or unnerving at times. That's understandable. You're bucking the system and there might be consequences; but to be blunt, you do yourself a huge disservice if you *assume* those consequences will all be negative (which is what we are told we should believe). You won't know until you try.

The amazing thing is that when we talk to women who have chosen to move forward with changes based on their anger, we run into very few stories of unhappy long-term outcomes. In the short run, you may have to go through the discomfort of confronting a friend, changing a lousy job, alienating an abusive family member, or convincing your partner to go to couple's therapy. But the truth is, you *can* just walk in and express your anger in almost any situation. You have the authority to do this. Why? Because you are as fundamentally entitled to your feelings as anyone else on the planet—all of your feelings, not just the pleasant ones. No one can negate your experience. You'll hear people say, "You shouldn't feel that way" or "Your perceptions of that situation are totally off base." Don't let these arguments convince you there's something wrong with the feelings you have. Anger is your personal advocate. Now that you have anger's wisdom for company, you can make choices about expressing your opposition, doing it wisely and honestly, and trusting yourself to say and do the right thing.

It is critical to break the rules, to walk into unfamiliar territory, and take some risks in order to make changes that are adaptive for you. That's because the traditional rules and parameters for women's anger have largely been oppressive and dysfunctional and have held women hostage in bad relationships, unfulfilling work lives, and self-doubt. Today, the old patterns need to be shattered. The women in the stories below have revolutionized old patterns and found themselves operating by a new system of emotional rules. Listen as they describe the emotional, intellectual, and relational benefits their anger has brought to them in this process of reworking outdated anger rules. Notice how far they've come. Imagine yourself doing the same kinds of things in your own life.

Monica: The Art of Anger

Monica is 42 years old, divorced, the mother of four, an artist, and a graduate student. Her talents are diverse and the ways in which she's learned to use them reflect her passion for beauty and excellence. Monica also feels keenly angry about certain things:

> *Most of my anger is about feeling like I'm not being heard or taken seriously.*

Being heard ranks as one of the most fundamental needs in life for Monica. She considers this to be so vital that she fights for the rights of children and adolescents to be heard as well. Surviving a family that abused, ignored, and negated her, she grew up knowing she would have to break old rules to become whole. Surviving a marriage that reduced her, she knew she would have to stand on her own two feet and do something extraordinary to heal, move forward, and find visibility.

Monica, like other emotionally successful women, finds she's developed her very own anger philosophy, one that's distinctively hers, different from her parents', even different from many of her friends'. Her philosophy is personally responsible, clear, direct, and all about fighting for what she treasures.

I think anger is a driving force. I think I can be angry—I think people can be angry—and if you process that with someone, they know where you are. You know where you are. I process out loud. I think anger's okay. I do believe that you need to hurt as few people in the process as possible. I try to separate the behavior from the person and tell them, "This is where I am. I am so angry with you. I'm so angry with this behavior." Or I'll tell my kids, "I am very angry. We need to talk about this later when I'm not so angry." So I try to be real up front with my anger. . . . And the guy I'm dating, I've used him as my sounding board. He's become closer to me because I've shared myself. I'm very real.

I learned to express my anger in other ways—different from my mother, who used rage to control us. I write; I write volumes and have ever since I was a young child. I noticed that when I was going through my divorce I had so much anger that I wrote a lot. I also exercised a lot to vent my anger because I didn't want to go into the rage that my mom did. I think that that has helped me because in any of my relationships, business or otherwise, I always start out by saying, "How am I feeling today?" I write and it will eventually lead me to the source of my feelings.

I allow my kids to know that it's okay to be angry. I have learned that passivity is not good. I don't care what people say. In our family, we throw eggs at a tree. Because it's kind of that cracking thing. My kids say, "I just need to go throw an egg." And I say, "Well, go right ahead." The dogs eat the eggs and they get a shiny coat, so that's good too. It works. All of us put so much force into throwing that egg. Sometimes we have to throw a dozen eggs. But I think that's okay. I'm thinking, "I am so damn mad. I am so damn mad. I am so damn mad." It releases a lot of frustration and emotion in a positive way. You're physically, mentally, emotionally using all your parts to throw this little egg. I've noticed it does the same thing in my kids.

When asked how she developed her anger philosophy, Monica talks more about her history, particularly with her mother and her ex-husband, Doug:

My mom's anger really has a lot to do with how I am. Her tongue could just cut me. I was a very sensitive child and I'm a very sensitive person. She was very physical with the rage, and I just knew that there was a different way. And so, when I was young, my anger forced me to move—I knew from a very young age that I was going to move away. I was the first one in my family to go to college. My dad tried to discourage me, but I said, "There's a better life out there." I knew it. I was a rebel in that way because I had to prove to myself that I was not like anybody else. That's been a driving force all my life.

When I married, I married the same type of person that was in my family. It was all about him. I felt like I never got any kind of recognition. He hated me as a mother. He never even noticed me—and I felt invisible. He was a doctor and we were in a small town. Everybody knew me as Dr. So-and-so's wife. That always got me angry.

During her marriage to Doug, Monica decided she wanted to spend most of her time with her children, as well as find an alternative way to work. Although she has a degree in journalism, when she had to make a career move, anger fueled her artistic passion and got her started in a new and unusual direction.

> *I knew I wanted to do something that would let me stay at home with my kids, but I had to ask myself, "What can I do? What are my skills?" I knew I didn't want to go back to an ad agency—because that's not a nine-to-five job, so I basically came up with my "Kid Art" business.*

Monica now produces stained-glass art and uses children's own drawings to create original glass designs. So, she bases her work on what she loves (her kids) to help her become visible in this unique way.

> *I just started expressing myself through my art about two years ago. There is a story behind every piece of art that I do. My art is very emotional.*

Additionally, personal rights, both her own and those of others, sit at the center of Monica's consciousness. Monica finds her outrage triggered by social injustice—preventable acts that hurt people. Think about how Monica's familial anger, her anger at her ex-husband, and her overarching anger themes come together to help her understand and take action on things that need to be changed about the world.

> *Part of it is about women being unheard. Because it's not just within my family—it's within the whole social context. Women have to prove themselves before they're even considered.*
>
> *And also kids' issues . . . I've made a commitment to my kids to help them work on their own selves, as opposed to worrying about what others think about them. I've gone up to the school many times and fought for kids' rights. I believe that kids have rights. For instance, my kids told me that they were not allowed to talk at lunch. They were not allowed to get up and go to the bathroom and when they wanted water,*

they would pour water into their used milk cartons! It just made me furious! I went up there and I asked the principal, who was very defensive, and she said, "Well, I don't do that." She wasn't giving me any information. I said, "You know what—this is inappropriate. These kids have the right to go to the bathroom when they need to go to the bathroom! These kids have a right to have fresh water!"

They did change. The principal would have never led me to believe that it would change. But the next day, she went in and talked to the kids and said, "This is how it is." So I was happy about that.

I'm always fighting for my kids, and not just my kids, but other kids. My new business that I really want to open is based on kids and how unappreciated kids' art is. I want to buy the kids' art, sell it, and pay part of the proceeds back to the kids. That's my next venture. This is what I want to do because kids are not appreciated and parents wonder why they in turn can't appreciate things when they grow up. I really believe in that.

Monica has transformed old messages about quieting her angry voice into the realization that she deserves to be heard by others. She knows now that anger is a route to justice, and that defending the rights of others is a positive use of angry energy. She and her kids know that when you feel like you'd like to strangle someone, it helps to go out and throw an egg; do something with your whole body and mind to express what's inside you. Monica has discovered that anger can create beauty.

Ann Louise: Overcoming Challenges with New Choices

Ann Louise remembers that early on her anger was stifled almost to the point of suffocation. She grew up in a Midwestern working-class family, where all the resources were directed toward the education and career development of her brothers, while she was groomed from the age of nine for housework and marriage, in spite of her aspirations and talent.

They remortgaged the house to send my brothers to college, but for me it was, "You'll get married anyway, so there's no point in spending the money." I definitely resented it.

As in most families, she was not allowed to express her anger and frustration directly to her parents. To cope emotionally, she learned a combination of externalizing and internalizing diversions. She acted out the anger she could not verbalize by going against her parents' will and marrying young, a choice that also gave her the chance to get out and leave her long-standing anger with her family behind.

The respite was short-lived, however. Her husband became physically abusive and Ann Louise found herself in a dangerous and enraging position. As extreme as her situation was, it was still difficult for her to point her anger in the right direction. While a part of her understood that what her husband was doing couldn't be right, the insecurities of youth and the messages society sent young wives in the 1970s made it impossible for her to hold her husband directly accountable. She used her anger in a way that secured her freedom, but at a terrible cost—Ann Louise didn't deny her anger, but chose to aim it more at herself than at her husband, her family, or society.

I was so angry, but I felt I couldn't leave. I thought my family must know, but they never said, they never did anything. I decided to make him mad enough to hurt me where it would show, then people couldn't ignore it. So I did; when I got mad I provoked him and my injuries got to the point where my sister-in-law stepped in and told him she'd call the police unless we separated. And I finally got to leave.

Later, after a stint in the interior design business, she moved to the West Coast and returned to college to obtain a bachelor's degree. There she began working for a man who sexually harassed her and baited her with promises of a bright career. As time went on and his behavior persisted, her fury mounted. Her long-term seething resentment drove her to leave the personnel job she loved, but not before she became quite ill over time with fibromyalgia, a chronic and painful disease. Today there is no doubt in her mind that her illness was directly related to the rage and stress she experienced over this extended period of time. She states that when she finally made the decision to leave her job, the pain from her illness left her upper body totally in the days following her resignation. Holding her anger in, as she had been taught as a child and encouraged to do as a woman, taxed her physical health and cost her the job that she so highly valued.

It wasn't until a few years ago that Ann Louise had a breakthrough experience with her anger. She held a human resources management position where she enjoyed both her colleagues and the work itself, but found some aspects of her responsibilities and the demands they made on her home life unbearable. Again, she felt her anger mounting, felt the pressure building, and began to think about using her anger to find a way out. This time, however, she realized she didn't want to sacrifice her job; she wanted to stay on and resolve the issues so she could continue working where she was. Instead of diverting her anger, Ann Louise found a way to tap into it, to decipher the messages it was sending about boundaries crossed and needs unmet, and to focus her efforts on achieving her goals. It took patience with herself and her employer and a willingness to tolerate her anger while she sorted out what was needed, what was possible, and what would work in the end. She came to believe that her anger was helping her to stay where she was, rather than pushing her out the door.

The important thing is to understand that making decisions should not be based only on the needs of others, they should be based on what makes me happy too. Anger kept me focused on where I was going and what I wanted even when I didn't know exactly what that was. Sometimes I didn't even believe things would change, but I still had the strength to stand up for what I wanted, and keep searching for it.

In addition, Ann Louise's employer responded respectfully to her needs.

I truly felt respected, and that he wanted me to stay there enough to make some changes. It's the first time I had been truly heard, not just listened to. I think it's all about mutual respect and trust. He knows that I would never ever do anything that wouldn't be in his best interest, and he values that. So he wants to be sure he's acting in my best interest as well. So this is the first time I was able to offer a creative solution that was accepted and it actually solved the problem. I got to keep my job instead of leaving out of anger.

The resolution proved to be a winning one for Ann Louise. Although she has moved on to a different career path, she takes with her lessons learned about how anger can empower and help to bring about much needed change. Her abilities to act effectively and productively earn her awards both professionally and as a volunteer. Recently named Businesswoman of the Year in her city, Ann Louise also holds the Community Leadership Award for her work with survivors of domestic abuse.

And that's another crucial and wonderful part of what happens when we broaden the focus of our anger to include things in our larger society—we begin to reach out to the world around us in ways that can make a difference. Ann Louise brought about important improvements in her community, in part because she learned how to move from blaming herself and silencing her anger to taking action to bring healing to herself and others.

PLAYING BY OUR OWN RULES

Once you make that marvelous step outside the lines a couple of times, you are likely to feel a mixture of exhilaration and fear. If the old rules don't apply, then what's left? It's up to you to create a new set of guidelines . . . to organize the disarray so that you don't feel adrift. We've found that amidst the turmoil, insights and creative solutions inevitably emerge.

Order out of Chaos

Chaos is commotion, disorder, the disruption of calm. When a partner is unfaithful or leaves us, when a friend betrays a sacred trust, when we are abused by someone we love, or when we fail at something we desperately want to do . . . all of these things bring chaos into our lives because they disarrange the parts of experience we expect and plan. And anger is a big part of this kind of chaos. Perhaps the most painful aspect of the kind of agony we experience when we lose a lover or a dream is the tumultuous sense of casting about, looking for a way to make meaning of, or organize a situation that feels like the end of the world. Where do we begin?

We can begin by letting our anger lead us through the most significant losses and to the most pressing issues—the most valued priorities we have. Anger organizes our thoughts and prepares us for the next steps. The things we're most furious about give us the opportunity to look into the future.

Think for a moment about the kinds of tremendously angry situations you've faced in your lifetime. Which ones stand out as most painful? Which ones continue to cause you to feel helpless or lost? Let your mind roam freely. Anything it finds will be exactly where you need to go. The following imagery exercise can be custom fit to your experience. Try it as often as you need to. Use the imagery to create some new images out of old hurts.

> *Find yourself sitting in a comfortable chair at home, where you have plenty of privacy. Hold a favorite blanket or throw, even a comfortable sweatshirt or some other kind of cloth. You can cover yourself with the cloth or hold it close to your cheek. Let your fingers sample the texture of the fabric. As you feel the softness of the cloth, close your eyes and let your attention go to your breathing and lengthen each breath just a bit until you find the deep breathing that feels best. Notice how your body is feeling and allow any tension to float out and away. And as you drift into a pleasant, relaxed state, you may find that your mind wanders . . .*

And as you continue enjoying how nice it feels to relax deeply and enjoy the pleasant weight of the cloth you're holding, you begin to see images of yourself as competent, strong, and perfectly woven together; all your feelings and thoughts coming together to form a beautiful tapestry . . .

. . . And you feel so glad to know that you can weave together all the parts of you that help you know the world, including all your emotions and all your thoughts. And isn't it nice to know that with every difficult emotion comes the clarity of mind to teach you what you need to know in order to thrive and to grow and to change. When you tear away the bindings you no longer need, you find yourself weaving new fabric that serves you better . . .

Can you see the old fastenings being torn away? What do they look like? What kinds of things do you make to put in their place?

. . . And you begin to see a woman who deserves your admiration because she gives herself credit and takes herself seriously and listens to her inner wisdom and anger and opinions because they make a difference in the world. Give yourself plenty of time to see her clearly in your mind's eye. She turns difficult experiences into powerful learning . . .

Can you see yourself being like her in some way? How? What would you be doing? What does your anger tell you about the world? What do you see that needs to happen? What needs to change?

And as you continue drifting and as you continue to enjoy weaving together the various parts of you that you've learned to love, you know the secret that helps you cut away the old and get what you want in life by creating the new.

And you begin to stretch your arms and legs and feel yourself emerging as you come from an important dream. You allow yourself to become fully alert and awake and glad you've taken the time to give yourself this important gift. Congratulations!

As you complete this imagery, you may find yourself having ideas that are new and drastic. Perhaps you decide to do something original with the pain you feel at this moment. Maybe you team up with all of the ex-girlfriends of your lying, cheating ex-boyfriend. Maybe you call them all together to your house for champagne, to celebrate what you've all learned about dating jerks. Or perhaps you decide it's time to write a letter to the college professor who shamed you in front of the whole speech class. You thoughtfully compose a letter that describes the feelings of anger you've carried since that happened and you tell her that you've done well for yourself in spite of her. Or possibly you even begin writing a book about your experiences in a family that was abusive. You put your life into your own words and help educate other women in similar circumstances. No matter what you devise, you use your voice to define yourself, to say to the world, "Like it or not, this is who I am. Love me as I am, or I will seek out others who can."

Defining Your Personal Anger Policies

Very successful women seem to make their own rules when it comes to their emotions. We've seen this across our focus groups and individual interviews with women who have pushed ahead to become leaders and those who have pushed themselves to do things radically different from what they once knew possible. In the next few stories, we hear real women developing their own anger philosophy, learning to live by it, and transforming their identities from helpless to triumphant. Listen to how these women take chaos and distress and revolutionize their lives by making meaning of the things that feel out of control.

Michal (36) tells the story about losing her partner to cancer a few years ago. She was "angry at absolutely everything." "Why has this happened to me?" Michal says she always has a "low level of anger current running through me. I've had a lot of losses." But this one really brought out feelings of rage. Going through this loss necessitated Michal using her emotion to create something new, to organize her painful experience and help her make sense of it. Michal says, "Once a year, I just have to break something." She makes her selection carefully (such as finding an old chair in the garage), gets out in the back-yard and smashes the thing to bits while focusing on her anger. She uses the strong waves of emotion to help her envision change, to "believe everything's going to be all right . . . to visualize it."

> *I can turn hurt into anger—because anger feels a lot bet-ter than hurt. Anger's more powerful and has a better energy. Hurt just seems to hurt and has no focus. But when it can transform for me into anger, then that gives me some more power and control over whatever's happening. It gives me the energy to change the situation or to address it in a more posi-tive way even though I'm angry.*
>
> *I'm in the middle of a relationship breakup. And when I'm just hurting, it's just sort of a non-functional, non-productive state of "ick." But when I can get above that and get angry about it, then I seem to be able to make better decisions—or any decision—and I feel stronger and I feel better and I think I get my focus back.*

Michal feels good about most of her angry decisions, even after the fact. As a result of getting mad, she changed careers, getting out of an administrative rut and into a more creative field. Her anger has given her the energy to get mobilized and do things she didn't want to do, but needed to do (like quitting a job that was stifling). Now she says she uses her angry energy to improve herself and spends more time and energy on self-care.

> *When I resigned from my company, there was anger. That really was the end result of a lot of frustration and anger that was already there and I just kept sort of putting it aside, "well, it will change . . . don't get carried away." And finally that sit-uation continued and didn't change, even though I was trying to effect change. I think finally I just reached a point where I was angry and fed up and quit. Finally I was able to say, "I can do this. I have given this enough time. I've worked on this enough."*

I think I do the same thing in relationships. I have patience. I don't just leave the minute things don't go right, but once I've given all the energy I can to change things and it doesn't change, then I get angry and I remove myself.

The anger helps me feel when I'm done.

When we asked her *how* anger becomes a positive, transformational force inside her. Michal had this to say:

I think I pull away from "feeling bad about whatever" to more of a sense of autonomy. "This is what I'm going to do and this is how I feel—versus how I think someone's making me feel." It's taking back control of my thoughts and my emotions—"this is what I'm going to do and this is how I'm doing it. And I don't care what you think about it." When I can pull out of being mired, depressed, and hurt to a more proactive stance—it really has to have some anger behind it for me.

I've channeled a lot of energy into getting involved in volunteer work because I just had to do something with the energy. You know, I feel that way a lot of times with anger— that I've got to do something with it. I have to get it out of me and channel it in some other way. I was working a lot and serving on some community boards, which helped for a while until I got frustrated with that process—a whole new anger develops (laughter) and then I stopped doing that, but it did work for a while.

It was historic preservation and it was something I was interested in and working in at the time. It was just a good place to take the energy and that's something I find that as I've gotten older—if I don't do something with the energy behind the anger, it just builds up on me in a negative way. So, whether it's working a lot or volunteering or maybe just taking a vigorous walk to get it out, I've got to do something constructive, work in the yard, cut wood, something major to get it out of my body.

- **Michal's Personal Anger Policies:** (1) Use anger to help you get unstuck. (2) Use anger to help you move from hurt victim to empowered survivor. (3) Do something active with the energy that comes with being angry. (4) Anger can help you switch your focus from what others are thinking to what *you* think, feel, want, and need.

Another success story comes from Vivian. At 46, Vivian is a very direct, forthright person who speaks her mind and is not afraid to ask for clarification or more information when she needs it. She makes little pretense and seems very comfortable just being who she is. Vivian really has a sense of boundaries—not wanting to give her anger to people who don't deserve it. She's very careful to take resentments to the appropriate person ("like a supervisor instead of someone who's just answering the phone"). Vivian knows how to pick her battles.

Vivian has used her anger to accomplish a number of things. First, she used anger to fuel her healing from childhood sexual abuse.

> *The anger itself angered me. That anger made me deter-mined to learn how to deal with it, to ask myself questions, to have a catharsis. "Hey, this shit's not going to control me!" I just started telling myself I need to recognize when I'm angry and then question why I am angry. Who am I really mad at? And what can I do about it? Is there something that I can change or is this just something I have to accept? Could I have changed the situation? Did I cause it? And then when I recognized that it was righteous anger, then I had that catharsis. I built dummies with clothing—beat them up. A tree that I had to cut for firewood, I would imagine that tree being someone I was mad at and I'd just cut him up into little pieces.*

Did she stay that angry at her perpetrators forever? No—in fact, going through the process of letting anger take this kind of physical form let her finally resolve something inside.

As a result of going through all that, I've learned; and I just don't get angry in the same way now. Sometimes I do, but I deal with it differently.

Second, Vivian used her anger to move into a new line of work when it was clear she would have trouble making a living in the area of her training. She decided to go into holistic health and is now studying to be a massage therapist. This instinctively seems right to her because she wants to do something that really helps people with their pain.

Vivian says that once she makes us her mind, she becomes very determined and pushes through until she accomplishes what she wants to do. She feels successful and empowered that she's done so many things through her angry energy—things that people told her she couldn't do and things that go *against the grain* for a woman's role in rural society. She raised a son by herself and he is now happy and successful with two master's degrees, a family, and a teaching job. Everyone told her that because she was raising him without a father, he would probably wind up a drug addict. She was so mad about that, she vowed to raise him to be strong. She also built her own house, with her own two hands! Again, people often wagged their fingers at Vivian and said she couldn't do it . . . "which pissed me off!" She took her time (a period of several years) but built the house to last. She's been furious with banks that didn't want to lend her money as a single woman on her own.

Being a single female, it was super hard to get financing. It was impossible at first. So it was a pay-as-I-go type of thing. Needless to say, I was angry about it. If I'd been a man doing the same thing, there wouldn't have been a problem. And I even had a couple of bankers tell me that. My anger over that said, "Well, hide and watch. I'm going to do it anyway with or without your help." And I did. I wanted it my way and I wanted it to last, so I designed it and built it. When I do something, it's done the way I want it done and it's done well.

Her struggles, and the anger she feels about them, make her more determined to help herself and help others too. As a result of this empowerment and attention to what matters, she joined forces with friends in her community and started an ambulance service there. Previously, the community had no access to emergency services; they had watched people go without the help they needed. "You have somebody sick and no one can come . . . it makes you mad!" She and her friends lobbied state and local governments, raised money for the ambulance, and worked as volunteers for four years to staff the service.

We went to the city council meetings and we went to the state meetings. We did all kinds of things. We even had fundraisers to raise money to buy an ambulance. Several of us went to school to become emergency medical technicians and we manned the ambulance after we bought it.

• **Vivian's Personal Anger Policies:** (1) Get clear about why you're mad and who has triggered that feeling. (2) Do something physical with the angry energy in your body. This will help you think differently about the situation. (3) Hang on to that frustrated energy. It will boost your success at achieving your goals. (4) Don't let anyone tell you that you can't do it because you're a woman; use your anger to prove them wrong.

A different anger achievement tale comes from Parker (36). She has a Ph.D. and teaches communications in a university in the Midwest. She says about anger, "I'm regularly pissed off about the world." What she means is that she feels constant anger about the oppression of women in general, and of lesbian women in particular in U.S. society and the effects these negative attitudes really have on all of us. Openly lesbian ("I told my parents I wasn't going to hide it."), she teaches students about race, gender, class, and sexual orientation. She helps naïve college students learn about how to end their own intolerance and become part of a new solution. "I make a difference here. I get frustrated but I use that energy. I don't give up. I make a difference."

Parker regularly taps into the anger she feels about *privileged oblivion*; that is, the benefits that money, status, or skin color bring to people even when they have zero awareness of these unearned perks. Parker uses her outrage at this injustice to sensitize her students through classroom activities and television criticism. Her anger informs everything she does. She's politically active, pro-choice, and she writes to her representatives. "I won't just sit there and listen to it. I'm always operating *on* it." She feels a responsibility to the public at large to help educate people about how bias, based on lack of education, exposure, and experience, can result in oppression and hate. The anger she feels about these things gives her the motivation and energy to persevere when it seems she's up against a difficult class of students in terms of their racism or sexism. "I don't allow it. I always challenge it."

I use that energy, I just don't give up. I use it to try to make the world a better place and it's in small ways, but it does make a difference. It's incremental, it's slow, but I think it does matter. I have students whose attitudes about the world and relationships and race, class, and gender and even sexual orientation change as a result of being in my class.

Our world really frustrates me. And this is an example: people always complained about the film Thelma and Louise *because it was about these two aggressive females using guns and causing violence and yet every other single film is about abusive men and the patriarchy [the system where men rule]. So I'm always frustrated with mainstream society in terms of television and just about everything. And I get frustrated with the notion that because I'm feminist, that my students are hearing "a perspective." But what they don't realize is that their everyday existence in the patriarchy is a perspective! It is a perspective. It is a worldview. They see me as the abnormal and themselves as the normal. And so I'm constantly frustrated at heteronormativity [the assumption that "heterosexual is the only right way to be"], gender bias, and racial bias. I mean it's just constantly there. I can't help but be reminded of it. And then I just try to do my part to make a difference. And not*

even because "I know it's better"—but because I can't survive
otherwise. I couldn't not say things. I couldn't not correct
people if they say something racist or sexist. I'm just always in
that mode.

It's the running joke among my students to not use the
word "girl" around me—they have to use "woman."

- **Parker's Personal Anger Policies:** (1) Anger obligates you to talk.
  This is especially true when it comes to issues of justice and
  human rights. (2) Talking about what gets you passionately angry
  makes the world a better place.

These three very different women have all authored their own
new anger rules, and, for each one, this act has brought rewards individually and to the family, friends, neighbors, patients, and students
around her. Other women have used their anger to fuel even broader
changes in their own lives and the lives of other women. In the stories
that follow, you'll hear about women whose impact extends to national
or even international levels—and anger helped them do it.

Change the World

Learning to acknowledge and live with our anger as a positive part
of ourselves is transformational in so many respects. As soon as we
accept anger as healthy and helpful, our perspective changes dramatically. We move from asking "What's wrong with me?" when we find
ourselves angry to asking simply "What's wrong?" The problem needing to be fixed suddenly does not exist *only* within. Certainly, it's
always worthwhile to engage in a little self-examination. But it's also
necessary for us to raise our heads and look around to the people and
communities surrounding us to find what needs change and improvement. We come to believe that anger is not a fault of ours and to know
that when we are angry it is no longer our fault. Instead anger
becomes a sign, an open door, a path that can lead us to effect change
in ways that go beyond our own small circle of experience to touch the
lives of many others.

We all have this potential for taking the anger advantage to a higher level. We can speak about it to our friends and family, explaining our new and different views on anger and how important it is to give up the idea that good women don't get mad. We can refuse to live within the rules our culture places on our anger, rules that push us to divert rather than experience and express our angry feelings. We can let others know it's okay to show their anger, that we will tolerate it and in fact welcome it, as long as it's delivered respectfully.

These actions allow the positive effects of constructive and healthy anger to ripple out from each of us, helping us to make our own unique and valuable impact on the lives of those we care about, as well as the world beyond. What kinds of things happen as a result? We turn now to the stories of two remarkable women whose anger played a key role in their significant accomplishments within their companies, communities, and around the world.

First, you'll hear from Jessica, who, like many women quoted in this book, requested anonymity. Even though (or perhaps *because*) Jessica is the highest ranked woman in her corporation, it is striking that she *must* consider the consequences of identifying herself or her company. This highlights the blunt realities and risks of declaring your anger publicly. Jessica is *personally* comfortable, confident, and competent with her anger awareness and assertive skills; they have taken her very far in a cutthroat, high-tech industry. But she, like many other smart women, knows that you can do everything right and still get negative press when you choose to be open with your anger. The context matters, and so does strategy.

In contrast, Nancy Gruver is happy to identify herself and her life's work, New Moon Publishing. *And she can.* She doesn't have a boss; she *is* the boss. She is openly dedicated to giving girls and women a forum for their voices, including hopes, fears, and, yes, anger. She feels free to say that repressed anger from her family motivated her to want to make societal changes for girls and women. Ironically, as up front as she is in the public world, she confesses she still struggles with anger diversion on a day-to-day level in her personal relationships, though she has vowed to keep working on it.

So Nancy and Jessica present an interesting study: one cautious to the public outside, but very secure on the inside; the other highly visible to the external world, but internally working to release old anger rules. Their differences highlight how there can be radically different paths to the same end—the anger advantage.

Jessica: An Anger Achiever

At age 40, Jessica occupies a top-level managerial position at one of the world's largest computer firms. Her division alone brings in $250 million a year, and she notes that she is the most senior woman executive in her division. How did Jessica arrive at this position of influence? What role has anger played in her success? Our interview with Jessica reveals just how well this emotion serves her.

Jessica recognizes the impact of her early family experiences. Both her parents worked, and she has a brother who is both disabled and has learning difficulties. Empowering her brother was a major focus in the family.

> *Saying "can't" was like saying the f-word. I never grew up with the experience of being told I couldn't do something.*

This familial attitude helped Jessica use her anger early on to assert herself in the defense of her brother at school, and today she feels good about her actions.

Following her own education, which included a bachelor's degree in industrial/organizational psychology, Jessica worked in an entry-level position in human resources as a paper-pusher until a woman came along who grabbed her attention:

> *She was pivotal in my development. She was non-traditional, a real professional businesswoman who could wheel and deal with the big boys; not soft and squishy. She mentored me and I left with her to join another company.*

In this intermediate stage of her career, she worked in international relations and operations as a project manager. Eventually, this company was bought out and she interviewed with and was hired by the firm that currently employs her. At her new job, Jessica eventually took on the role of restructuring a floundering division of the company.

> *It was like working in a sandbox with little boys throwing sand at each other. They needed somebody tough who could stand up to them, and I was good at fixing things.*

After four years, she moved up to her current position, where Jessica wields her considerable authority with self-assurance and a sense of humor. How does she do it?

> *I'm very different from most women. A lot of women are motivated by the need for approval and feel they need to be nice all the time. I never worry about that at work. I care about being respected and adding value. I've never believed the top line of my job description says "be nice." Most women feel they have to be collaborative all the time. It's hard to be this way in business and be a good leader. Sometimes you have to be willing to be unpopular to make the best business decision.*

Another key element in Jessica's success is not just how assertive she is, but how she uses her anger:

> *I get very high manager ratings from my employees and people stay with me. I'm super up-front with people. I just tell people when I am mad and then it's over. I'm not passive-aggressive like a lot of women. Passive-aggressive is the worst. You end up tiptoeing around on pins and needles. Nobody likes to work around that. People don't like to guess where you are coming from.*
> *Sometimes anger is a good motivator; you stop whining and go do something. I sit and figure out why I am mad and what I can do to fix it. If I am particularly angry sometimes I will jokingly just tell people, "My bitch meter is in the red zone today, it's not a good time to ask me for money." People*

know to let me cool off and then they come back and it's "I hear you." I'm decisive and people who know me know when I can be pushed and not. When it's negotiable and when it's not. People who know me well sometimes say "Jessica, you've got that walk." Fast and determined.

Jessica doesn't divert her anger. She is conscious of her anger and how it looks and feels in her body. She lets others know about it. She may sometimes think tank it, suspending action until she has clarity about how she'd like to move on her annoyance. Jessica expresses her anger clearly and directly and decides on the best course of action. She knows when it's important to listen to others (and when to hold her ground); and she knows *when* she is ready to listen to others.

For someone in as powerful a role as Jessica's, it is interesting that she says she is just beginning to realize the true scope of her influence. She notes:

I think I underestimate it and sometimes I take it for granted. I've realized that if I don't support an idea or program at work, it's perceived as the kiss of death and as a result, I have to be very careful about the comments I make. Sometimes a minor comment from me causes changes and people will later say, "We changed this based on what you said." The length to which people will prepare to meet with me still is surprising. I get annoyed when I ask for a product demonstration and find out a team of ten people spent two days preparing, when a quick 15-minute demonstration is all I was looking for.

Jessica reports that her awareness about how being a woman impacts her own career, and those of other women around her has also grown in the recent past. While long conscious of the fact that the computer industry is, in her words "a man's world," her role with other women is evolving:

I didn't have a sense until a couple of years ago that being a woman was a big factor. This company is a big boys club. My last boss was threatened by me and I was "worked out" of a particular project. A lot of women were offended and came to me saying "this is blatant sex discrimination—maybe you should have joined the football pool earlier." They saw me as a role model and felt I had been wronged. After enough comments from women in the group, I went to the executive VP and said, "I just want you to know that women perceive the division as being sexist." I was surprised, but it really bothered him that women felt that way and since then, several women were named into director positions. I'd like to think my talk with him had some influence.

Regarding sexual harassment, Jessica indicates it has never happened to her directly:

I don't present myself like that would be okay. Some women use sexuality to sell—it's very effective. But it's not okay for me. I'm no nonsense. I think it's possible to have fun at work and maintain good relationships without being unprofessional or offensive.

While indicating that she is not super-conscious of her responsibility to other women, Jessica has taken actions and has ideas about empowering other women. She says:

People have brought it to my attention that I am a role model for other women so it's in the back of my mind. I try to be fair and treat all people with respect, but running the business comes first—that's what they pay me to do. The best thing I can do for other women is to do a great job. People will see that women can do well because we are doing well. Someday, I'd like to do volunteer work with abused women to help them develop self-confidence and professional skills. I brought my niece up for "Take Your Daughter to Work Day" so she would think about the possibilities in business.

It's clear, however, that other women within her company look to Jessica as an outstanding example of what a woman can achieve when she's not afraid to be assertive and to use her anger for advancement and constructive change. She is someone they seek out because she can use her outrage effectively when they cannot:

> *If it's a women's issue, women don't feel comfortable complaining to a man—even if he is really nice and approachable. We had an event that was very successful and had a party afterward to celebrate. The guy who planned the party hired women in skimpy costumes to hand out cocktails. The women in the office were outraged. One of them pulled me aside and said, "If they strip, I'll go ballistic!" I went to the guy and said, "What were you thinking?" And he sent out an e-mail apologizing. They wouldn't have gone to him directly. They went to me.*

Jessica talks about another incident in which she was instrumental in voicing the anger of her whole division to the chairman and the CEO of her company. Her division had developed a product they were certain would catch on, but the big bosses disagreed. Listen to Jessica's account of courage—and effectiveness—fueled by anger:

> *At a big planning meeting, the CEO dismissed our product as wrong without hearing any of the data. I argued with him in front of 300 people. I was mad and I didn't care about sticking my neck out. I had better data and our proposal was the right thing for the company. And I won.*

She concludes:

> *Those are the people who get something done. The ones who are willing to get mad and use that passion to take action.*

At the end of the interview with Jessica, we asked if there was anything she would like to add. She said:

> *If I could say anything to women, I'd say they're too hung up on being nice, on not being controversial. They're afraid they won't be respected and admired. They'll still respect and admire you, but just in a different way. People may say, "She's not girly enough." I say, "Do you really care what they think?"*

Jessica shows just how far an assertive woman who uses anger consciousness and adaptive anger skills can go in the high-powered, male-dominated world of technology and corporate business. In doing so, she provides resources and a great model for other women in her company. Moving in a different context, but in an equally empowering direction, read on to hear how Nancy has made her own global impact on girls and women.

Nancy: Anger and Activism

At 48, Nancy Gruver is married and has 21-year-old twin daughters. She is the founder of *New Moon: The Magazine for Girls and Their Dreams*, a remarkable journal for pre- and early-adolescent girls that reaches out, empowers, and creates real change in the lives of contributors and readers alike. First published in 1993, Nancy wanted to create "a resource for all girls who want their voices heard and their dreams taken seriously." As noted on the *New Moon* website (www.newmoon.org):

> *The problem with most magazines for girls is that the images in those magazines tell girls what they should be.* New Moon *is where girls tell the world who they are, without adults or advertisers as interpreters. Other publications for girls portray a "perfect girl" for readers to measure themselves against. By contrast,* New Moon *challenges stereotypes by accepting girls as they are, listening to them, and celebrating their diverse experience and dreams.*

Focusing on girls aged 8 to 14, Nancy and her family developed not only the publication, but a *process* in which girls work as equals on the editorial board of the magazine, right along with the adults. They strive to give girls a voice about the full range of their ideas and emotions—including anger. For example, the magazine has a regular feature called "How Aggravating!" where girls write in about what makes them mad and can express their opinions about what's unfair to them, as well as to other girls and women.

When asked what role anger has played in her decision to create *New Moon*, Nancy says:

> *Concern for my daughters specifically, and other girls and women in general, motivated me. My anger at the sexism I'd experienced and seen and particularly my anger at the way our culture silences girls and women motivated me. My personal experience as an incest survivor caused a lot of anger that is a big part of my drive to make the world a better place for myself and others. It also helped me believe that I had the inner reserves and creativity to do something risky that I didn't know how to do—start the magazine. Surviving incest made doing something like starting the magazine feel like a manageable risk. And the possible benefits for me and others was a great potential reward for taking the risk. I knew that I could survive failure if it didn't work and I knew that I had a lot of coping skills developed by dealing with difficult situations. I felt confident that whatever happened I could handle it. Having been literally silenced as a girl by not being able to speak about the abuse I experienced created a great awareness for me of the importance of girls and women speaking out. It also deepened my commitment to helping girls do that.*

In her own family, women and girls were actively discouraged from voicing anger:

> *I learned not to express anger directly in my own family. I still have difficulty with anger and how to experience and*

express it constructively and I work on this a lot. It's a struggle because of what I learned as child. I learned to ignore and bury my angry feelings as a child—girls weren't allowed to express anger—that was inappropriate. In my family expressing anger was a privilege, not a right. The people with the most power (men) could express their anger most directly and those with less power (women and kids) were blamed and seen as responsible for making the more powerful angry.

For example, when I was 12 or 13, I was taken on a weekend trip to visit relatives by the family member who had abused me when I was much younger (I didn't remember the abuse at the time). While on the one-and-one-half-hour drive home, I started reading a teen magazine. The relative seemed annoyed by this but didn't say anything about it. He just used body language and sighs to express his annoyance. But I felt rebellious, ignored the signals, and just kept reading. He fumed and I resisted and the tension in the car built silently for the rest of the drive. When we pulled up to my house, without saying a word he got out of the car, took my suitcase out of the trunk, and drove off in a huff without stopping in to talk with my parents or say good-bye. My mother got scared because she knew this meant he was very angry. She asked me what had happened and what I'd done to upset him. When I told her she screamed at me, saying that if he had a heart attack it would be my fault.

So, like many women and girls, Nancy learned early on to divert her anger. However, her anger didn't go away—it became an undercover agent, fueling her passionate devotion to social change:

It became a hidden motivator (hidden to me, at least) for my deep interest in justice and in listening to girls. But I never learned how conflict could be resolved openly and then left in the past.

Today, Nancy recognizes her anger, how it has helped her, and lets it operate more out in the open. She has had new experiences with healthy anger; she is now not only using her anger to motivate the continuation of *New Moon*, but is seeing the benefits of adaptive conflict in her personal and professional life.

A friend and colleague has shown me how to use anger constructively by being aware of it and then deciding what to do about it. This was a big change for me from keeping the anger repressed and then just using the energy it had generated to do something else rather than do something directly about the source of the anger. I'm still working on this on a nearly daily basis.

One of my coworkers at New Moon amazed most of the rest of us by saying that she thinks conflict can be a positive thing. She said that in her family conflicts lead to resolution and not to long-simmering tension. We've made a group commitment to work on bringing up conflicts with each other but it's still difficult for most of us. However, when we do, we find that she's right and we can resolve them openly.

In the work of the Girls Editorial Board we strive to teach them how to disagree with each other respectfully and express their true opinions. At the same time, they need to learn how to accept that even though they express a strong feeling, the group decision might go a different way. This is something that few girls experience growing up and that is really valuable for them to learn. I wish that I'd had the opportunity as a girl to learn respectful disagreement and how not to take it personally when someone disagrees with my idea.

Even though *New Moon* now reaches an estimated audience of 75,000 to 100,000 readers, with subscribers in 45 countries across the globe, Nancy's anger-powered drive to improve the world for girls and women has expanded even further. In addition to the original magazine, New Moon Publishing now has a parenting newsletter, a number of books, and professional speakers available to present at conferences and conventions.

One of the neat things about Nancy Gruver is that she's in the process of growing into her anger at a personal level, while already using it to make an impressive impact at the societal level. She shows us that we can accomplish so much without having it all down perfectly, and that's an inspiration. The important thing is to start the journey.

But Nancy's story is just one example of activism sparked, fueled, and sustained by healthy anger. What is it that you see in the world around you that causes your blood to boil? Have you been sitting on your outrage, hiding it, and placating yourself with distractions like food, overworking, shopping, too much TV? What would happen if that energy was released and pointed in the direction of the offending agent? Monica, Ann Louise, Parker, Vivian, Michal, Jessica, and Nancy show us just a few of the possibilities. Imagine what can happen when a multitude of women join together in anger and determination to create a change.

Activist movements, including feminism and many others (e.g., Mothers Against Drunk Driving), teach us the power in numbers. One woman's anger flowing uninhibited toward its target can be a powerful agent for change. But when joined with the anger of 100 or 1,000 other women, the force can become unstoppable. Whether its women's fight for equality, protection of the environment, political corruption, crime and violence, children's rights, discrimination and harassment—whatever our cause—anger can help us fight for a better world, and win!

Weaving Your Anger Tapestry

Each of our emotions is a vital thread in our lives; these threads are intimately interwoven with the warp and woof of everything we think and do. From these threads, integrated into a whole cloth, emerges the tapestry of each of our lives. If a thread is dropped, the fabric is uneven; pulled, pinched, or frayed. Each thread is essential.

Imagine your anger as bright and glowing sun-yellow thread. At the core of the experience of anger, these glowing threads are woven together to form a basic pattern of pure anger. This is the raw emotion that you were born with, that our species developed out of thousands of years of successful evolution. This is the fiber of a true acknowledgment of anger to self. The sun-yellow thread represents all the adaptive power of anger; to clarify who you are, to set your boundaries with others, to motivate change, to strive for connection in relation to those you love, to walk out on bad situations, to cue you when it's time to shift into a new gear, to make a difference in the world.

Now imagine weaving other colors among the shining yellow, forming a circular tapestry. With dazzling yellow at the center, imagine the threads of anger radiating outward, streaming to the edges of your circle like the rays of sunshine you used to draw when you were a child. Weave in the reds of your most intimate friends, family, and lovers. Weave in the purples of your acquaintances and coworkers, your peers. Weave in the greens of your boss and others who have power over you, and over whom you have power yourself. Each color wraps over and under the golden yellow spokes of your tapestry, but the bright, sunny threads are always visible; your guide to meshing the anger advantage into all other aspects of your life.

There will be other threads too; the orange of happiness and the blue of sadness, the blackness of fear. Each emotion is a critical strand in your tapestry, but always weaves in and around your beautiful, powerful, yellow threads. Your tapestry—even as a work in progress—should be on display, in your permanent collection, in the spotlight and prominently on exhibit for all to admire and respect. It is a glorious creation of your sweat, your insight, your faith in the truth of your own emotional experience, your courage, your voice, and your love. Your anger is part of your whole cloth now, lovely and intricate. Revel in it. Wrap yourself up in it. Claim it. Flaunt it. Dream with it. Go forward with it.

There are so many levels on which you can use your anger advantage, from enhancing your most intimate relationships with family and friends to creating international change. Make the choices that feel right for you and that fit with your new anger rules. Let your anger advantage add a strand of color in the tapestry of your life, intertwined with everything else you are and can be.

Bibliography

Arber, S., & Ginn, J. "Women and aging," *Reviews in Clinical Gerontology 4*, 349–358, 1994.

Atkins, D. C., Baucom, D. H., & Jacobson, N. "Understanding infidelity: Correlates in a national random sample," *Journal of Family Psychology 15*, 735–749, 2001.

Averill, J. R. "The emotions: An integrative approach," In R. Hogan, J. Johnson, & S. Briggs (eds.), *Handbook of personality psychology*, pp. 513–543. San Diego, CA: Academic Press, 1997.

Bar-On, R., & Parker, J. D. A. *The handbook of emotional intelligence: Theory, development, assessment, and application at home, school, and in the workplace*. San Francisco: Jossey-Bass, 2000.

Bernardez, T. "Women and anger: Cultural prohibitions and the feminine ideal." *Working paper # 31*. Stone Center, Wellesley College, MA, 1988.

Bowen, M. *Family therapy in clinical practice*. Northvale, NJ: Aronson, 1994.

Bowlby, J. *A secure base: Parent-child attatchment and healthy human development*. New York: Basic Books, 1988.

Brondolo, E., Masheb, R., Stores, J., Stockhammer, T., Tunick, W. & Melhado, E. "Anger-related traits and response to interpersonal conflict among New York City traffic agents," *Journal of Applied Social Psychology, 28*, 2089–2118, 1998.

Brown, L. M. *Raising our voices: The politics of girls' anger*. Cambridge, MA: Harvard, 1998.

Buntaine, R. L. & Costenbader, V. K. "Self-reported differences in the experience and expression of anger between girls and boys." *Sex Roles 36*, 625–637, 1997.

Bushman, B. J. "Does venting anger feed or extinguish the flame? Catharsis, rumination, distraction, anger, and aggressive responding," *Personality and Social Psychology Bulletin* 28, 724–731, 2002.

Cox, D. L., Stabb, S. D. & Bruckner, K. H. *Women's anger: Clinical and developmental perspectives.* Philadelphia: Taylor & Francis, 1999.

Cox, D. L., Van Velsor, P. & Hulgus, J. F. "Who me, angry? Patterns of anger diversion in women." Paper presented at the 110th Convention of the American Psychological Association, Chicago, IL, August 2002.

Cox, D. L., Van Velsor, P., Hulgus, J. F., Weatherman, S. R., Smenner, M. L., Dickens, D. & Davis, C. "What's the use in getting mad?" Anger and instrumentality in women's relationships (forthcoming).

Donelson, F. E. *Women's experiences: A psychological perspective.* Mountain View, CA: Mayfield Publishing Company, 1999.

Droppelman, P. G. & Thomas, S. P. "Anger in women as an emerging issue in MCH," *MCN: American Journal of Maternal Child Nursing* 20, 85–94, 1995.

Ekman, P. "All emotions are basic." In P. Ekman & R. J. Davidson (eds.), *The nature of emotion: Fundamental questions,* 15–19. Oxford: Oxford University Press, 1994.

Fehr, B., Baldwin, B., Collins, L., Patterson, S. & Benditt, R. "Anger in close relationships: An interpersonal script analysis," *Personality and Social Psychology Bulletin* 25, 299–312, 1999.

Fields, B., Reesman, K., Robinson, C., Sims, A., Edwards, K., McCall, B., Short, B. & Thomas, S. P. "Anger of African American women in the South," *Issues in Mental Health Nursing* 19, 353–373, 1998.

Fitness, J. "Anger in the workplace: An emotion script approach to anger episodes between workers and their superiors, co-workers and subordinates," *Journal of Organizational Behavior* 21, 147–162, 2000.

Fitzgerald, L. F. "Sexual harassment: Violence against women in the workplace," *American Psychologist* 48, 1070–1076, 1993.

Fivush, R. "Gender and emotion in mother-child conversations about the past," *Journal of Narrative and Life History* 1, 325–341, 1991.

Galen, B. R. & Underwood, M. K. "A developmental investigation of social aggression among children," *Developmental Psychology* 33, 589–600, 1997.

Gersick, C. J. G., Bartunek, J. M. & Dutton, J. E. "Learning from academia: The importance of relationships in professional life," *Academy of Management Journal* 43, 1026–1044, 2000.

Gjerdingen, D., McGovern, P., Bekker, M., Lundberg, U. & Willemsen, T. "Women's work roles and their impact on health, well-being, and career:

Comparisons between the United States, Sweden, and the Netherlands." *Women & Health 31*, 1–20, 2000.

Goleman, D. *"Emotional intelligence*. New York: Bantam Books, 1995.

Gottman, J. *Marital therapy: An empirically-based approach*. Professional Seminar, Dallas, TX, October 2001.

Gottman, J. M., Katz, L. F. & Hooven, C. "Parental meta-emotion philosophy and the emotional life of families: Theoretical models and preliminary data," *Journal of Family Psychology 10*, 243–268, 1996.

Izard, C. E. "Innate and universal facial expressions: Evidence from developmental and cross-cultural research," *Psychological Bulletin 115*, 288–299, 1994.

Greer, S. & Morris, T. "Psychological attributes of women who develop breast cancer: A controlled study," *Journal of Psychosomatic Research 19*, 147–153, 1975.

Harmon-Jones, E. & Allen, J. B. "Anger and frontal brain activity: EEG asymmetry consistent with approach motivation despite negative affect valence," *Journal of Personality and Social Psychology 74*, 1310–1316, 1998.

Haynes, S., Levine, S., Scotch, N., Feinleib, M. & Kannel, W. B. "The relationship of psychosocial factors to coronary heart disease in the Framingham study. Part I: Methods and risk factors," *American Journal of Epidemiology 107*, 362–383, 1978.

Jack, D. C. *Behind the mask: Destruction and creativity in women's aggression*. Cambridge, MA: Harvard University Press, 1999.

Jack, D. C. *Silencing the self: Women and depression*. Cambridge, MA: Harvard University Press, 1991.

Kassinove, H., Sukhodolsky, D. G., Tsytsarev, S. V. & Solovyova, S. "Self-reported anger episodes in Russia and America," *Journal of Social Behavior and Personality 12*, 301–324, 1997.

Kennedy-Moore, E. & Watson, J. C. *Expressing emotion: Myths, realities, and therapeutic strategies*. New York: Guilford Press, 1999.

Kiely, M. C. *The meaning and experience of desire: An analysis of women's narratives*. Doctoral Dissertation, University of Massachusetts. Published by UMI Dissertation Services, Ann Arbor, Michigan, 1997.

King, J. L. & Mallinckrodt, B. "Family environment and alexithymia in clients and non-clients," *Psychotherapy Research 10*, 78–86, 2000.

Lewis, K. M. "When leaders display emotion: How followers respond to negative emotional expression of male and female leaders," *Journal of Organizational Behavior 21*, 221–234, 2000.

Maume, D. J. & Houston, P. "Job segregation and gender differences in work-family spillover among white-collar workers," *Journal of Family and Economic Issues* 22 (2), 171–189, 2001.

Miller, J. B. "The construction of anger in women and men," *Working paper # 4*. Stone Center, Wellesley College, MA, 1985.

Miller, J. B. & Surrey, J. "Revisioning women's anger: The personal and the global," *Working paper # 43*. Stone Center, Wellesley College, MA, 1990.

Mills, P. J. & Dimsdale, J. E. "Anger suppression: Its relationship to b-adrenergic receptor sensitivity and stress-induced changes in blood pressure," *Psychological Medicine* 23, 673–678, 1993.

Moustakas, C. E. *Heuristic research: Design, methodology, and applications*. Newbury Park, CA: Sage, 1990.

Nowack, K. M. & Pentkowski, A. M. "Lifestyle habits, substance use and predictors of job burnout in professional working women," *Work & Stress* 8, 19–35, 1994.

Nyhlin, H., Ford, M. J., Eastwood, J., Smith, J. H., Nicol, E. F., Elton, R. A. & Eastwood, M. A. "Non-alimentary aspects of the irritable bowel syndrome," *Journal of Psychosomatic Research* 37, 155–162, 1993.

Oesterman, K., Bjoerkqvist, K., Lagerspetz, K. M. J., Kaukiainen, A., Landau, S. F., Fraczek, A. & Caprara, G. V. "Cross-cultural evidence of female indirect aggression," *Aggressive Behavior* 24, 1–8, 1998.

Patton, M. Q. *Qualitative research and evaluation methods*. Thousand Oaks, CA: Sage, 2002.

Pennebaker, J. W., Kiecolt-Glaser, J. K. & Glaser, R. "Disclosure of traumas and immune function: Health implications for psychotherapy," *Journal of Consulting and Clinical Psychology* 56, 239–245, 1988.

Pinhas, L., Toner, B. B., Ali, A., Garfinkel, P. E. & Stuckless, N. "The effects of the ideal of female beauty on mood and body satisfaction," *International Journal of Eating Disorders* 25, 223–226, 1999.

Richards, J. M. & Gross, J. J. "Emotion regulation and memory: The cognitive costs of keeping one's cool," *Journal of Personality and Social Psychology* 79, 410–424, 2000.

Rind, P. "Beyond Betty, Veronica, Thelma, and Louise: An exploration of best friendship among heterosexual women," *Dissertation Abstracts International Section A: Humanities and Social Sciences* 60 (9-A), 3556, 2000.

Ross, C. *The trauma model: A solution to the problem of comorbidity in psychiatry*. Richardson, TX: Manitou Communications, Inc., 2000.

Rusting, C. & Nolen-Hoeksema, A. "Regulating responses to anger: Effects of rumination and distraction on angry mood," *Journal of Personality and Social Psychology* 74, 790–803,1998.

Scherer, K. R, Banse, R. & Wallbott, H. G. "Emotion inferences from vocal expression correlate across languages and cultures," *Journal of Cross-Cultural Psychology* 32, 76–92, 2001.

Silverstein, J. L. "Origins of psychogenic vaginismus," *Psychotherapy and Psychosomatics* 52, 197–204, 1989.

Sternberg, R. J. "Triangulating love," in R. J. Sternberg and M. L. Barnes (eds.), *The psychology of love,* 119–138. New Haven: Yale University Press, 1988.

Swinford, S. P., De Maris, A., Cernkovich, S. A. & Giordano, P. C. "Harsh physical discipline in childhood and violence in later romantic involvements: The mediating role of problem behaviors," *Journal of Marriage and the Family* 62, 508–519, 2000.

Taylor, G. J., Bagby, R. M. & Parker, J. D. A. *Disorders of affect regulation: Alexithymia in medical and psychiatric illness.* Cambridge: Cambridge University Press, 1997.

Thomas, S. P. "Women's anger: Relationship of suppression to blood pressure," *Nursing Research* 46, 324–330, 1997.

Thomas, S. P. & Atakan, S. "Trait anger, anger expression, stress, and health status of American and Turkish midlife women," *Health Care for Women International* 14, 129–143, 1993.

Thomas, S. P., McCoy, D. & Martin, R. "Men's anger: A phenomenological exploration of its meaning," Poster presented at the 108th Annual Convention of the American Psychological Association, Washington, DC, August 2000.

Thomas, S. P., Smucker, C. & Droppleman, P. "It hurts most around the heart: A phenomenological exploration of women's anger," *Journal of Advanced Nursing* 28, 311–322, 1998.

Thomas, S. P. & Williams, R. "Relationships among perceived stress, trait anger, modes of anger expression, and health status of college men and women," *Nursing Research* 40, 303–307, 1991.

Thompson, R. A. "Emotional regulation and emotional development," *Educational Psychology Review* 3, 269–307, 1991.

Tiedens, L. Z. "Anger and advancement versus sadness and subjugation: The effect of negative emotion expressions on social status conferral," *Journal of Personality and Social Psychology* 80, 86–94, 2001.

Tucker, J. "Everyday forms of employee resistance," *Sociological Forum* 8, 25–45, 1993.

Venable, V. L., Carlson, C. R. & Wilson, J. "The role of anger and depression in recurrent headache," *Headache 41*, 21–30, 2001.

Weinstock, J. S. & Bond, L. A. "Conceptions of conflict in close friendships and ways of knowing among young college women: A developmental framework," *Journal of Social and Personal Relationships 17*, 687–696, 2000.

White, J. W. & Kowalski, R. M. "Deconstructing the myth of the nonaggressive woman: A feminist analysis," *Psychology of Women Quarterly 18*, 487–508, 1994.

Whitesell, N. R. & Harter, S. "The interpersonal context of emotion: Anger with close friends and classmates," *Child Development 67*, 1345–1359, 1996.

Acknowledgments

The three of us, first and foremost, wish to thank our agent, Laureen Rowland, whose immense energy, crucial feedback, and ongoing support have been invaluable throughout the whole process of this book. We have learned so much from you and appreciate your faith in us more than you can ever know. We also wish to thank our editor, Ann Campbell, for her careful guidance and wonderful enthusiasm for this project. We have felt tremendously lucky to be in the hands of someone who shares our vision for this book and is so dedicated to its success. The three of us additionally wish to acknowledge all the women who participated in our interviews and surveys, either in our research or through our clinical practices. You have openly shared your struggles, your perceptions, and, ultimately, your wisdom. We are grateful for your courage and your words.

FROM DEBORAH L. COX

Many wonderful people have supported me since my research into women's anger began and have continued to encourage, advise, and sustain me through the writing of this book. First among them, I wish to thank my partner, Joe Hulgus, who listens so well and sees so clearly. His own expertise has been an invaluable source of ideas, words, and research methodology. Joe not only knows me well, he knows this project well and his inside understanding has fueled much of its evolution.

I would like to thank the rest of my family for their unwavering support of this research and writing and their constant emotional nurturance. My mother, Patricia Cox, has been especially helpful in listening and cheering me on when I have needed it most. My sister-in-law, Carol Hulgus, has provided helpful mentoring. My aunt, Carolyn Cox-Barton, has inspired me, taught me about our family anger history, and made me laugh a lot too. My sister Leah Cox has provided a listening ear and has devoted much time and energy to watching A. J. so I could write.

Additionally, some close friends and colleagues have been major contributors to my work as well as to my development as a person. Sally St. Clair, Dick Schaeffer, Suzanne Weatherman, Deb Larson, and Jillian Cummings have spent countless hours with me discussing the ins and outs of emotional experience, providing consultation and advice, sharing laughter, tears, consternation, creativity, and insight. They have broadened my vision and enriched my life. My colleagues in the Department of Counseling at SMSU, Chuck Barke, Leon Bradshaw, Leslie Anderson, and Paul Blisard, have provided tremendous backing and encouragement for this work. Specifically, Patricia Van Velsor has helped me clarify many of the foundational ideas for our anger research and continues to be a valued collaborator in this effort. My graduate assistants and research team members have conducted interviews, transcribed tapes, collected survey data, and performed myriad tasks, all of which have furthered my research in women's anger. Among them, thanks goes to Marcia Smenner, Denise Dickens, Carol Davis, Suzanne Weatherman, Carolyn Williams, Valerie Harter, Marti Marlin, Paul Wickersham, Lola McClarnon, Dee Ann Stidham, Lynn Gooch, and Shandra Head.

Finally, heartfelt gratitude goes to Laureen Rowland for her consistent leadership and encouragement in this process. Her insight and valuing of *The Anger Advantage* has helped me clearly articulate a set of ideas in which I am deeply invested.

From Karin H. Bruckner

Without the support of family and friends, my interest and my work in women's experiences with anger would most certainly have remained a private pursuit. Throughout the challenging process of bringing my personal beliefs and theories into a more public arena, I have turned time and again to those close to me for courage and faith, which they inspire abundantly. Endless thanks to my family—Joan Gilman, Harry and Judith Hoglander, Bruce Hoglander, Gail Hewins, Paige Holman—and to *their* families as well for rallying to the cause as often and as heartily as needed.

Special thanks to Diana Boone, a dear friend who helps me take a look at who I am and then gets me laughing about what I see—a valuable perspective for any writer. Many thanks as well to Shannon Pheiffer, Janet Beeler, Judy Claybrook, and Märta Christina Nilsson, who graciously and repeatedly welcome me back into friendship after allowing me to disappear into my research and writing for months at a time.

Finally, I wish to acknowledge the sacrifices and support of my children, Lorin, Benjamin, and Gailynn, who have unselfishly moved over to make room for this literary sibling. And after I swore I wouldn't mix book-writing and mothering again until everyone was well launched on their own life adventure! Thank you with all my heart for so generously sharing your love, your energy, and your pride in the work I do.

FROM SALLY D. STABB

First, I wish to thank my loving partner, Martin, for his unfailing devotion to me and his patience during this project. He has sacrificed much. He has generously given me time and space and has generally put up with a lot of kvetching. There are many nights when he went to sleep alone while I was glued to the computer keyboard, and he never complained once. He also brings me treats and makes an excellent cup of tea.

I want to thank my Middle Eastern–dance friends, Julie Winans (photographer and designer extraordinaire), Pat Meyer, Maury Ballenger, and Cecile Labega and my dance teachers, Tambra and Vashti—you all have kept me sane through this process and reminded me that there is more to life than writing. Likewise, my other long-standing friends who sustained me in so many ways; especially Alison Mack, Greta Brinkman, Jeanette La Fontaine, and the Schnurrs, Carla and Carl.

I wish to thank my colleagues at Texas Woman's University who have supported me throughout this project, especially my department chair, Dan Miller, for allowing me to cut back on administrivia, my good friends Linda Rubin and Roberta Nutt for their understanding when I was fried, and Carmen Cruz for encouraging conversation and drumming. I also wish to acknowledge the students who have participated on my women's anger research teams: Faye Reimers, Ashley Williams, Barbara Hokamp, Jan Seltzer, Angelina Maynard, Shanti Majefski, Cindy Spoonts, Debra Wagner-Johnson, and Dave Popple. I could not have completed this work without your help. Last, but not least, I wish to thank my two brothers, Jon and David, for periodic comic relief. There's nothing like an inane, freewheeling conversation or some surfing pictures of Costa Rica to keep one from getting too obsessed with a book.